D1237289

FLORIDA STATE
UNIVERSITY LIBRARIES

NOV 3 1998

TALLAHASSEE, FLORIDA

Kistiakovsky

UKRAINIAN RESEARCH INSTITUTE
HARVARD UNIVERSITY
HARVARD SERIES IN UKRAINIAN STUDIES

Editorial Board

Michael S. Flier
George G. Grabowicz
Lubomyr Hajda
Edward L. Keenan
Roman Szporluk, *Chairman*

Robert A. DeLossa
Director of Publications

Cambridge, Massachusetts

Kistiakovsky

The Struggle for National and Constitutional Rights in the Last Years of Tsarism

Susan Heuman

Distributed by Harvard University Press
for the
Harvard Ukrainian Research Institute

KKY
110
.K57
H48
1998

Publication of this volume has been made possible by the Alex Woskob Family Foundation Endowment for Ukrainian Studies at Harvard University

© 1998 by the President and Fellows of Harvard College

All rights reserved
ISBN 0-916458-61-X (cloth)
ISBN 0-916458-65-2 (pbk)

LC Number 98-6667

Printed on acid-free paper
Printed in Canada by Transcontinental Printing/Best Books

The Ukrainian Research Institute was established in 1973 as an integral part of Harvard University. It supports research associates and visiting scholars who are engaged in projects concerned with all aspects of Ukrainian studies. The Institute also works in close cooperation with the Committee on Ukrainian Studies, which supervises and coordinates the teaching of Ukrainian history, language, and literature at Harvard University.

To my parents,

Lily Mamlock Heuman
and
Joseph Heuman,

whose lives and principles
taught me the importance of
respecting and protecting
human rights.

Contents

Usage Note   viii

Preface and Acknowledgments   ix

Illustrations
   1. Bogdan Kistiakovsky, 1903   xi
   2. Bogdan Kistiakovsky, 1910   xii
   3. Kistiakovsky with his son George, 1903   xiii
   4. Kistiakovsky with his sons George and Alexander, 1910   xiv

Introduction   1

Chapter 1. *A Cosmopolitan in Three Worlds*   7

Chapter 2. *Neo-Kantianism and the General Theory of Law*   39

Chapter 3. *Human Rights: A Pre-Revolutionary Model*   59

Chapter 4. *Constitutionalism and the Rule-of-Law State*   75

Chapter 5. *The Role of the Intelligentsia*   93

Chapter 6. *The Ukrainian Movement within the Multinational Russian Empire*   113

Chapter 7. *The Debate on the Ukrainian National Question: Kistiakovsky vs. Struve*   129

Conclusion   147

Notes   153

Select Bibliography   193

Index   211

Usage Note

The usage of forms herein conforms to the standards of the Harvard Series in Ukrainian Studies: place names are given in the form of their current territorial jurisdiction, with relevant forms as necessary. Thus L'viv (L'vov) and Chełm (Kholm). Transliteration is modified from the Library of Congress ALA Standards by the omission of ligatures.

The transmission of personal names from this period reflects a difficulty arising from the political and social circumstances of the times. In general, those individuals that clearly self-identified as Ukrainians have been given with the Ukrainian form of their name, which is supplemented by the Russian form to aid cross-referencing in the literature. For Kistiakovsky himself and his family, Anglicized forms have been used as a compromise arising from the fact that although he identified as Ukrainian, during his cosmopolitan life he never publicly used the Ukrainian form of his name, and, indeed, his offspring, settling in Russia and the United States, went on to use *only* Russian or Anglicized forms, respectively.

Preface and Acknowledgments

Transforming the study of Kistiakovsky's life and work into a book has taken many years. When I first worked on the subject of his life in Germany, Russia and Ukraine, there was little interest in a turn-of-the-century liberal who advocated national rights, constitutionalism, and human rights. This was before the era of Gorbachev and perestroika, when revolutionary ideas were still in vogue and issues of national autonomy had not yet reached the consciousness of most historians specializing in the region. I finished the draft and put the manuscript in my trunk when I traveled to Africa to teach at the University of Zambia for three years. Far away from the worlds he inhabited and wrote about, I was invited to speak about Kistiakovsky's ideas on constitutionalism, social justice, and human rights at the universities in Zambia and later in Zimbabwe, a few months after independence had been declared in 1981. The discussions ensuing were lively attempts to understand these concepts for the new African situations. In newly independent countries, the question of establishing a representative form of government that was based on human rights and democratic principles was a pressing reality.

Few people knew about Kistiakovsky's "arrival" in Africa, but somehow a German scholar, Ditmar Dahlmann, who was one of the editor's for the collected works of Max Weber, tracked me down in Zambia to ask about the correspondence between Kistiakovsky and Max Weber. It was the German inquiry about Kistiakovsky and his relationship to Max Weber that rekindled the idea of publishing the work. The demise of the Soviet Union and the formation of an independent Ukraine contributed further to the growing interest in the fresh urgency of Kistiakovsky's devotion to the development of rule of law and respect for the rights of nationalities, which he first articulated more than ninety years ago.

I am most grateful to those who have supported my efforts during the many years that I have worked on this topic. The generous assistance from the International Research and Exchanges Board, the National Endowment for the Humanities, the American Philosophical Society, the City University of New York–Baruch College, and Manhattanville College made it possible for me to complete the research on the manuscript.

In addition, I am especially grateful for the support of my colleagues who read all or part of this manuscript and who offered invaluable comments—Richard Wortman, who encouraged me to return to the project after my years abroad in Africa and Europe, William Wagner, Theodore Friedgut, Peter Juviler, George Fisher, the late John Hazard, the late

George Kistiakowsky, Marcia Wright, Ditmar Dahlmann, Eugene Huskey, Vadim Khazin, Edward Kasinec, and Olga Andriewsky. The Kistiakovsky family in Moscow—the late Andrei and his widow Marina Shemekhanskaia, and Hennadii Boriak of the Mykhailo Hrushevs'kyi Institute of Ukrainian Archeography at the Ukrainian Academy of Science were most helpful in locating materials and photographs. Sergei Kazantzev of the Law Faculty at St. Petersburg University in Russia was most helpful with his own insights and in arranging discussions with Russian scholars in the law faculty. Robert DeLossa of the Ukrainian Research Institute at Harvard saw the book through to print and Julia Vaingurt edited the manuscript for style. I am appreciative to both of them for their efforts. My thanks also to the freedom fighters of the African National Congress who were my friends during my years in Zambia; their insights into the problems and practical aspects of establishing a new state based on a constitution brought some of this work to life.

My deepest thanks go to my husband Michael Trencher. His astute editorial comments and unflagging support and patience were essential to the completion of this long and sometimes difficult process.

Susan E. Heuman
February 1998

1. Bogdan Kistiakovsky, 1903.

2. Bogdan Kistiakovsky, 1910.

3. Kistiakovsky with his son George, 1903.

4. Kistiakovsky with his sons George (right) and Alexander (left), 1910.

Kistiakovsky

Introduction

> It is not enough to indicate that law delimits interests or creates a compromise between them; it must be firmly stressed that there can be law only where there is freedom for the individual. In this sense the legal order is a system of relationships in which all persons of a given society possess the greatest possible freedom of activity and self-determination.
>
> *Bogdan Kistiakovsky, 1909*

In 1903, Bogdan Kistiakovsky* railed against Vladimir Lenin's concept of a vanguard party to lead the revolution, remarking that he did not want to see the despotism of the Romanov autocracy replaced with the despotism of Lenin in the name of the dictatorship of the proletariat. As if he were able to see into the future, Kistiakovsky made clear his fear that state dogmatism could develop into a police state. Throughout his life, Kistiakovsky voiced his moral vision for a constitutional governmental order based on individual liberties and social justice; his concept of socialism was based on individualism rather than on an authoritarian system. It was his hope that a democratic movement representing all classes and estates as well as nationalities would develop into the challenging force leading to the end of the autocracy and the beginning of a democratically elected government.

Bogdan Kistiakovsky's rich scholarly, yet politically active cosmopolitan life (1868–1920) presents the reader with a wide-ranging pre-revolutionary insight into the problems of human rights, constitutionalism, and federalism in a legally based state, a *pravovoe gosudarstvo*. His ideals were characteristic of the turn-of-the-century Russian intelligentsia who rejected *laissez-faire* liberalism and instead proposed a constitutional system in a socialist context that would allow for a just relationship of the individual to society to be established. In all three spheres of his life and work—in what is now Ukraine, Germany, and Russia—Kistiakovsky's intellectual path was dictated by his dedication to establishing a social, economic, and political order in which the individual could be self-determining and eventually enjoy human rights, that is, the combination of political and economic rights that he articulated in his 1905 article, "Prava cheloveka i grazhdanina" [The Rights of Man and the Citizen]. His modern view of human rights predated the formulation of political and economic rights in the United Nations Universal Declaration of Human Rights by forty-three years.[1]

Kistiakovsky was not considered a central figure in any one of the three worlds in which he lived and worked. Instead, he was often seen as an idiosyncratic outsider, a maverick, by his contemporaries in the liberal movement; the circles of Petr Struve's friends in the Moscow and St. Petersburg intelligentsia called him a Kyivan.[2] Though Kistiakovsky worked closely with Struve on the publication of *Osvobozhdenie* [Liberation] and participated in the central debates and activities of the Russian liberal movement, he remained the outsider— the Ukrainian who educated the Russian intelligentsia about Ukrainian issues and history. Similarly, Ukrainian nationalists did not accept his anti-separatist position—his belief in cultural autonomy for nations based on a federal state structure. Among legal thinkers Kistiakovsky was not known for his brilliant speeches in the courtroom; a creative theorist rather than a practitioner, he focused on the social foundations of law and the process of formulating an original method for integrating law and the social sciences.

As a product of the Ukrainian movement, Kistiakovsky recognized that universal values and truths, such as natural laws, had to be expressed in the social and political language of a specific society. Ukrainian culture and language were the center of the world in which he grew up. His father, Alexander, had diligently collected and studied Ukrainian customary legal practices for decades and was an active member of the Ukrainian movement. As an outcast from the Russian Empire's university system because of his Ukrainian political activities (see chapter 1), Kistiakovsky completed his university studies in Germany and earned his diploma in philosophy rather than law. On the basis of his Ukrainian experience and his studies in Germany, he advocated reformulating the ideas of human rights and constitutionalism in order to effectively apply them to a particular society. He understood that there was no perfect model applicable to all societies. As the late Isaiah Berlin explains in his collection of essays, *The Crooked Timber of Humanity:*[3]

> The idea of a single, perfect society of all mankind must be internally self-contradictory, because the Valhalla of the Germans is necessarily different from the ideal of future life of the French, because the paradise of the Muslims is not that of the Jews or Christians . . . But if we are to have as many types of perfection as there are types of culture, each with its ideal constellation of virtues then the very notion of the possibility of a single perfect society is logically incoherent.[4]

Kistiakovsky's sociological studies led him away from the conventional search for a linear approach to progress and perfection. He focused on sociology and sociology of law to construct a method for discovering the sources of the law and establishing a viable democratic political structure for the multilayered and multifaceted social fabric of the Russian Empire. One had to avoid the danger of wholesale borrowing of foreign legal forms and codes; Kistiakovsky recognized that constitutions in Western countries, such as England, the United States, or France developed over time through political and legal struggles as well as revolutionary upheavals. Furthermore, Kistiakovsky was unafraid of disavowing the idea that universal truths were valid for all men in all contexts. Instead, he dared to forge the path to a new methodology for developing a legal structure based on specific cultural and social realities.

In the Soviet era, Kistiakovsky's work was virtually unknown. He was considered a pre-revolutionary liberal bourgeois theorist of law and sociology whose work had nothing to offer those building a new communist society. His name, along with that of Pavel Ivanovich Novgorodtsev, Lev Iosifovich Petrazhitskii, and Anatolii Fedorovich Koni, among other turn-of-the-century theorist and activist lawyers, is currently of great interest due to growing curiosity about Russian legal traditions. Many pre-revolutionary era essays of political and legal thought are being revived in reprinted editions, such as Mykhailo Drahomanov's *Sobranie sochinenii* (Kyiv, 1991) and *Vlast' i pravo, iz istorii russkoi pravovoi mysli* (Leningrad, 1990) that included the works of Boris Nikolaevich Chicherin, Vladimir Sergeyevich Soloviev,

Bogdan Kistiakovsky, Pavel Ivanovich Novgorodtsev, Sergei Nikolaevich Bulgakov, and Nikolai Aleksandrovich Berdiaev.[5] Numerous republications of *Vekhi* [Landmarks] have become available, and numerous articles on pre-revolutionary life and culture have appeared in the journal *Nashe nasledie* [Our Heritage], among others. Students can now study the works of pre-revolutionary liberal philosophers and lawyers and write about them in non-ideological terms.

Only in the last two decades have Western scholars taken a serious look at Kistiakovsky's extensive range of written works. Russian historians readily recognize Kistiakovsky as the author of the well-known, provocative essay "V zashchitu prava. Intelligentsiia i pravosoznanie" [In Defense of Law. The Intelligentsia and Legal Consciousness], published in *Vekhi* in 1909.[6] The critique here of the intelligentsia's failure to understand the importance of legal guarantees for individual rights and a general lack of legal consciousness, however, does not show the entire scope of Kistiakovsky's thought. Reading his other works reveals his hope to both discover and integrate existing legal ideas into the various layers of society in order to develop a new democratic constitutional order. The chapter on Kistiakovsky's sociology of law in Alexander Vucinich's 1976 book *Social Thought in Tsarist Russia*[7] was one of the first Western articles dedicated to Kistiakovsky's thought. My own short article, "A Socialist Conception of Human Rights: A Model from Prerevolutionary Russia," appeared a few years later. Andrzej Walicki reviews and analyzes Kistiakovsky's writings in a chapter of his comprehensive work, *Legal Philosophies of Russian Liberalism*.[8] Kistiakovsky's work and influence on the life of his friend, the sociologist Max Weber, is discussed in the 1989 volume *Zur Russischen Revolution von 1905,* which is volume ten of the *Max Weber Gesamtausgabe*.[9]

After the declaration of Ukrainian independence in 1991, Ukrainian scholars have been even more interested in documenting the achievements of their own national heroes such as Drahomanov and Kistiakovsky. A study of the connection between Bogdan Kistiakovsky's achievements and his devotion to the Ukrainian national cause and federal ideas constitutes an important chapter of the heretofore unwritten Ukrainian history.[10] With the growing interest in Ukraine's and Russia's common constitutional tradition, Kistiakovsky's legacy is taking on a renewed importance among scholars in both countries. This interest in Kistiakovsky is exemplified by the recent work of Larysa Depenchuk, who has written an impressive narrative of his life, and also the republication of the 1909 article "In Defense of Law. The Intelligentsia and Legal Consciousness," which originally appeared in the famous volume *Vekhi* [Landmarks].[11]

In addition, the distinguished careers of the Kistiakovsky family have been receiving fresh attention. Kistiakovsky's father, Alexander, was a noted jurist and a professor at Kyiv University who wrote serious studies on customary and criminal law. His diaries are being published by the Ukrainian Academy of Sciences in Kyiv. One of Bogdan Kistiakovsky's two sons, George Kistiakowsky, was a scientific advisor to President Eisenhower (1959–1961), a member of the United States Arms Control and Disarmament Agency (1961–1969), and a professor of chemistry at Harvard University for over thirty years. In fact, the Kistiakovsky family produced three generations of distinguished scholars and scientists.

Because of the complex pattern of Kistiakovsky's life, a thematic structure has proved most useful in analyzing his contributions to Russian and Ukrainian thought. Chapter 1 begins with a biographical overview, followed by chapter 2, which offers a discussion of the philosophical bases of human rights—particularly Kistiakovsky's involvement with neo-Kantianism. Chapter 3 focuses on his concept of human rights. Chapters 4 and 5 turn to his engagement in the constitutional movement and the role of the Russian intelligentsia. Chapter 6 defines his devotion to federalism and its roots in Drahomanov's thought. The study concludes with Kistiakovsky's clash with the Russian intelligentsia just before the outbreak of World War I.

CHAPTER ONE

A Cosmopolitan in Three Worlds

Bogdan Kistiakovsky's lifelong commitment to individual rights, constitutionalism, and federalism developed in the context of dramatic changes unfolding in the three worlds that he inhabited during his cosmopolitan life—centered in Ukraine, Russia, and Germany. He was born in 1868, in the era just following Tsar Alexander II's Great Reforms of 1861—the emancipation of the serfs—and the Judicial Reforms of 1864. Though a restructuring of the legal order and the establishment of local government organs were major parts of the reforms, the focus on legal and socioeconomic problems of the Russian Empire did not extend to the national problems of non-Russian peoples. Russian political dominance combined with the tsarist rejection of any type of constitution that would allow pluralism made it impossible for national and regional self-determination to develop.

The Kistiakovsky Family and Ukrainian Cultural Heritage

Bogdan Kistiakovsky (1868–1920) was one of three sons born in Kyiv to a prominent Ukrainian family descended from peasants.[1] Kistiakovsky's lineage has been traced to 1808, when his great grandfather was granted freedom from serfdom. Thereafter, his grandfather attended Chernihiv Seminary and became a village priest. His father, Alexander Kistiakovsky (1833–1885), was a distinguished legal scholar and professor of criminal law at Kyiv University.[2] The elder Kistiakovsky was known for his work on death penalty and juvenile delinquency; he worked on the legal sources of peasant customary law and recorded them in his voluminous notebooks.

Alexander Kistiakovsky's research on the hetmanate's legal system revealed an order that was based on a contractual relationship between the monarch and the subjects.[3] The Ukrainian legal tradition, which was a composite of proclamations of the hetman, the General Military administration, and village customary laws, contained practical complications. The overlapping and contradictory laws and customary practices caused lengthy and confusing judicial proceedings. A Ukrainian juridical commission active from 1728–1743 compiled and integrated the existing codes to establish a unified legal code, *Prava, po kotorym suditsia malorossiiskii narod* [Laws by Which the Little Russian People are Judged]. Even though it had never been formally adopted as an official code, it laid the basis for the law used in Ukrainian courts during the second half of the eighteenth century. Nevertheless, the Ukrainian code was first published only in 1867, by Alexander Kistiakovsky.[4]

His father's interest in customary law and academic law career clearly influenced Bogdan's own career and intellectual development. Developing a Ukrainian identity was a pivotal point for intellectual life in the sophisticated Kistiakovsky home. In fact, Kistiakovsky grew up in the company of the great intellectual leaders of the Ukrainian movement, such as Mykhailo Drahomanov (1841–1895), the renowned Ukrainian scholar, activist, and publicist, who later, after his exile, became the editor of the journal *Hromada*, and Kistiakovsky's uncle, Volodymyr Antonovych, who was a distinguished professor of Ukrainian history at Kyiv University. These two scholars together wrote one of the classics of Ukrainian ethnography—the two volume *Historical Songs of the Little Russian People* (1874–1875). The world of the cultural and intellectual leaders of the Kyiv *Hromada* [community] permeated the environment in which Kistiakovsky was raised and later deeply influenced his *weltanschauung*.

The Hromada *Movement*

The political and cultural oppression of Ukraine by the tsarist government served as a catalyst in the formation of secret, underground societies of nationalists as early as 1845 when the Cyril and Methodius Brotherhood was organized in Kyiv. Among the founding members were the poet Taras Shevchenko, Panteleimon Kulish, and Mykola Kostomarov who, together with about nine other members of the intelligentsia, advocated the emancipation of the serfs and the creation of a federated Slavic state based on the principle of national autonomy. The idea of nationalism was expressed in broad Pan-Slavic terms—all Slavic peoples should have the right to foster their cultures. This group, imbued with nineteenth-century romanticism, Western utopian socialism, and German idealism, idealized the Cossacks and their egalitarian social organization. The Cyril and Methodius Brotherhood concentrated on promoting Ukrainian (Little Russian) literature and publishing educational materials in Ukrainian language to make them available to the people. The organization's populist goals and activities were considered subversive and the Brotherhood was forcibly closed in 1847 when most of the members were arrested and exiled by Nicholas I's police.[5]

The organization only revived after Nicholas I's death in 1855. After their release from exile, some of the leaders of the Brotherhood, such as Shevchenko, Kostomarov, and Kulish, went to live in St. Petersburg where they formed a *hromada* [community]. This group was joined by a small group of younger scholars including Alexander Kistiakovsky, who moved to St. Petersburg after the Kyiv *Hromada* was banned in 1863 in the wake of the Polish rebellion.[6] The organization was devoted to Ukrainian national matters and the improvement of the situation for Ukrainians within the empire, including popular enlightenment of the Ukrainian masses.[7] The Ukrainian intelligentsia's activities were supported by the Russian intelligentsia who looked favorably on all popular enlightenment programs in the Russian Empire.

The Kyiv *Hromada* was organized to support the Ukrainian national revival in 1859 and closed by the authorities in 1863. In 1869 it was revived by scholars and activists such as Antonovych,[8] Viliam Berenshtam (the father of Bogdan Kistiakovsky's future wife), and Drahomanov. Among the activities of the Kyiv *Hromada* was the establishment of a network of Sunday schools for Ukrainian peasants and the assumption of the leadership of the Southwestern Branch of the Imperial Russian Geographic Society. Further, the Kyivans transformed the Southwestern Branch into a center for Ukrainian studies which published archives and research in Ukrainian ethnography, geography, and statistics.

Although the Kyiv *Hromada* tried to emphasize that its activities were cultural and educational and not dangerous to the ruling Russians, the movement was nevertheless perceived as a political threat. Consequently, the tsar reacted resolutely to the growth of Ukrainian national activities by issuing the 1876 Ems Ukaz, which banned any publication of Ukrainian language books as well as any use of Ukrainian language in schools and theater. For the Ukrainian activists, the Ems Ukaz served to stimulate the struggle against tsarist policy toward non-Russian nationalities.[9] Threatened by the tension created by the Polish national uprising of 1863 and the Ukrainian renaissance, the Russian government proclaimed the *ukaz* to prevent a possible liaison between the Ukrainian populists and the Polish nationalists, or an Austrian-German plot against the Russian Empire.

It was his parents' involvement with the *Hromada* that led to Kistiakovsky's first exposure to the Ukrainian movement and set the stage for his lifelong commitment to human rights and establishing a government in which social justice could become the norm.[10]

When he was just nine years old, Kistiakovsky witnessed the intensification of the Ukrainian movement after the tsarist government's Ems Ukaz. The ban on the use of Ukrainian language made a vivid impression on him and his classmates, when as students they were forbidden to sing Ukrainian songs unless the lyrics had been translated into other languages.

At thirteen Kistiakovsky joined the Kyiv *Hromada* group and, as a gymnasium student, he became an organizer for the Ukrainian cause. He was expelled from two *gimnazii* for circulating illegal Ukrainian literature. Kistiakovsky was admitted to a third gymnasium in Ukraine where he finally earned his diploma.[11] In the fall of 1888, he entered Kyiv University to study Ukrainian language and history with his uncle, Professor Antonovych.

Although Kistiakovsky was imbued with the goals and principles of *Hromada* members, he and other younger activists in the Ukrainian movement considered the purely cultural activities of *Hromada* ineffective.[12] *Hromada* limited its activities to the cultural and linguistic spheres of Ukrainian national rights because the group feared that involvement in other more political aspects of Ukrainian life might lead to more severe repression by the Russians. The younger members of the movement, however, sought a more direct, less timid approach. The 1876 linguistic proscriptions combined with the repressive atmosphere following the assassination of Tsar Alexander II in 1881 and the spirit of the Russian populist movement of the late 1870s nurtured a political, activist response to the problem of attaining political and cultural rights. The younger Ukrainian populists pursued work outside of their underground study groups as political organizers in the midst of the peasants and workers. Kistiakovsky and other members, therefore, broke with *Hromada* in the second half of the 1870s and joined a politically active circle of Ukrainians. This group carried out its activities under the tutelage of Mykhailo Drahomanov, who left Kyiv for Galicia (then under the Austro-Hungarian Empire) at the time of the repression of 1876 in order to continue his Ukrainian political activities.

Drahomanov's Influence

Mykhailo Drahomanov opposed a separatist movement and feared the authoritarian tendencies in a centralized state. His vision for the Russian Empire was the creation of a loose confederation of autonomous regions in which local decision making was the rule. The younger activists were attracted to Drahomanov's federalist, constitutionalist, and socialist goals for Slavic peoples in addition to his activity as a political organizer in Galicia. Given the repressive atmosphere in Russian Ukraine, Kistiakovsky and his circle considered political organizing among the Ukrainian peasantry a task for the future. They believed work among the Galician Ukrainians was more feasible and productive toward establishing a new base for their political activities.

Drahomanov was a proponent of constitutionalism and federalism who understood that individual freedoms had to be the basis of a democratic constitutional order. Throughout his life, Kistiakovsky dedicated a considerable part of his scholarly activity to Drahomanov's life and work in his effort to present the legacy of the Ukrainian national movement to Russian readers. Drahomanov's influence among the Russian intelligentsia was minimal as a result of his principled stance against the use of terrorist activities, even in support of revolution; this position caused many among the Russian intelligentsia to treat him with disdain. In addition, his belief in the right to national cultural autonomy for Ukrainians and other non-Russian nationalities made him an opponent to the centralist programs set forth by Russian revolutionaries. Because of his forced emigration—the result of his "illegal activities" in the Ukrainian *Hromada* movement in the Russian

Empire—he was most influential among Galician Ukrainians ("Ruthenians") in the Hapsburg Empire.

Drahomanov pointed out that the power of the state had to be limited so that the freedom of individuals and nationalities could be increased. In Drahomanov's words,

> Mankind's goal, which is completely unlike present-day States, is a condition where both larger and smaller social bodies will be composed of free men, united voluntarily for common work and mutual help. This goal is called anarchy, i.e., the autonomy of each individual and the free cooperation of men and groups.[13]

Drahomanov explained that he adopted the term *anarchy* as it was first used by Pierre Joseph Proudhon to counter theories that led to a centralized government: "Proudhon says that the synonym for anarchy is the English word 'self-government.' In its practical application the theory of anarchy leads to federalism."[14] Autonomy was a way of attaining real federalism since it meant having basic freedom from governmental interference. For a theorist who started with the inviolable freedom of the individual and rejected authoritarianism, it was natural that a concept of federalism was the answer to social organization. Individuals with equal rights would belong to groups, associations, and communities that would cooperate through larger unions and in this way prevent the atomization of society.[15] Drahomanov believed that federalism had two main practical advantages: First, it would allow the courts and administration to be closer to the population as well as to help in the process of education. Second, administrative matters would be handled by those people whose interests were most directly affected. Drahomanov suggested that a comparison of social and political life in centralized states and federal states, such as Switzerland and the United States of America, would support his argument.[16]

Moreover, Drahomanov was the first Ukrainian activist to firmly state that the rights of the Ukrainian people could only be satisfied in a federally organized government; he was the first to advocate federalism for Ukraine since the Cyril-Methodius Brotherhood developed its broad program for a federal government.[17] Drahomanov's views on federalism were most clearly expressed in his "Draft Constitution for the Ukrainian Society Free Union," which was first published in 1884. The basic idea of the Free Union was to form in Ukrainian territory of the Russian Empire an organization that would fight for political freedoms as well as inviolability of nationality. The latter meant the recognition of native languages in private and public life. Drahomanov projected the goal of formulating statutes to regulate the relationship between local self-government and the central governing apparatus. In an 1889 letter to George Kennan, Drahomanov admitted that it would be naive to think that federalism *à l'américaine* in Russia was possible. Federalism has opponents among the conservatives, as well as among the revolutionaries. But the idea of Russia's decentralization—at least administrative decentralization—and of self-government for local and provincial *zemstva* (*uezdy* and *oblasti*) is very widespread, especially among the . . . activists in the *zemstvo* institutions. Drahomanov suggested a form of local self-government or home rule instead of federalism for Russia. He alluded to his position as moderate "Girondist-American ideas."[18]

Drahomanov did not support a combative political stand to achieve federal goals. The Ukrainian people were not in a position to protect themselves from the imperialist designs of the Great Russians or the tendencies toward annexation that, he felt, were developing among the Poles. While he supported the Poles in their quest for self-determination, Drahomanov was wary of the Polish nationalists' attitude to Ukrainians, even after the 1863 uprising against Russian rule was crushed. He knew that the Polish nationalists' dream was to reestablish an independent Poland within the 1772 boundaries that included Ukrainian territory in the Russian Empire as well as territories lost to Austria and Prussia.

Bogdan Kistiakovsky became a convinced Drahomanovite. Imbued with Drahomanov's federalist and democratic ideas, he endorsed his predecessor's militancy in demanding the end of the subjugation of non-Russian nationalities when he quoted Drahomanov's comment in an 1892 article, "Observing the history of all civilized nations, we must come to the conclusion that the system of compulsory nationality is the same universal phenomenon of social life as the system of compulsory religion."[19]

Galicia and the Beginning of Political Activism

The Ukrainian population in Galicia, the Ruthenians, were adherents of the Greek Catholic Church and considered themselves

"Ruthenians," distinct from "Ukrainians" who lived in the Russian Empire.[20] While the Polish population's national identity was reinforced by its link with a historical Polish nation, the Ukrainian population did not have a nation with which to identity after the Treaty of Periaslavl' of 1654. Nationally conscious Ukrainians considered the Treaty of Periaslavl' to be a symbol of the rights and privileges that Ukrainians lost to the Russians. The dominant Russians, on the other hand, thought of Ukrainians as "Little Russians" who naturally were part of the empire's historical mission to consolidate the "Russian lands."[21] Given the lack of an existing Ukrainian nation, Ukrainians identified themselves either with the Russian or Polish nation, depending on their place of residence. Although the Poles were temporarily without a state because they had been incorporated into the Russian Empire, they had a "historical nation" to identify with, while Ukrainians, Czechs, Slovaks, and Belarusians did not have a state tradition, and were without a "history."[22] However, Ukrainians did have a sense of their own national, cultural identity, which was more freely and legally expressed in the Hapsburg territories than in the Russian Empire.

Galicia, an ethnically mixed area populated mostly by Ukrainians and Poles with a substantial Jewish minority, included the western section of Ukraine that the Austrians had ruled since the first Polish Partition in 1772.[23] Under the terms of the 1867 Austro-Hungarian Constitution, Galicia was one of the regions of the empire that enjoyed a broad range of cultural and political autonomy. This permitted the Ukrainians considerable freedom, despite the recognition of the cultural and political supremacy of the Polish upper class in Galicia. In this way, the Hapsburg monarchy carried out its deliberate policy of counterbalancing politically subordinate nationalities against the ruling elite to prevent any separatist inclinations: Ukrainian nationalism in Galicia was used as a counterweight to Polish nationalism. By the end of the nineteenth century, there were Ukrainian political parties, schools and *gimnazii*, two Ukrainian-language chairs at the University of L'viv as well as a legal Ukrainian press. Nurtured in the context of the Hapsburg constitutional government, the growing Ukrainian national movement in Austrian Galicia had given the west Ukrainians— the Ruthenians—the opportunity to bring their national and socioeconomic interests into the parliament. The Ruthenians were able to develop a clear national identity supported by their right to form political parties and organizations as well as to publish in Ukrainian.

As one of Kistiakovsky's friends, the Marxist Pavlo Tuchaps'kyi [Pavel Tuchapskii], described in his memoirs, the young activists of the 1880s were afraid that the Ukrainian movement in Russia would end in disastrous arrests, as had the Russian populist endeavors of 1873–1874:

> We looked skeptically at direct work with the Ukrainian peasants because of memories of the populist movement and the realization of how difficult it would be to win a political battle with the help of the *zemstvo* organization in Russia as prescribed by Drahomanov. Here was our rationalization: we felt that the organization of the Galician Ukrainian peasants would certainly strike an echo among our Russian Ukrainian peasants, and then . . . what would occur after this we did not really know. But, in any case, the Galician radical movement was for us the only way to influence the Ukrainian peasantry. We thought their work would overflow into our Ukrainian area.[24]

These Ukrainian activists were advocates of rights for the peasantry in both the Russian and Austro-Hungarian empires. In addition, on the basis of their readings of Marx and Drahomanov, they professed political and economic change that, they hoped, would ultimately result in the formation of a socialist system. To achieve their goals, the Ukrainian activists formed study groups in Ukrainian history and language, though they devoted most of their energies to analyzing the social and economic structure of Russian Ukraine and Galicia. They strove to prepare themselves for political activity among the workers and peasants to promote the liberation of the oppressed Ukrainians. By cultivating both a national and class consciousness, these activists hoped to establish a common ground for solidarity between the Ukrainians in Galicia and those in the Russian Empire.[25]

In August 1889, Kistiakovsky, his friend Sergei Degen, and Degen's two sisters traveled from Kyiv to Galicia to vacation and develop closer ties with the Galician Ukrainian Peasant Radical Party organized in the late 1870s by two of Drahomanov's students—the activist Mykhailo Pavlyk and the distinguished Ukrainian writer Ivan Franko.[26] Though the visitors did not have a clear-cut political mission, the Austrian foreign minister was informed that they were arriving in Galicia to carry out Drahomanov's instructions—to stir up hatred for the Polish landlords among the Ukrainian peasantry.[27] Degen's and his friends'

introduction to the work of the Ukrainian Peasant Radical Party was cut
short when Kistiakovsky and other Kyivan as well as Galician radicals
were arrested by the Austrian police for subversive activities.
Kistiakovsky had already spent two weeks in prison when he wrote his
mother on September 4, 1889: " . . . and how could I know that I would
arouse suspicions of having Pan-Slavic tendencies? By the time the
interrogations were over, I realized that Austria feared losing control
over Russian Galicia; yet, I could not have ever imagined what the
police suspected me of doing—being a Russian spy."[28] After he was
held in prison for nearly ten weeks, the charges against Kistiakovsky
were dismissed. However, the Austrian police did not let the case drop
before they notified the Kyiv *Guberniia* police administration. As soon
as Kistiakovsky and his companions returned to Kyiv, they were inves-
tigated again by the police because of the Austrian report which stated:

> . . . the students in question (Kistiakovsky, Marshynskii, and Degen)
> were found in possession of letters from Kyiv, Paris, Geneva, and
> Bulgaria; among these were a few letters from émigrés, and the
> contents of these indicated that these persons were possibly partici-
> pating in revolutionary activity. The majority of the letters were
> addressed to Kistiakovsky, and in one of them the émigré
> Drahomanov informed him about the mailing of printed works
> through Bucharest. He recommended that a storehouse . . . be orga-
> nized for such future mailings and even indicated the areas in Galicia
> in which he could find aid and sympathy for the cause.[29]

In Kyiv the police searched Kistiakovsky and his colleagues and con-
fiscated books and pamphlets in Ukrainian. Among them was "Pomich
narodu" [Aid to the People] that advocated the building of socialism
and the organization of a federation of nationalities with equal rights.
Therefore, the Kyivan police concluded that Kistiakovsky was circulating illegal Ukrainian literature as a member of a circle of Ukrainian
revolutionary activists.[30] As a result, Kistiakovsky was arrested for a
short time and subsequently expelled from Kyiv University. In 1890 he
left Kyiv to continue his studies in Kharkiv. After only a few months at
the historical and philological faculties of Kharkiv University, he again
was expelled for political activities. Following this, Kistiakovsky was
placed in the "untrustworthy" category by the police.[31]

Dorpat University and the Activist Years

The only university in the empire that remained open to Kistiakovsky was Dorpat University (now Tartu University) in Estland Province (now Estonia). In the interest of Russification of the essentially German university, even students expelled from other universities in the Russian Empire were accepted at Dorpat.[32] When Kistiakovsky enrolled in the law faculty of Dorpat University in August 1891, he joined the most cosmopolitan student community in the empire. One of the Polish students, a radical named Stanisław Stempowski, described his first encounter with the Ukrainian intelligentsia:

> I grew up amidst the Ukrainian villages and knew the language, songs, and culture very well, but I only encountered the Ukrainian intelligentsia in the German-Baltic Dorpat [Tartu]. This was during the student unrest of the 1880s and the beginning of the 1890s. Every year large groups of students who had been thrown out of universities with "wolves tickets" [a stamp forbidding them to enter university] from Petersburg, Kharkiv, Kyiv, and Tomsk were knocking on the door of this famous German university. Dorpat University had no limitations on students from the Russian Empire, because of its long tradition of autonomy.[33]

The students had little contact with the local population and dressed like classical nihilists of the 1860s with long hair, beards, long peasant shirts, and capes. Kistiakovsky's style was in sharp contrast to the peasant style of the others:

> ... there was an enormous sensation when a student from Kyiv appeared for matriculation in evening clothes. This student was Bogdan Kistiakovsky, the son of a famous professor of criminal law. He did not make friends with the Russian students and stayed far away from the local students. He only visited professors and devoted all his time to studies. He was always dressed neatly in European-style dress, shaved his beard and mustache, and had a short haircut. In life and work he was extremely (pedantically) systematic. Every day he had his timetable planned in advance and did not deviate from it.[34]

It was in this setting that the twenty-two-year-old Kistiakovsky joined a Marxist study group composed mainly of Polish students and became deeply involved with Marxism. Kistiakovsky asked his fellow student Stempowski to take him to a meeting place of radical Polish students called the "kitchen." He was accepted and quickly learned

Polish as well as German and English.[35] In return Kistiakovsky introduced the Polish students to his Ukrainian friend named Kosach who
was a talented raconteur. As Stempowski described:

> In the bathhouse (*bania*), [Kosach] told stories about priests, police-
> men, Gypsies, Jews, the Polish *szlachta*, and Russians—he gave
> lessons in Ukrainian language and humor. Those who wanted to get
> deeper into the Ukrainian atmosphere went to Yeghen Degen, the son
> of a general from Poltava Region. He lived with his wife—a typical
> and convinced Ukrainian. Her head was surrounded by her braids
> forming a type of wreath . . . The inside of the house was filled with
> ethnographically Ukrainian things—embroidered towels, portraits.
> There I for the first time heard Shevchenko's poems, the last works of
> Franko. The Poles coming to such parties at Degen's said, "We are
> going to Ukraine."

Meeting in the "kitchen" with the Polish Marxists, the group read
and discussed the first volume of Marx's *Das Kapital* in German and
French and arranged for the reprinting and distributing of *Neue Zeit*, the
major theoretical journal of the German Socialists.[36] Since censorship
in Dorpat was not as strict as in other parts of the Russian Empire at
that time, the group was able to publish leftist writings that were
forbidden by the censors elsewhere. There Kistiakovsky participated in
such projects as the translation of the *Erfurt Program*[37] into Ukrainian
and its illegal publication in L'viv.[38] During the summers of his Dorpat
years, Kistiakovsky returned to Kyiv to work as a propagandist of
Marxism. In describing Kistiakovsky's student life in Dorpat University,[39] Tuchaps'kyi wrote:

> In Iur'ev [Dorpat], Kistiakovsky was close with Polish students who
> were Marxists. In their company he read Social Democratic litera-
> ture, published by the Liberation of Labor Group. So, when
> Kistiakovsky came to Kyiv in the summer of 1892, he was already a
> Marxist.[40]

Although he was not formally a member of a Marxist party,
Kistiakovsky received Marxist literature and distributed it to his many
leftist contacts and acquaintances on a regular basis.[41]

In 1890, Ivan Franko and Mykhailo Pavlyk joined other left-wing
"Ruthenian" Ukrainians in L'viv to form the Ukrainian Radical Party.
That same year they started to publish a journal—*Narod* [The People].
Ukrainian students in Dorpat received copies of the journal, disguised
as private letters, in sealed envelopes through the mail. *Narod* was

distributed throughout Galicia in this way. Since the journal was cleverly concealed, the police did not notice and the mass distribution of the Ukrainian papers was not blocked.[42] Kistiakovsky, who kept up with the latest Polish and German radical literature, tried to transport to Russian Ukraine and there distribute *Narod* as well as other Ukrainian and foreign publications legal in Austrian Galicia in such closed envelopes. As Stempowski recorded:

> . . . we established conspiratorial contacts with Riga that by sea allowed us to transport whole trunks of Polish literature and so we no longer needed the frontier with Ukraine at Radziwiłłów [Radziviliv] in Volhynia. I proposed that Bogdan use these connections in Radziwiłłów and . . . I would give him the connection . . . to our colleague, an officer of the Border Guards named ZH.[43]

To produce leaflets in Kyiv, Stempowski also gave Kistiakovsky a lithographic stone that had been used by the Polish activists. In the middle of July 1892, Bogdan went to Radziviliv (now Chervono-armiis'k) and appeared at the apartment of Zh (a pseudonym), but didn't find him home. The servant told Kistiakovsky that his employer would return in two days. Kistiakovsky was invited to live in Zh's house; Stempowski described that:

> Unfortunately there were full moon and summer nights and Bogdan, instead of prudently sitting at home and not making himself seen in an unknown border town, went out to look at the city and the surroundings. He did all this in his usual elegant dress and his unusual shaved face. Of course he didn't know that a major spy ring of the Austrian General Staff was discovered there a month earlier and the police and gendarmes were on alert.[44]

Kistiakovsky seemed to be unaware of the impact his striking appearance had on his surroundings—he ignored his surroundings and his comportment revealed that he did not concentrate on the fine points of subversive behavior. His political activity once again led to his arrest in Volhynia on July 4, 1892, when he was charged with not being registered (*bezpis'mennost'*).[45]

Kistiakovsky was held overnight in the police station to be transported to Kyiv by train the next morning. That night he escaped and fled through fields and forests for several days until he was captured with the help of Ukrainian peasants. The visit to Radziviliv ended tragically. Zh was distraught by the police surveillance and harassment, which involved the repeated searching and sealing of the contents of his apartment. Furthermore, consumed with the fear that his friend and colleague Stempowski had been arrested (which was the case), Zh fell into a deep depression and committed suicide by taking poison.

Kistiakovsky never betrayed the Ukrainian national cause, though he was never a reliable and skilled revolutionary. Stempowski stated that:

> I should emphasize that this episode from the revolutionary practice of the future professor is evidence of the inadequacy of his conspiratorial abilities. During the investigation, however, Bogdan conducted himself brilliantly: he refused to confess and didn't name anyone.[46]

Just three years after his first two arrests, Kistiakovsky was again accused of engaging in subversive activities and served several months in prison, from late 1893 to early 1894.

By the time he was twenty-six, Kistiakovsky had been expelled from three of the six major universities in the Russian Empire and exiled from his native Kyiv. Following his last arrest, he was expelled from Dorpat University and, consequently, was forced to continue his studies abroad.[47] However, for the period of one year after his release from prison, Kistiakovsky was placed under official police surveillance (on parole) and could not leave the Russian Empire legally. He decided to spend that year in Libava (Liepaja, Libau), Estland, a German-speaking city on the Baltic coast, to improve his German.[48] His days as a political activist were over at this point and he limited himself to attending meetings and writing articles.

Doctoral Study in Germany and the First Scholarly Works

When he was granted a passport to go abroad in January 1895, Kistiakovsky traveled to Berlin. From 1895 to 1897—the two years between his arrival in Berlin and his official enrollment in the University of Berlin—he devoted most of his time to study and writing. In 1896 his first published work, an introductory article for the new edition of his father's book *Issledovanie o smertnoi kazni* [Research on the Death Penalty], appeared in Moscow. Bogdan Kistiakovsky's extensive introduction served as a supplement, which outlined the new studies and major trends in research on the question of capital punishment since 1867, the year his father, a strong opponent of the death penalty, had first published his book.[49] In 1905 Bogdan collaborated with his mother in writing a letter to the publisher Longin Fedorovich Panteleev, hoping that distributing the book would support public outrage about the death penalty. As Kistiakovsky explained, "In the last year there have been so many executions . . . that it is essential to revive active propaganda against the use of the death penalty and fight for its abolition."[50]

Kistiakovsky's first years in Germany also marked his initial contacts with the Russian Liberation movement and the beginning of his work as a political journalist and editor of Russian journals. Through his acquaintance with the charismatic Russian legal Marxist Petr Struve (1870–1944) and other political refugees in Germany, he learned of such forums for his ideas as the legal Marxist periodical *Novoe slovo* [The New Word].[51] The term "legal Marxist" was first used derogatorily by Lenin after his political break with Struve. The legal Marxists were so named once they made a practice of legally publishing their works inside Russia along with others who strayed from orthodox Marxism and revolutionary socialism. It was in this St. Petersburg-based journal that Kistiakovsky published his first articles in Russian in 1896 and 1897. These articles were noteworthy in that they were the only works where Kistiakovsky explicitly acknowledged the influence of Marxism on his analysis of society and art. The first article comprised a Marxist view of the 1897 retrospective exhibition of the works by the Swiss artist Arnold Böcklin (1827–1901).

Kistiakovsky's descriptions of Böcklin's landscapes were expressed in Marxist terms of social criticism:

> Already Marx, following Hegel, said that it is a mistake to see in evil only evil, for it contains the elements, which when carried to the realm of reality, will create a new more optimistic future. That very bourgeoisie which deprived art of its color and took from art its real character by its purely utilitarian attitudes to nature, established heavy capitalist industry, and at the same time furthered the development of new needs. The tremendous growth of large cities, factory complexes, city smoke, grey tones, . . . all this filled contemporary man with the desire to attain the real quality of untouched nature.[52]

In this same period, Kistiakovsky first got involved in the study of neo-Kantianism, an intellectual school then fashionable among Marxists who sought the ethical aspects of their predominantly materialist approach to knowledge. Among the Russians, the interest in German neo-Kantianism peaked in the late 1880s and early 1890s as an integral part of the philosophical debate on the contradiction between free will and determinism.[53] Kistiakovsky retained a respect for Marxism as a methodology for social analysis even when he stopped considering Marxism the basis for his *weltanschauung* and political views. His conception of Marxism was modified and eventually overshadowed by neo-Kantian idealism which was a dominant philosophical trend among the Russian *intelligenty* and those scholars with whom he came in contact in Western Europe.

Kistiakovsky first read German idealist philosophers, such as Kant and Hegel, when he was imprisoned in Dorpat for his political activities in 1894. He continued his studies at the University of Berlin with the leading neo-Kantians—the sociologist Georg Simmel and, later, the philosopher Wilhelm Windelband in Strasburg. Kistiakovsky established his reputation as a neo-Kantian social and legal theorist when, in 1899, he published his dissertation *Gesellschaft und Einzelwesen* [Society and the Individual] in Berlin.[54] In his study he concentrated on clarifying the methodology for conducting research on society to reveal the relationship between ideals and law. The dissertation, in which the author employed neo-Kantian methodology, constituted a break with Marxism. Kistiakovsky and other neo-Kantians were working to develop the epistemological and theoretical bases for social sciences. Kistiakovsky sought a theory of society that incorporated individual value judgments or ideals that, the neo-Kantians claimed, were missing in the Marxist, empiricist, or positivist approaches to the study of society and the development of social ideals. He was praised for contributing to the formulation of a precise conceptual framework by defining the distinction between the state in the juridical sense and the state in the sociological sense.[55] *Gesellschaft und Einzelwesen* was read widely by members of the German intellectual community at the turn of the century.[56]

Return to Russia and Russian Neo-Kantianism

After receiving his doctorate in philosophy from the University of Berlin in 1899, Kistiakovsky returned to the Russian Empire, where he planned to teach law. Unlike other law students who went abroad to enhance their studies and complete doctorates, such as the legal philosophers Pavel

Ivanovich Novgorodtsev (1866–1924) and Lev Iosifovich Petrazhitskii (1867–1931),[57] Kistiakovsky was not a candidate for a professorial position in law. In order to teach at the university level, he needed both a degree in law and a proof that he had passed the master's examination in state law required by the State Commission.[58] Although it was not ever overtly stated, his political activities in the Ukrainian movement provided yet another obstacle to his career.[59] Kistiakovsky consulted with many friends and colleagues on how to go about finding a position in Russia. Petrazhitskii made Kistiakovsky an unexpected offer—a teaching job in philosophy of law at the Iaroslavskii Lyceum, which Kistiakovsky accepted. Petrazhitskii was impressed with the importance of Kistiakovsky's work in the general theory of law and tried to get him a professorial position in his area of specialization.[60]

To cultivate and deepen his ties with the neo-Kantians in Germany, Kistiakovsky went abroad several months of each year from 1901 to 1917. During his first few annual trips he lived in Heidelberg, where he frequently met with Max Weber and attended the well-known seminars of the neo-Kantian legal theorist Georg Jellinek.[61] At the weekly café meetings that grew out of Jellinek's seminars, Kistiakovsky met Russian lawyers and students of neo-Kantianism such as Fedor Stepun, Sergei I. Gessen, the son of Iosif Gessen (the publisher of *Pravo*), and Sergei I. Zhivago, who was a close friend of Kistiakovsky and Stepun.[62] Once back in Russia, some of the Russians Kistiakovsky met abroad became his colleagues in the unofficial circles of liberal lawyers who discussed possible solutions to the problems of establishing a constitutional system in the Russian Empire.

In this same period, Kistiakovsky's contacts with Russian students of neo-Kantianism in Germany, including Pavel Ivanovich Novgorodtsev and the legal Marxists, Petr Berngardovich Struve, Sergei Nikolaevich Bulgakov (1871–1927), Nikolai Aleksandrovich Berdiaev (1874–1948), and Semen Liudvigovich Frank (1877–1950), led to his involvement with debates on the role of idealism in Russian progressive thought. By 1902 their neo-Kantianism was most clearly expressed in the collection of essays, *Problemy idealizma* [Problems of Idealism]. Among the participants were Kistiakovsky, Struve, Bulgakov, Berdiaev, Frank, and Novgorodtsev, the editor of the volume.[63] Taken together, the articles provided an overview of contemporary criticisms of positivism, materialism, and populism of the past and present intelligentsia. The former

Marxists and Marxist-influenced authors turned to idealist philosophers to find a way to resolve the contradiction between the Marxist conception of determinism and the idea of free will and individualism.[64] These former Marxists' interest in moral ideas was in sharp contrast with their earlier, largely deterministic views of history and social and economic growth of society. In Kistiakovsky's own words, the most pressing problem was " . . . the basic contradiction between the spontaneous path of social events and the conscious strivings of the individual."[65]

In *Problemy idealizma*, both Struve and Kistiakovsky concentrated on the populist spokesman Nikolai Konstantinovich Mikhailovskii (1842–1904) and revealed their concern that their idealism remain distinct from that of the populists.[66] Mikhailovskii, the chief spokesman for populism during the last quarter of the nineteenth century, as well as his predecessor, Petr Lavrov (1823–1900), were also opposed to deterministic views of society or history. In fact, the neo-Kantians' new idealism encompassed some points shared with the populist stance— particularly, concerning free will. Nevertheless, Struve and Kistiakovsky continued to reject the populist views of Russian philosophers and their concept of a development particular to Russia that would avoid capitalism. However, idealism did allow the authors to modify their extreme Westernizing stance. Prior to the publication of *Problemy idealizma,* the writings of both Struve and Kistiakovsky contained few, if any, references to Russian authors.[67] Their neo-Kantian idealism generated interest in the idealist tradition of Russian philosophy. At the same time, Struve and Kistiakovsky sought Russian foundations for their philosophical idealism.

Kistiakovsky's article in the collection was his earliest Russian work where he applied his neo-Kantian approach to the debates among the Russian intelligentsia. (Though he had made his reputation as a neo-Kantian in Germany, in 1899, when his dissertation was published, *Gesellschaft und Einzelwesen* was neither translated into Russian, nor widely read and discussed in Russia.) In his article on the Russian Sociological School, Kistiakovsky asserted that neo-Kantianism could contribute to the solution of the major problem in Russian philosophy, the failure to develop a systematic theory of knowledge. Using the neo-Kantian method to criticize Lavrov and Mikhailovskii's (subjective) sociological method, he elaborated his fundamental rejection of the notion that there could be an exclusively Russian "subjective" ethic on which to base sociological methods of analysis. Although Russian populist sociologists staunchly defended subjectivism against objectivism and possibility against necessity, their idea of subjectivism had been defined as a possible acceptance of the Kantian concepts of *Sein* and *Sollen*. However, Kistiakovsky asserted that a scientific approach cannot ignore the category of necessity and ethics cannot rely only on subjective judgments. He explained that neo-Kantian idealism attempts to establish the objective existence of values and locates inner necessity in the realm of moral duty.[68] With this 1902 article on the "Russian sociological method," which the sociologist Georgii Gurvich claimed " . . . must be regarded as a classic," Kistiakovsky established his position as the leading spokesman for neo-Kantianism in the Russian Empire.[69]

Marriage and Internal Exile

Though his professional life was far from secure and well defined, Kistiakovsky married the Ukrainian activist Maria V. Berenshtam in the first year after his return to Russia. Her father, Viliam Berenshtam, was one of the founding fathers of *Hromada*. Maria Berenshtam Kistiakovsky was active in the Ukrainian women's movement that blossomed after the closing of the Advanced Courses for Women in Kyiv in 1881.[70] She was a prominent organizer of the movement's activities in the form of study circles, whose purpose was to develop national consciousness, political awareness, and community work. Their work continued to the beginning of the 1900s when Ukrainian women organized a women's *hromada* that met under the guise of a women's tea group to circumvent the ban on Ukrainian organizations.[71]

The marriage added further complications to Kistiakovsky's life— Maria was arrested on March 13 for her activities in the Ukrainian movement. "They came to the house with a search warrant and searched from 2:00 A.M. until 8:00 P.M." The police found no connections to organizations, but they did find a compromising letter.[72] When the authorities realized she was pregnant, they released her from prison and subsequently exiled her from all capital cities in the empire. The period of exile forced the Kistiakovsky family to leave their home in St. Petersburg for the remote town of Vologda.[73] In his letters to Georg Jellinek, Kistiakovsky vividly described the practical difficulties of life

in the exile community. On February 5, 1903, he expressed his frustra-
tions, "Life in the Vologda region was difficult because of arbitrary
administrative acts as well as food shortages and unpaved roads that
became impassable during the continuous rains . . . If one understands
the circumstances in which an intelligent Russian is forced to live, then
it is understandable that all educated Russians become neurasthenic
and suffer from weak will."[74]

The Publishing of Osvobozhdenie *and the*
Russian Liberation Movement

In Germany, Kistiakovsky's association with Struve extended to editorial work on the Russian journal *Osvobozhdenie* [Liberation], which
Struve started publishing abroad in 1902 and which was smuggled into
Russia to avoid the heavy hands of the censors. Publication of dissident
material inside Russia was illegal, and *Osvobozhdenie* was considered
the major voice for constitutionalist forces and a projected forum for a
national liberal party. Kistiakovsky's involvement was natural given
that Struve's *Osvobozhdenie* was conceived of as the continuation of
the work of Aleksander Herzen's *Kolokol* [Bell] and Mykhailo
Drahomanov's *Vol'noe slovo* [Free Word]. The journal followed their
tradition of spreading the spirit of anti-government struggle for liberal
constitutionalism and freedom for the individual.[75] Indeed, there was a
real sense of continuity provided by the participation of the radical
zemstvo constitutionalists Ivan Il'ich Petrunkevich and Fedor
Ismailovich Rodichev—they were also involved in backing both the
journal edited by Drahomanov in the 1880s.[76]

During his annual trip to Germany in 1903, Kistiakovsky joined
Russian activists in a trip to Schaffhausen, Switzerland for one of the
first meetings of the Union of Liberation—a coalition of liberal constitutionalists and leftists, including both Marxist and populist socialists.
This meeting was attended by members of the intelligentsia, half of
whom were *zemstvo* constitutionalists, including S. A. Kotliarevskii, N.
N. L'vov, Petrunkevich, and Vladimir Ivanovich Vernadskii, among
others. The other half were writers and publicists—mostly former Social Democrats who had either broken with Marxism (Struve, Berdiaev,
Bulgakov, and Frank) or continued to consider themselves socialists,
" . . . but could find no place in the Social Democratic party dominated

by Plekhanov and Lenin" (E. D. Kuskova, S. N. Prokopovich, and V. Ia. Bogucharsky [Iakovlev]). The participants were hoping to unify the Russian dissident movement into a party or union that would promote the formation of an effective force against the autocracy.[77] They shared the basic goal of ending the autocracy and establishing a liberal constitutionalist (Novgorodtsev) or socialist constitutionalist (Kistiakovsky, Berdiaev, Bulgakov, Frank) regime. Although Kistiakovsky was committed to the constitutional program of the Union of Liberation, he did not become a full-time political activist in the Russian Empire because of his involvement with academic work and the neo-Kantian circle, which he visited each year in Germany. However, considering himself a "socialist-liberationist" within the Union of Liberation, he did maintain contact with the members of the Union of Liberation and other Russian liberals in Germany and Russia through his writing and editing for *Osvobozhdenie*.[78]

In 1904, when he was again in the Russian Empire, Kistiakovsky and his wife Maria received permission to reside in Kyiv. Urban life in Kyiv and other major cities in Ukraine was bustling with the activities of opposition parties. Upon their return to Kyiv, both Kistiakovsky and his wife created the "Banquet Movement" to spread the liberal constitutionalist program of the Union of Liberation. Together with Berdiaev and Bulgakov, among other members of the Kyiv branch of the organization, Kistiakovsky and his wife organized a political banquet at which the first public demand for an end to the autocracy and the establishment of a new government based on a constitution was voiced in Ukraine.[79]

Kistiakovsky's Return to Germany and Collaboration with Max Weber

Kistiakovsky did not stay to follow through with the political demands of the Kyiv-based section of the Union of Liberation. After a mysterious fire in Kistiakovsky's summer home near Kyiv had destroyed all of his manuscripts and notes, he returned to Heidelberg for the winter of 1905–1906 to recover some of his lost research and to complete his project, the publication of the collected political writings of Mykhailo Drahomanov. Kistiakovsky encouraged Struve to publish Drahomanov's political writings that appeared in Russian editions published in Paris in 1905 and

1906. Kistiakovsky's comprehensive introductory essay on Drahomanov acknowledged the importance of the initiative and resources of Ukrainian democrats and revealed his commitment to making Drahomanov's writings available to educated society. In the first volume on the "Center and Periphery," Kistiakovsky hoped to emphasize the failure of both liberals and the central government to recognize the particular problems and national development of the Lithuanian, Belarusian, and Ukrainian peoples—Russians looking at the western borderlands usually would see only Poland and Polish issues. Struve had edited the first volume by the time Kistiakovsky returned to Germany. To continue the project, Kistiakovsky edited the second volume of Drahomanov's political works, which was thematically organized to include Drahomanov's articles on "Political Freedom and Individual Rights." Kistiakovsky also wrote an extensive essay on Drahomanov's life and political activities for the second volume, which he completed and published in Paris during the spring of 1906.[80] A few years later, in 1908, he resumed the project—in Moscow he wrote an introductory essay on Drahomanov for a third volume, emphasizing his desire that Drahomanov's work be available to Russian and Ukrainian readers.[81]

The intense discussions on the Russian Liberation movement among the Russian students and refugees in Germany aroused the interest of their German professors and colleagues. Max Weber, the leading sociologist in Germany, stopped what he was working on and " . . . with bated breath followed the Russian drama for months."[82] At this time, Kistiakovsky became Weber's Russian-language teacher and helped him collect materials on the constitutional movement in the Russian Empire. He and Weber had met in the Heidelberg circles of neo-Kantians through mutual friends, including Kistiakovsky's professors Simmel, Windelband, and Jellinek. As an activist in both the Ukrainian national movement and the Russian Liberation movement, Kistiakovsky was an effective and well-informed source on the social and political currents in the Russian Empire. For instance, he familiarized Weber with the unenviable status of the non-Russian nationalities in the multinational empire and introduced the German sociologist to the writings of Drahomanov. Based on the materials and experiences Kistiakovsky shared with him, Weber wrote two book-length monographs, *Zur Lage der bürgerlichen Demokratie in Russland* [On the Situation of Bourgeois Democracy in Russia] and *Russlands Übergang zum*

Scheinkonsitutionalismus [Russia's Transition to Pseudo-Constitutionalism].[83] In a remarkably short time, Weber produced two serious monographs that surveyed and evaluated the Russian situation, discussing the spectrum of political groups and leading activists. As is evident in the titles of these articles on the Russian constitutional movement and constitutional experiment—though he hoped that liberalism and liberal leaders would be triumphant—Weber was pessimistic about the prognosis for the new regime, which he characterized as only "pseudo-constitutional." In the first place, major groups of the industrial and financial bourgeoisie were not supportive of a liberal order. However, Weber's focus on the future dominance of the bureaucracy did not ever become a reality in the last years of the empire. Kistiakovsky, too, was well aware of the shortcomings of the new constitutional monarchy defined in the October Manifesto of 1905. However, he still clung to the hope that the nominal legal beginnings articulated in this controversial document could be the harbinger of a vital popular movement for constitutional democracy that would soon eliminate the autocracy.[84] When the news of the Russian Revolution of 1905 reached him, Kistiakovsky was back in Heidelberg, closing the offices of *Osvobozhdenie* for Struve, who had already returned to Russia. He and other Russians in Heidelberg started a series of active discussions on the meaning of the October Manifesto and its future.

Educator-Activist in the Post-1905 Period

Kistiakovsky returned to live in Russia after the 1905 revolution and continued to participate in the debates with the neo-Kantians both at home and in Germany on the Ukrainian movement and on law in the Russian Empire. Just before the opening of the First State Duma in 1906, he began his career as a teacher of law at Moscow Commercial Institute where he lectured on governmental and administrative law.[85] He also taught at the special Advanced Courses for Women (*Vysshie zhenskie kursy*), a fashionable cause for liberal academics in the first decade of the twentieth century, since women were not permitted to attend Russian universities.[86]

By 1907 he joined the faculty of Moscow University as an instructor (*privat-dotsent*) in public law. By this time Kistiakovsky was forty-one and feared that he would never get a better position as a professor. He wrote, " . . . I will be an eternal *privat-dotsent* and evidently a 'loser' on the surface." [87] Kistiakovsky admitted that he was now becoming more ambitious and would have liked the satisfaction of getting a more prestigious teaching appointment. Moscow offered no possibilities to head a department of state law, since he only had a master's degree in law and there were younger competitors with both master's and doctoral degrees. His ideal would have been to get a position at Iur'ev University. He thought he had a chance in Iaroslavl', where they would have to take a candidate from outside since the institution offered no master's program. Besides, he wrote that, " . . . in Moscow there was much to distract me from my work and I simply was not made for big cities."[88] In his letters to his mother, he often complained that his health was deteriorating. In fact, Kistiakovsky never did establish a stable academic career and attain the title of professor in the tsarist Russian Empire.

Though he continued to support the constitutional thrust of the Union of Liberation and maintained contact with members of that organization who later became Constitutional Democrats (*Kadets*), he never joined a political party in the newly formed constitutional monarchy. Aware of the lack of sufficient numbers of citizens equipped to participate in the new constitutional system, Kistiakovsky focused his political activities on popular political education. To educate the people of the empire in the rights and duties of citizens and the principles of constitutionalism, in 1906 and 1907 he wrote articles on individual rights, popular representation, the state, and the relationship between state and society. These articles appeared in short-lived liberal publications edited by his friends Struve and Frank—*Duma*, *Poliarnaia zvezda* [The Polar Star], and *Svoboda i kul'tura* [Freedom and Culture].[89]

In addition, along with other liberals, he devoted much of his time to the projects for popular education under the auspices of the Moscow Commission for the Organization of Reading at Home (*Moskovskaia Komissiia po organizatsii domashnego chteniia*), which produced handbooks for subscribers in rural as well as urban areas.[90] He wrote brochures on public law and government as well as the introductory article, entitled "Nashe politicheskoe obrazovanie" [Our Political Education], to the *Politicheskaia èntsiklopediia* [Political Encyclopedia]. In this article Kistiakovsky first defined the basic flaws in Russian political education, the lack of legal or civic consciousness and the lack of government based on law; he felt that the *Politicheskaia èntsiklopedia* would be useful in preparing the citizens of the empire to become self-determining individuals and to replace the pervading tradition of popular helplessness in the face of practical governmental problems.[91] By 1907, Kistiakovsky took on more responsibility in the work of the Commission for the Organization of Reading at Home when he became the editor of the organization's new journal, *Kriticheskoe obozrenie* [The Critical Review], which was designed to provide short synopses of and review current books on politics, state, and society for the lay reader. From 1907 to 1910 he edited and wrote reviews for this journal. In the same period Kistiakovsky arranged for the publication of European neo-Kantian works translated from German into Russian. The works that he edited and introduced comprised books on sociology and law; some titles were Georg Simmel's *Sotsial'naia differentsiatsia* [On Social Differentiation], Georg Jellinek's *Konstitutsii, ikh izmeneniia i preobrazovaniia* [Constitutions, their Changes and Transformations], and Gustav Radbruch's *Metodologicheskaia priroda nauki o prave* [The Methodological Nature of the Legal Sciences].[92]

Through his editorial and journalistic work directed at popular education in government, Kistiakovsky met the literary historian Mikhail O. Gershenzon (1869–1925). Gershenzon asked him to contribute an article to the symposium on the intelligentsia published in 1909 under the title *Vekhi. Sbornik statei o russkoi intelligentsii* [Landmarks: A Collection of Essays About the Russian Intelligentsia].[93] Through this celebrated collection—published in five editions in the course of just one year, 1909—Kistiakovsky's name became widely known in Russian educated society.[94]

After his controversial article, "V zashchitu prava; Intelligentsiia i pravosoznanie" [In Defense of Law; The Intelligentsia and Legal Consciousness], appeared in *Vekhi*, Kistiakovsky continued to publish extensively on law, legal consciousness, and legal theory in a constitutional system. Reinforcing his reputation as one not afraid to stand up for principles, he resigned from the university in 1911 in an act of protest against government interference and repressions in the Moscow University community. [95] Shortly thereafter, Kistiakovsky accepted an invitation to teach in Iaroslavl' at the Demidov Lyceum, a post which allowed him to spend a substantial amount of time in Moscow. He continued at that post until 1917, when he returned to Ukraine.

Iuridicheskii vestnik *and Legal Activism*

Kistiakovsky was an active member of the liberal organization of lawyers that became the Moscow Juridical Society after it was officially reopened in 1912.[96] The organization had originally been founded in 1863 at the time of the Great Reforms. Sergei Andreevich Muromtsev, a law professor at Moscow University from 1877 to 1884 was the leading figure in the organization in its first incarnation shut down in 1891 by Nikolai Pavlovich Bogolepov, the minister of popular education. Kistiakovsky respected Muromtsev as a leader of the Moscow Juridical Society, the editor of *Iuridicheskii vestnik* [Juridical Courier] from 1878 to 1892, and the founder of sociology of law as a discipline.[97] *Iuridicheskii vestnik* under Muromtsev's guidance was "the only Russian journal dedicated to social theory" in the broad sense of the term.[98] This juridical organization and its periodical served as the precursors to the liberal lawyers' organizations dedicated to popular enlightenment prior to the legal reopening of the Moscow Juridical Society. Its journal was once again named *Iuridicheskii vestnik*. Kistiakovsky became the journal's editor at the time of its reincarnation in 1912. From 1912 to 1916, he edited and contributed articles to the journal, and prepared his book *Sotsial'nye nauki i pravo,* which was published in 1916.[99]

Yet, Kistiakovsky did not limit his scope to law and legal theory, for he was seeking the connecting links between the fabric of society and its laws. He enriched his perspective on Russian society and its intellectual life by taking part in lectures, discussions, and debates sponsored by the Moscow Philosophical Society, the Moscow Psychological Society, and the Ukrainian section of the Moscow Society of Slavic Culture, where he gave lectures in both Russian and Ukrainian.[100]

Caught in the Russian-Ukrainian Conflict

Kistiakovsky, who advocated Ukrainian cultural autonomy, was referred to as a "Ukrainophile" by the more nationally conscious Ukrainian intelligentsia, who emphasized the importance of a separate Ukraine. He and other advocates of national cultural rights, such as Volodomyr Naumenko, Mykola Vasylenko, and Mykhailo Mohylians'kyi, did not support the political aspect of the movement; in fact, many were members of the Kadet Party (Constitutional Democratic

Party) and saw Ukrainian interests as part of the quest for a constitutional democracy.[101] Although Kistiakovsky emerged as a major source of information on the Ukrainian movement in Moscow, his anti-separatist approach to the question of Ukrainian national rights made Ukrainian activists living in Kyiv suspicious that he in fact was pro-Russian, or even a Russian agent.[102] Given his sacrifices for the Ukrainian cause, which included his expulsion from universities in Ukraine and Russia as well as his exile, one would assume that he would be treated differently. However, the fact remained that he appeared closer to Russian political activists than to Ukrainian ones because of his political stance. Besides, he had not lived in Ukraine after his student years and was considered a bystander, or an outsider, to the everyday activities in the Ukrainian national movement.

The period following the 1905 revolution unleashed national movements among many of the non-Russian nationalities in the Russian Empire, especially among the Ukrainians. An informal liberalization of the official ban on the use of the Ukrainian language took place. Based on the constitutional rights granted all citizens of the empire in the October Manifesto, the open publication of books and periodicals in the Ukrainian language was allowed *de facto*. This liberal period was reinforced in 1905 by a decision of the Imperial Academy of Sciences that the Ukrainian language was an independent language rather than a dialect of Russian. Though the Ems Ukaz was never formally repealed, the Ukrainian language did acquire official status with the October Manifesto and the temporary press regulations that were issued on November 24, 1905, by the Chief Department of Publications.[103] Daily newspapers began to appear in Ukrainian in major cities such as Kyiv, Ekaterinoslav (now Dnipropetrovs'k), and Poltava. At the same time, a Ukrainian bookshop was opened in Kyiv and the new periodical, *Literaturno-naukovyi visnyk* [The Literary Scientific Herald], published in Ukrainian was launched in both L'viv and Kyiv.[104] This period of liberalization ended with the increase of renewed Russian oppression of the nationalities after 1907. The government reaction to the developing constitutional crisis was to suppress the growing unrest in the empire. In response to the burgeoning pressures from "Great Russian" nationalist elements,[105] Ukrainian nationalists began to reveal anti-Russian sentiments along with their intensified feelings on the subject of ending the autocracy.

Once the brief period of *de facto* greater freedoms for minority nationalities following the 1905 revolution had come to an end and the ban on the use of the Ukrainian language was reimposed,[106] Kistiakovsky found himself profoundly at odds with the Russian constitutionalists. After 1907, Kistiakovsky's identity as both a Ukrainian nationalist and a Russian constitutionalist became more difficult to maintain. Though he shared the Russian liberal goals of ending the autocracy and building a democratic, constitutional system of government, he was disappointed with their failure to note the need for federalism as much as constitutionalism in replacing the Russian autocracy with a democratic form of government in the multinational empire.

Russian nationalism increased dramatically during the constitutional crisis marked by the tsar's arbitrary dissolution of the Second Duma and the promulgation of the new electoral laws for the Third Duma by Petr Stolypin on June 3, 1907. These controversial laws reduced both the left-wing and minority national representatives and proclaimed that the Third Duma should be "Russian in spirit."[107] The Russian national spirit that dominated the Duma only confirmed that Russian society paid little or no attention to the Ukrainian movement. Kistiakovsky and other "Ukrainophiles" followed the rise of Great Russian chauvinism among some of the Russian intelligentsia with horror and worked to counter the trend.

Kistiakovsky worked energetically to inform the Russian intelligentsia of the Ukrainian national movement, its history, its goals, and its contributions to the Russian Liberation movement of the nineteenth century. In 1912, he wrote the book *Stranitsy proshlogo* [Pages from the Past][108] and a series of articles in *Ukrainskaia zhizn'* [Ukrainian Life], a new Russian-language journal organized by the Ukrainian section of the Moscow Society of Slavic Culture. In particular, Kistiakovsky stressed the federalist and constitutionalist traditions of the Ukrainian national movement, presented in Drahomanov's works, and political activities; in this way, he used the history of the movement to point out the flaws in the present constitutional monarchy's policy toward non-Russian nationalities.

In the same period, 1911–1912, Kistiakovsky entered a bitter and impassioned debate with Petr Struve, his old friend and colleague, that started with Struve's Russian chauvinist statement on the nationalities. In response, Kistiakovsky spoke out for national rights for Ukrainians and other non-Russians (see chapter 7). During and after his debate with Struve, which started on the pages of the journal *Russkaia mysl'*, Kistiakovsky's ambivalence and distance from the Ukrainian movement changed; he became more militant about the Ukrainian issue. Just a few years later, after the outbreak of World War I, Kistiakovsky joined other Ukrainian intellectuals and activists in Moscow to save the Galician Ukrainian community, which was caught in the crossfire of the war. This group, which included Volodymyr Naumenko, the editor of the journal *Ukraina*, again failed to find an adequate solution.[109]

After 1914, as the war effort strained the resources of the crumbling Russian Empire, the ruling circles paid even less attention to the needs of the nationalities. By 1915, the growth of Russian chauvinism led Kistiakovsky and other non-Russian members of the intelligentsia to join forces and resources in publishing a Russian-language journal called *Natsional'nye problemy* [Nationality Problems]. The journal aimed at informing the peoples of the empire of the problems and goals of the nationalities. In the spirit of Drahomanov's "Free Union," a draft constitution for a reconstructed Russian Empire first published in 1884, Kistiakovsky advocated federalization within the boundaries of the Russian Empire. That meant the transformation of the Russian regime from an autocracy to a democratic constitutional government with the greatest degree of regional and communal self-government. As Drahomanov explained:

> The independence of a region and people can be achieved either by secession and the creation of an independent state (separatism), or by attaining self-government without that separation (federalism).[110]

Though Kistiakovsky supported co-operation between the Ukrainians living in different states (the Russian Empire and the Austrian Empire), he did not advocate an independent Ukrainian state that encompassed the Ukrainian populations in all surrounding states. He focused on the establishment of individual rights and democratic political institutions based on a foundation of cultural rights for non-Russian peoples in the Russian Empire. Exclusive national concerns were never to override basic universal human values; so Kistiakovsky did not support independence for non-Russian nationalities. He considered the issue of national rights a part of the transnational struggle to end the autocracy and guarantee individual rights to all citizens in the empire.[111] Given the context of an increasingly volatile society and the pressures connected with the Russian Empire's entry into World War I, the rights of the non-Russian nationalities were curtailed even more. After only three issues of the militant new journal on nationalities had appeared, its publication was closed by the authorities as a possible threat to social stability.[112]

From 1915 to 1917, in addition to his work as editor of *Iuridicheskii vestnik*, Kistiakovsky contributed to scholarly journals on law and collected archival materials for a history of the Russian revolutionary movement. As he was collecting documents during the chaos of the revolution, Kistiakovsky was arrested briefly for taking down a list of rules posted by the Temporary Administration during the 1917 events. He was released a day later after one of his students intervened on his behalf.[113] In 1916 Kistiakovsky published his collected essays on sociological method, *Sotsial'nye nauki i pravo* [Social Sciences and Law], in Moscow. He based these articles on the neo-Kantian methodology he first elaborated in his 1889 German dissertation, *Gesellschaft und Einzelwesen* where he attempted to clarify the relationship between social research and law. His 1916 collection on social sciences and law extended the earlier work into a "multifaceted" sociological method for developing a general theory of law.[114]

Revolution and Nationalism

Just after the February Revolution, Kistiakovsky sent his mother an enthusiastic card from Germany dated March 31, 1917: "I congratulate you on the establishment of political freedom in Russia."[115] Later that year he returned to his native Ukraine from Moscow, deeply disappointed with the increasing pressure against the rights of nationalities. Once in Ukraine, he became an active participant in the Ukrainian scholarly community's activities. He first qualified himself as an academician in Kharkiv University on February 5, 1917, when he successfully defended his book *Sotsial'nye nauki i pravo* as his dissertation and earned his second doctoral degree.[116]

Once news of the uprising in Petrograd reached Kyiv on March 1, 1917, the Ukrainians started to organize themselves for self-government. A coalition of the Society of Ukrainian Progressives, the pro-

Kadet Ukrainian Democratic Radical Party as well as Ukrainian socialists created the Ukrainian Central Council, or *Rada*, which became the
designated center for Ukrainian affairs in the Kyiv region. Ukrainian
political figures started returning from tsarist exile, the front, and other
cities to take part in forming the new Ukrainian government. One of
those people was the historian Mykhailo Hrushevs'kyi, who, while on
his way to Kyiv from Moscow, was elected president of the Rada *in
absentia*.[117] He pronounced the end of the Ukrainian problem as the
Rada demanded autonomous status for Ukraine within a federalized
Russian democracy.[118]

During this revolutionary period, Kistiakovsky withdrew completely
from the Russian intelligentsia and focused his energies on the Ukrainian national cause. In 1918 Kistiakovsky was elected professor of law
at the newly established Ukrainian State University of Kyiv. He also
co-authored the first citizenship law for Ukraine, enacted on July 3,
1918. According to the new law, Ukrainian citizenship was conferred
on all Russian imperial subjects residing in Ukraine, subject to their
acceptance.[119]

Meanwhile, Kistiakovsky's life had been complicated by his brother
Igor's activities as minister of internal affairs for the controversial
Skoropads'kyi government. In 1918, when Ukraine was occupied by
the Germans, Igor [Ihor] Kistiakovsky was one of the Ukrainian Kadets
who worked for the separatist Pavlo Petrovych Skoropads'kyi, the
hetman renowned for his reliance on German support of his regime.
The food crisis sparked by German requisitions of Ukrainian supplies
and the harsh penalties delivered by the courts-martial system against
peasants who took up arms against the German command generated
resentment against the Kadets and Hetman Skoropads'kyi. The overseer
of this brutal system was the Kadet "state secretary" and then minister
of internal affairs, Igor Kistiakovsky.[120]

Needless to say, Bogdan Kistiakovsky was not on good terms with
his brother. As Stempowski describes his last meeting with
Kistiakovsky in 1918:

> His younger brother Igor was then the minister of interior and I hoped
> that through his position I could have two Jewish Socialists, who were
> arrested in Vinnytsia, released from prison. Bogdan had just recently
> moved from Moscow and lived with his family amidst unpacked
> baggage in the home of his mother on Kuznechna Street in Kyiv. He

listened to my stories about the cruel behavior of the hetman authorities in the provinces. He said that he would be glad to help me, but his
relationship with his brother concerning their political views was such
that his involvement could only worsen the situation of my clients. He
advised me to turn to our colleague from Dorpat, Mykola Vasylenko,
who then was a representative of the prime minister. And, really, that
advice was good. After I returned to Vynnitsia I found my clients
free.[121]

No doubt, the Kistiakovsky name was not a popular one after the fall
of the Skoropads'kyi Hetmanate. Once the troops of the Central Powers
had withdrawn, the hetmanate was overthrown and Igor Kistiakovsky
and the other Skoropads'kyi government officials fled to the West.[122]

Bogdan continued his scholarly work and devoted much of his time
to research on the history of the Ukrainian national movement. He
worked on the *Rosiis'ko-Ukraïns'kyi slovnyk pravnychoï movy* [Rus-
sian-Ukrainian Dictionary of Legal Terms], which was published post-
humously in 1926.[123] In 1919, he was elected a member of the newly
established Ukrainian Academy of Sciences' Socioeconomic Division,
where he continued his work on the Ukrainian national movement.[124]
One month later, in February 1919, when Kyiv fell to the Bolsheviks
during the turmoil of the Civil War and a state of anarchy ensued,
Kistiakovsky and the president of the Academy, V. I. Vernadskii fled to
Rostov.[125] From there, Kistiakovsky, who had left his family in Kyiv,
traveled to Ekaterinodar (Krasnodar). For a short time, he taught at the
Polytechnic Institute there, until his untimely death at the age of 52. He
died on April 29, 1920, from a heart condition that became acute after
an operation.[126] His unfinished manuscript on the Ukrainian movement
has never been recovered.[127]

CHAPTER TWO

Neo-Kantianism and the General Theory of Law

> For us, "Back to Kant!" signifies, above all, "A return to serious philosophical education." Such education was lacking in the recent era when people were captivated by positivism, and it is necessary to revive it . . . Only a broad philosophical education will help us correctly define the essence of science and its limits; only this can save us from a pernicious dogmatism which fetters thought with the narrow restrictions of time bound formulae and schemata.
>
> Pavel Novgorodtsev[1]

The defense of the freedom and dignity of the individual was a focal point for Russian ethical and social theories from the 1840s until the 1917 Revolution. Many prominent Russian theorists tried to construct an intellectual framework that would allow the development and protection of individual rights and freedoms. In Western Europe and England the proponents of rights, such as John Locke, John Stuart Mill, and Montesquieu were reformers of an existing social and political order, while the Russian intellectuals who defended individual rights were confronted with the arbitrary autocracy and often became radical proponents of abolishing the existing government. The preoccupation with rights was expressed by thinkers who ranged from political conservatives to liberals, from radicals to early Russian Marxists, from individualist Nietzscheans to Kantian-oriented ethical individualists.[2] Among the vocal defenders of rights were the liberal legal theorist Boris Nikolaevich Chicherin (1828–1904), and those influenced by

Kant—the ethical individualist Nikolai Ivanovich Kareev (1850–1931), the neo-idealist and advocate of natural law Pavel Novgorodtsev (1866–1924), and the former Marxists Kistiakovsky, Petr Struve, and Nikolai Berdiaev.

Bogdan Kistiakovsky's goal was to formulate a legal system that would withstand the strains of fundamental systemic transformation and simultaneously provide the framework for the new order. He hoped that a state based on law would be formed and thus, the ultimate chaos of revolution could be avoided. It was to that end that he composed his sociologically based, neo-Kantian theory of law.

Individualism and Neo-Kantianism

Kistiakovsky's interest in the concept of individualism developed during the years he worked with neo-Kantians in Germany. The Heidelberg neo-Kantians with whom Kistiakovsky studied and collaborated were largely scholars of democratic, liberal or even socialist inclinations who were protesting the semi-authoritarian monarchic government in Germany. Because the majority of German scholars at the turn of the century accepted the existing governmental form as an ideal and carried this view into their work, the dissenting neo-Kantians developed a crusading zeal in their methodological studies which were their forum for stressing the vital distinction between fact and value.[3]

Kistiakovsky's own discontent with the existing legal and state system in the Russian Empire was reinforced when he came in contact with his German counterparts involved with the implementation of the newly codified German Civil Code, *The Bürgerliches Gesetzbuch*, which was enacted in 1896 and went into force in 1900.[4] In defining his approach to law, Kistiakovsky noted the discrepancies between the legal forms and practical, historical problems in Germany and in the Russian Empire where he hoped to implement his ideas. By the end of the nineteenth century the dream of German national unity was fulfilled and a new unified government of the German Reich was established. The major task of German jurisprudence was to study the positive law and logically refine it in order to apply it; this meant that the focus of the German school of public law, in Kistiakovsky's eyes, was mainly directed at the analysis of *quid est juris*—"what is"—from the legal point of view.[5]

Kistiakovsky and other Russian legal theorists sought to create a system that could respond to fundamental changes in their society without leading to the total disintegration of the legal order. Russia had outgrown its forms of law and the arbitrarily exercised power of the autocratic government. By the turn of the century, the progressive forces in society strove to institute a legal system based on principles of democracy and constitutionalism. For Kistiakovsky, the law was an expression of a social process; he believed that, "All legal ideas take on their own coloring and shading in the consciousness of each separate nation."[6] In Germany he concentrated on the sociological method for developing laws that were based on the context for which they were written, and in Russia he took into account the specific needs of the empire. While in Germany the emphasis was on improving the existing system—"what is" (*Sein*)—in the Russian Empire the task of legal theorists was to establish a law-based system to express justice, "what should be" (*Sollen*).[7]

The neo-Kantian insistence on individual value judgments as an integral part of any social or philosophical study attracted Kistiakovsky since it was a reaction to the prevailing trends—positivism and materialism. If the individual was to perform a self-determining and morally self-conscious function in guiding the laws of society, as Kistiakovsky hoped, then the role of the individual could not remain obscured as it did in Marxist and positivist analyses of society and social change.

His break with Marxism was best explained in his dissertation, *Gesellschaft und Einzelwesen* [Society and the Individual], which was published in Berlin in 1899. Kistiakovsky noted the influence that two major contributions of Marxism had on his work. First, Marxist writings had addressed the methodological and epistemological characteristics unique to social sciences; second, they had incorporated many aspects of the social sciences that had been overlooked by scholars earlier.[8] Yet, he criticized the Marxist approach to social-science analysis; it relied so heavily on causality in the explanation of social phenomena that it became, in effect, an overly deterministic world view. Social theorists who came from positivist or positivist-influenced Marxist traditions subscribed to the "pure scientific method": 1) empirical sensory observation, 2) measurement, and, 3) inductive reasoning based on the two former processes. This approach precluded the theorists from incorporating personal value judgments in the study.

Influenced by the leaders of the Heidelberg School of the "Back to Kant" movement identified with the philosopher Wilhelm Windelband (of Strasburg University), Kistiakovsky believed that the study of society required both the examination of empirical facts and events and the application of judgment about their significance. The German neo-Kantian movement included a very broad group of intellectuals—as many as twelve contending schools have been identified. The two major schools of neo-Kantianism were the Marburg and Heidelberg Schools. The Marburg School, under the leadership of Hermann Cohen, whose work focused on natural science, concentrated on developing a system of moral norms that transcended both the limits of history and scientific scrutiny. The Heidelberg School (also known as the Baden School), founded by Windelband, focused on the philosophical and methodological foundations of the social sciences.[9] As the legal theorist Arnold Brecht explained, the factors that gave rise to neo-Kantianism in the context of the nineteenth-century intellectual reactions against positivism (the German *Methodenstreit*) were " . . . not to be sought in the emergence of different ideologies, but in what preceded this event by about two decades, the rise of the theoretical opinion that no scientific choice between ultimate values can be made."[10]

Though the neo-Kantians shared a common approach to the distinction between the natural and social sciences, they differed from one another in the definition of the social sciences and, particularly, sociology. Kistiakovsky, like most of the Russian students, was closer to the Heidelberg neo-Kantians since his interest in law and philosophy led him to study society (and later sociology of law), a discipline which was more empirical than idealistic in its focus. In his quest for a social-science methodology, Kistiakovsky insisted on separating empirical studies of "what is" (*Sein*) from normative, subjective conceptions of "what should be" (*Sollen*).[11] Neither science nor formal logic alone could provide an effective method for studying society, the individual and, more generally, the creative, subjective human realm; there was a distinction between studies of natural phenomena in the pure sciences and of non-observable human values in the social sciences.[12]

Kistiakovsky maintained that the social sciences could and should be exact to the point of providing developmental guidelines for the object of the study. He called his philosophical approach "scientific idealism," in which both idealism and science played equally important roles. In his search for a science of society, Kistiakovsky pointed out that the greatest precision in social science could only be possible if the methodology of the pure sciences was used as a model for sociology.[13]

In his conception, the empirical world was based on the interrelationship and compromises between the normative realm of ideas and the exigencies of daily life. Kistiakovsky focused precisely on the problem of the interaction between scientific studies of empirical reality and social and juridical values that could not be judged scientifically.[14] The discrepancies between the empirical world and the realm of values and expectations provided Kistiakovsky with the most fruitful area for studying social change and the social foundations of law.

The individual's role in doing social research and potentially formulating social policy on the basis of sociological studies was explicit (rather than implicit) in his neo-Kantian approach. Kistiakovsky explained, "The evaluation or justification of one alternative and the condemnation of the other could only be conducted by the individual . . . "[15] Kistiakovsky's colleague Max Weber, the neo-Kantian with whom he shared many views on sociology and law, made the same point in the introductory article to the journal *Archiv für Sozialwissenschaft und Sozialpolitik* [The Archive for Social Science and Social Politics] in 1904, when he, Edgar Jaffe, and Werner Sombart took over the editorship:

> To apply the results of . . . (social) analysis in the making of a decision, however, is not a task which science can undertake; it is rather the task of the acting, willing person; he weighs and chooses from among the values involved, according to his own conscience and his personal view of the world.[16]

Kistiakovsky named his approach to social analysis "scientific philosophical idealism." His form of neo-Kantian idealism did not have a metaphysical or mystical implication; instead, he justified the injection of idealism into the study of society in pragmatic terms—by asserting that only through the active participation of the individual could constructive ideals and norms for society be established.

The word *scientific* in "scientific philosophical idealism" indicated that Kistiakovsky shared with the positivists the belief in the power of science to explore all of human life, though, at the same time, he opposed the self-sufficiency of the positivists.[17] He felt that the positivist social theorists, including one of the founders of positivism, Auguste Comte, " . . . have overrated society and thus denied any independent value to the individual (*lichnost'*)."[18] Similarly, he argued that Marxist materialism, like positivism, negated the actions of the individual by attributing all human initiatives to a causal connection with social and economic conditions:

> . . . scientific socialism or Marxism concluded that all human life is determined with natural necessity by social conditions, which are moving and developing according to the law of causality. Even conscious strivings, according to this theory, are only reflections of ripening new social conditions, and therefore the social ideal should in the last analysis be realized only as a result of social necessity.[19]

Kistiakovsky defined the individual as a self-motivated agent in society and sought to balance the determining forces of the state and society with the force of the individual's independent actions and ideals:

> Establishing special laws of evaluation or of norms testifies to the autonomy of the individual, and this autonomy indicates the freedom of the human being in general and the individual in particular. Further, from the fact of independent evaluation and autonomy follows the principle of the intrinsic value of the individual person and the equal value of persons among themselves. Finally, by making freedom and autonomy the basis for individual behavior, an individual creates ideals for himself and demands their fulfillment in reality.[20]

Subjective Sociology

At the turn of the century Russian sociology was just beginning to gain its stature as an academic discipline. Although there were no university chairs in sociology, it was taught in some of the technical schools such as the St. Petersburg Psycho-Neurological Institute.[21] Sociology was a popular discipline among members of the intelligentsia, such as Nikolai Konstantinovich Mikhailovskii, Sergei Andreevich Muromtsev, Petr Struve, and Kistiakovsky, because of their dedication to social change. The intelligentsia traditionally had contributed to *Obshchestvennaia mysl'* [Social Thought] by writing articles that criticized the present social structure and systemic injustice in Russia. The people involved in the social debates of their time, populists, Marxists, and liberals, rejected the sociologists whose studies focused on traditional society. As Judith Zimmerman notes in her article "Sociological Ideas in Pre-Revolutionary Russia":

> This was as true of the populists, who wished to see the peasant commune completely restructured on a freer basis, as it was of the Marxists, who wished to abolish it altogether. The thinkers who attracted attention were those like Gabriel Tarde and Georg Simmel who attempted to explain the processes of social change, and not those whose vision was essentially conservative or reactionary.[22]

Kistiakovsky's concern with how individual evaluations were made in the context of sociological analyses prompted him to take Mikhailovskii to task for not approaching sociology as an area for serious scientific inquiry.[23] After the populist debacle of the 1870s, in which students who tried to educate the peasantry or incite rebellion among it, or both, were arrested, Mikhailovskii grew critical of the populist movement's failure to address the question of individual freedom. He wrote:

> Since we were skeptical . . . of the principle of freedom, we were ready to refrain from demanding any rights for ourselves; not only privileges—that goes without saying—but even the elementary rights that were in the old days called natural rights . . . and we did all this for the sake of one possibility into which we put our whole soul, the possibility of immediate transition to a higher order, leaving out the middle stage of European development, the stage of bourgeois government.[24]

By the beginning of this century, Mikhailovskii became a passionate defender of the freedom and integrity of the individual; society was the major threat to the full development of the individual.

Mikhailovskii and his fellow populist theorist, Petr Lavrov, were both convinced that sociology should be grounded in the phenomenology of Kant's *Critique of Pure Reason* and the ethicality of Kant's *Critique of Practical Reason*. Predecessors to the Marburg and Baden neo-Kantian schools of philosophy, they felt that a synthesis of two Kantian traditions should be developed within the framework of science and a combination of epistemological and historical relativism. They struggled to free sociology from metaphysical dogmatism and improvisation.[25] Mikhailovskii rejected the very idea of a dispassionate appraisal in a sociological investigation; he advocated a sociology immersed in and guided by values—the "subjective method" rather than a passive observation of social phenomena. The sociologist was to identify with the object he was observing by understanding the possibilities of a given situation and thus forming an intellectual bridge that would enable him to go directly from the "real to the ideal."[26]

Kistiakovsky's neo-Kantian sociological method included both normative and empirical (causal and positive) dimensions. He rejected Mikhailovskii's failure to recognize causal necessity as an integral part of sociological studies. The lack of a clear distinction between the categories of the empirical (*Sein*) and the normative (*Sollen*) arose as a consequence when Mikhailovskii substituted the subjective category of "the possible" for causal necessity—objective causes.[27] Mikhailovskii's method incorrectly limited the conclusions that could be drawn from the study of society because it constrained the material of the analysis in an arbitrary and ideologically unsound way. In his approach, the role of values was misunderstood and hence observations of society and its elements were distorted. Kistiakovsky proposed that the formation of ideals should not be derived solely from a populist, empiricist base, but rather, that the ethical realm was to preserve an independence as well as a relation to the empirical. Mikhailovskii confused the justification for "what should be" with its empirical possibility.

Having considered the limitations Mikhailovskii's ideologically based sociological method placed on the individual studying society, Kistiakovsky concluded that the subjective method also could restrict the potential development of individual freedom and self-determination. Mikhailovskii's perceptions of the empirical world were distorted by his populist justifications of particular Russian social and historical conditions.

By 1902, when he wrote his article on the Russian sociological school, Kistiakovsky considered himself an individualist and humanist who could not accept the predominance of the collective, the commune, and the underdeveloped state of civil and political awareness as a given Russian condition: "It is most accurate to recognize the interests of the state and the interests of the individual as having equal value . . . there is no basis for reducing the real foundation of the state and society—the individual—to naught."[28] Though Kistiakovsky hoped to end arbitrary state controls over individuals and groups in the Russian Empire, he never found a resolution to the problem of the relationship between the individual, society, and the state.

In his criticism of Mikhailovskii and the Russian Subjectivist School, Kistiakovsky failed to mention that he shared Mikhailovskii's own concern about the position of the individual in society. This may have been a result of Kistiakovsky's perception or, perhaps, a statement of his political attitude toward the populist world view.[29] In fact, there were certain similarities in his and Mikhailovskii's approaches to social analysis. As Nikolai Ivanovich Kareev (1850–1934), the liberal historian and disciple of Mikhailovskii, wrote, "B. A. Kistiakovsky's introduction of the notions of duty and justice into the study of social phenomena makes him akin to the 'Russian Sociological School,' which some fifty years ago came to be known as sociological subjectivism and which he has subjected to unjust or, at least, unwarranted criticism."[30] Kareev, who was trying to make Mikhailovskii more acceptable to liberals, concluded, "Kistiakovsky differs from the positivists-objectivists who view the historical process strictly as a mechanical or organic evolution . . . in that he recognizes the creative role of the individual in social life. This, too, brings him close to the views of the Russian Sociological School."[31]

Positivism and Natural Law

Unlike the individualism of the subjective sociologists, Kistiakovsky's individualism was steeped in neo-Kantian philosophy. He explained the sources for his position on individualism and an active self-determining role for the individual as follows:

> The recent rebirth of individualism was accompanied by, or more precisely, was conditioned by the rebirth of philosophical idealism. For it was at all times closely connected with individualism. This tie was again confirmed with the recent return to philosophical idealism, which became prominent at the beginning of the sixties of the past century, and gushed forth at first in a call for a return to Kant, and later was channeled into the neo-Kantian movement. This performed a great service for the rebirth of individualism . . . it led to the revitalization of the idea of natural rights, an idea that in the previous era was considered disposed of once and for all.[32]

The revival of the idea of "natural rights" accompanied a growing awareness that the inalienable rights of the individual remained largely nominal rather than practical in existing constitutional governments. Nevertheless, "natural laws"—the absolute standard defining justice and the rights of the individual—were accepted as the basis for continental legal codes. In practice the emphasis was actually on the positive laws rather than the normative "natural laws"—the overall principles creating the foundation for a legal code.

In the theories of major legal philosophers, such as Hegel, Kant, Rousseau, Locke, and Hobbes, the positive laws—the laws applied to society—had been juxtaposed to "natural laws." "Natural laws" were those fundamental, rational principles of public behavior that served as the guiding force for legislators who formulated laws in particular societies. In other words, nature was governed by "natural laws," while civil society possessed a government that framed and applied the positive laws.[33]

For the neo-Kantian legal theorists, such as Emil Lask, Georg Jellinek, and Kistiakovsky, law was a cultural phenomenon comprised of the empirical, positive *Sein*—a part of the fabric of society and law in the juridical sense, and *Sollen*—a complex of norms.[34] The cultural phenomenon called "law" consisted of two aspects: jurisprudence and the social theory of law. Following the example of Jellinek, the first legal theorist to introduce this methodological dualism into his inquiry on law, Kistiakovsky was skeptical of any legal system which presented itself as an absolute set of laws that were not in some way indicative of the social and political conditions of a given society. In his view, continental systems of jurisprudence had failed in practice because those who applied the law to a society tried to make the codified laws into abstract and absolute rules for all times, by merging the positive laws of a society with the values and the norms that the law ought to encompass.[35] The neo-Kantian separation of "what is" and "what ought to be" represented a radical departure both from the scholastic hierarchy of values, in which positive law was only an emanation of a higher "natural law," and from the fusion of the philosophy of law and the science of law in a Hegelian system. The separation of *Sein* and *Sollen* did not imply any contempt for the importance of values in law, but it did assign both to different fields.[36] Kistiakovsky realized that organic theories of society were problematic, but he felt that they were valuable for setting up a system for researching the laws of society.

Kistiakovsky stressed the neo-Kantian distinction between the methodology of the natural and cultural sciences. To embark on a study of the law as a cultural phenomenon, he stressed, it was crucial to eliminate any absolute concepts of law, for they were efforts to make law an emanation of a law of nature. He pointed out that in recent decades it had become fashionable to use Natural Laws to define social phenomena:

> . . . the idea was that the same laws were relevant to society and nature. But this is a superficial use of the words "law" and "Natural Law." There actually are no general natural laws. What science has achieved is revelations about the mechanical, astronomical, laws of physics, chemical and physiological laws. The concept of Natural Law just places all these types of laws into one common group. But there is no higher form of Natural Law . . . If we examine what is common to separate, different types of Natural Laws, only then can we sort out the causal connection of these phenomena as such. This common trend of all Natural Laws is not a law in itself, but rather a norm of human thought.[37]

Based on his understanding of the neo-Kantian distinction between the empirical and normative aspects of scientific inquiry, he recognized the possibility of a person's value judgments coloring his perception of nature or any aspect of empirical reality. That confusion could then carry over into sociological studies if those normative judgments perceived as laws of nature were applied to society. Kistiakovsky explained that the only laws existing in nature were limited, predictable phenomena in the pure sciences; therefore, he insisted,

> . . . one must eliminate laws of nature from consideration in order to remove all misunderstandings, for none of the laws of nature we know in the narrower sense, whether mechanistic, physical, chemical, or physiological can be applied directly to social processes. If we ever discover the laws of social life, then they will in the first place be laws of society, and as such may they be subsumed under a higher methodological concept that perhaps also will be called a law of nature.[38]

The search for general principles of law that might later be called laws of society had to be based on a study of the social foundations for the law. Kistiakovsky explained that:

> . . . in a scientific-social study of law one must . . . proceed from the examination of law as embodied in legal relations. Hence, one must look at the law that lives within the people and reveals itself in the nation's behavior, actions, and circumstances—and not (exclusively) the law that is established in the articles of legal codes.[39]

A sociological analysis of the substance of the law should pursue a theoretical and practical goal: to contribute to the understanding of the legal relations—how the law is carried out in practice—and, on the theoretical plane, to insure that the law is an expression of justice.[40]

When a sociological theorist focused on the articles in legal codes, as the positivist school of jurisprudence did, the structure of legal norms could present unchangeable features that could be described as belonging to the essence of law. Because such an approach to law treated the formal principles of legal systems and the internal logic of the laws as the main elements in legal science, it was not easily applied to situations in which social change was in question. In fact, that approach was dedicated above all to the preservation and justification of the existing governmental order.[41] The more frequent use of analytical positivism in jurisprudence was accompanied by the rise of the modern national state as the progressively exclusive repository of political and legal power.[42]

Analytical jurisprudence, the predominant legal form in nineteenth- and early-twentieth-century continental law, functioned as a closed, self-generating system of values; as such, it required no regular interaction with the empirical world to test the values on which it was based and, hence, to modify the existing system in form or content. Kistiakovsky characterized dogmatic jurisprudence as primarily a descriptive science: for the codified norms were constant in form and were adjusted to meet the needs of a particular society and situation.[43] Since Kistiakovsky rejected the notion that positive laws themselves embodied a standard of justice by which they systematically could be evaluated, he and other legal theorists—particularly, the neo-Kantians—sought a moral authority that could establish a standard of justice for the positive laws applied to society.[44] In fact, he argued that the moral authority should be found inside the people themselves. Instead of using a nation's history as an excuse, individuals should be responsible for it.

Just as neo-Kantianism was a reaction to positivism in philosophy, so the renewed interest in a new sociologically based form of law evolved as an antidote to the reign of analytical positivism in jurisprudence. At the same time, the search for legal ideals expressed a protest against the arbitrary powers of the state which issued positive laws as if they were based on inherent principles of justice.[45]

Sociological Jurisprudence

Kistiakovsky's neo-Kantian legal theory was characterized by his initial methodological dualism—between the normative and empirical realms—combined with an innovative linkage between jurisprudence and a social theory of law. His particular neo-Kantian approach to law provided the basis for a science of sociological jurisprudence. His position was a combination of the positivist commitment to discover the laws of social structure and change and the neo-Kantian claim that the social sciences must discover the characteristics of particular societies and historical eras rather than general laws for all times.[46] In other words, Kistiakovsky considered law a cultural science, *Kulturwissenschaft*, endowed with both a purpose and a meaning. The purpose of law was to become an expression of justice—a concept based on both an intellectual comprehension and human value judgments for a given society.[47]

Kistiakovsky's concept of justice was similar to the neo-Kantian legal theorist Rudolf Stammler's notion of "right law"; in *Die Lehre von dem Richtigen Recht* (translated as *Theory of Justice*), Stammler noted that positive law should be part of the attempt to create "right law"; for "law as a means in the service of human purposes requires for its justification . . . that it is a right means for a right purpose."[48] Similarly, Kistiakovsky wrote, " . . . that which concerns people and occurs among them, can and must be judged from the moral point of view, establishing the justice or injustice of this or that phenomenon."[49] But Stammler, more closely affiliated with the Marburg school of neo-Kantians, was most concerned with creating a codified system of moral norms that were universal rules; and hence, his concept of justice had no systematic relationship with the social realities of a specific society. Kistiakovsky, nevertheless, shared with Stammler the idea of "just," or "right law," but he always referred that ideal concept of "just law" to the context of a specific empirical realm. He explained:

> The process of the realization of justice in the social world is explained by the fact that the human being always and everywhere is inherently striving for justice. For that reason, for each person there exists a given need not only to judge about the justice or injustice of this or that social phenomenon, but also to recognize that the idea of justice should realize itself in the social realm.[50]

Kistiakovsky elaborated Kant's distinction between critical knowledge ("pure reason") of the things perceived by the senses, and goals established by beliefs and volition ("practical reason").

The initial form of Kistiakovsky's social-science method for discovering and formulating social norms in *Gesellschaft und Einzelwesen* " . . . was particularly concerned with clarifying the complex relationship between research in the philosophically based normative sciences (law)." He grounded this approach to the legal sciences in Georg Jellinek's neo-Kantian-based two-faceted theory of the state. That approach encompassed separate studies of the social (positive) and juridical (normative) nature of society and the state.[51] He defined the state as a social phenomenon made of positive and normative elements that actually enacted two sides of the same thing:

> The rules and norms are just the later, already crystallized form of this [social] process, they are the ripe fruits of the same . . . the state was at the same time a society. And in every society, one can find the signs that will later lead to the state organization."[52]

The state was a richly textured social fabric that represented much more than codified laws. The limited conception of the state and law as exclusively positive or normative was not adequate; the broader conception of the laws of the state and society had to bear the capacity for both mirroring (in the sense of *Sein*) and transforming (in the sense of *Sollen*) a specific society. In that dual capacity the law expressed the values that could guide the social transformation as well as mirror the existing reality.

A General Theory of Law

In his collected essays, *Social Sciences and Law*, Kistiakovsky developed his two-faceted approach to the law and the state into a multifaceted sociological method for formulating a general theory of law. He based his methodology for the projected general theory of law on a synthesis of the major trends in jurisprudence, which he subjected to extensive criticism. That multifaceted general theory of law was comprised of four parts—the analytical, the psychological, the normative, and the sociological approaches, which he derived from the four major schools of jurisprudence in the nineteenth- and early- twentieth-century legal theory. Analytical jurisprudence, which Kistiakovsky also called analytical-dogmatic jurisprudence, defined the major task of legal science as the proper application of the formal legal precepts embodied in the existing codes. The psychological approach was presented by his friend Lev Petrazhitskii, who had become a professor of law at St. Petersburg University. In its most coherent form it stressed the intuitive, instinctive, and emotional bases for legal behavior. The normative approach to jurisprudence was most clearly elaborated by Pavel Novgorodtsev, Kistiakovsky's colleague on the Moscow University law faculty and a fellow neo-Kantian, who perceived law as an expression of universal and transcendent values of life. Law in Novgorodtsev's conception was limited to the ethical normative realm, or, in neo-Kantian terms, the realm of *Sollen*—"what should be."[53] And lastly, the sociological approach to jurisprudence was to be based on sociology and a general theory of law.

The sociological school of jurisprudence was first articulated by Professor Sergei Muromtsev, who taught law at Moscow University. Muromtsev was a guiding figure in the Moscow Juridical Society; his political activities caused his dismissal from the university. The Juridical Society's meetings formed a place where constitutional ideas were discussed actively and law became part of the realm of politics.[54] Years later, Muromtsev became the chairman of the First State Duma (1906), where he demonstrated his devotion to proper parliamentary procedures and democratic processes.[55]

Kistiakovsky acknowledged his intellectual debt to Muromtsev, the first person to articulate the importance of sociology of law as a discipline.[56] Muromtsev argued that legal studies must address both the universal characteristics of law and the unique legal formations in specific societies. It was Muromtsev who first considered law a system of social relations. Kistiakovsky shared with Muromtsev the conviction that the basic fallacy of most contemporary studies of law (in their respective eras) was the objectivization of abstract legal principles when the focus should have been on the positive law—a study of the social processes in the formulation of the law.[57]

As pointed out above, Kistiakovsky considered the analytical school inadequate in dealing with social change or those legal situations whose conditions do not lend themselves to abstract generalizations or precise logical formulations. Though he valued Petrazhitskii's contribution in bringing attention to the subjective psychological factors that affect the formulation and the implementation of the law, he objected to Petrazhitskii's failure to incorporate positive or social foundations into his conception of the law.[58] Similarly, he criticized Novgorodtsev's failure to acknowledge the importance of the empirical foundations of the law. In fact, Novgorodtsev, his fellow neo-Kantian, pointed out the limitations of an empirical study of society based on the epistemological approach. Kistiakovsky, on the contrary, considered the social foundations of law a progressive orientation that aimed at explaining the bases for social integration, cohesion, and evolution.

Kistiakovsky subjected each of these orientations in jurisprudence to extensive criticism. He clearly was only interested in utilizing those aspects of the approaches that he felt would enhance and broaden the scope of his own methodological problems inherent in the social sciences.[59] Kistiakovsky hoped to discover the laws, or consistent patterns, revealing the interaction of juridical norms and the social fabric of the environment. While he was opposed to the neglect of the empirical foundations for the law in society, he did not merely support the sociological approach to law proposed by Muromtsev. Law was not only a social phenomenon that could be discovered as part of a social structure. Kistiakovsky pointed out that it was essential to study the normative aspect of the law. The way in which ideal values are expressed in a society could reveal how human ideals influence a society and its social evolution.[60] Furthermore, the law's expression of justice could not be discovered through a purely empirical approach.[61]

By incorporating normative, analytical, psychological, and sociological approaches to jurisprudence in his sociologically based method, Kistiakovsky believed he could accomplish two goals—both broaden the empirical base and make the theoretical design of the sociological approach more precise.[62] It was essential both to isolate specific components of society and nature for a serious study of the empirical foundations of law; at the same time, on the normative plane, the connection between the meaning of law and its duty to express justice could not be overlooked.[63]

Kistiakovsky's commitment to law based on social science research led him to assign social science and law a significant role in the process of change. He insisted on combining no fewer than three quite distinct factors: the empirical-descriptive, the logical-analytical, and the moral-normative.[64] In other words, the process for developing laws consisted of two factors conventionally considered part of scientific activity in combination with one factor drawn from philosophy—the moral norms. At this point, the neo-Kantian dualism was to take the form of first clearly separating and then closely integrating science (closer to *Sein*) and philosophy (closer to *Sollen*). Kistiakovsky's social science method, when applied by the legal researcher—the law finder and law maker—was to function as the intermediary between "what is" and "what should be" of a specific time and place. In this way, the methodology applied by the legal researcher would act as the connecting force between the empirical and normative factors in the relationship of the individual to the society.

Kistiakovsky shared with his colleague Max Weber the view that lawyers and other legal practitioners (activists) would play a leading role in the formulation, implementation, and legitimization of the laws of state and society.[65] His basic sociological orientation was similar to Weber's in that they both maintained that a social scientist should neither ignore causality nor accept the method of analysis used in the natural sciences as a dogma for sociological method. Causality in sociological terms had to be free of any anthropomorphic and metaphysical implications as well as ideological considerations. That form of causality was best described by Weber's term "objective possibility," which meant that it was logical to conceive of it as an empirical entity.[66] To enhance his own description of "objective possibility," Weber referred to Kistiakovsky's incisive critique of the ideological use of the "possible" by the Russian subjective sociologists who actually eliminated causality from their method by identifying "the possible" with their ideological goals. Though they did differ on some details in their proposed approaches to ascertaining the nature of causal relations,[67] they both clearly rejected any type of "unconditional necessity" for the social sciences.[68]

Though Kistiakovsky claimed his study was confined to setting forth a methodology, he went beyond his stated goals when he stressed the importance of discovering a unifying element that would make it possible to perceive a specific society as if it were an integrated, individual social entity. He claimed, "The unity of society is based on the creation of various groups of persons who in their emotional life are assimilated . . . " In fact, he explained, "The character of the unified social spirit that binds the society together is similar to the individual spirit."[69]

Kistiakovsky cited an example of such a natural unifying spirit in the German people during the wars of liberation in 1813 and 1871, when they identified themselves and their goals with those of the existing state. At those times, during the Napoleonic and Franco-Prussian wars, a commonly accepted aim was considered primary by both the state and the society.[70] To Kistiakovsky, this common goal expressed a form of general will grounded in social reality rather than a general will based on an absolute universal concept of law. His search for a "unifying spirit" in society revealed his concern with finding evidence of the individual's goals expressed in the government and state, and the state's goals reflected in the individual and society. To solve the problem of harmonizing the individual's interests and social position (or role) with the projected goals of the society and state, he sought a way to reconcile the society with the goals of the government and state of a (hypothetical) social order. He never resolved the theoretical problem of the relationship between the individual and society other than to conclude hopefully that the individual and the society must be ends in themselves through the "ultimate merging of the individual and society into one harmonious whole, whereby each of them, as an end in itself, would complement the other, and not suppress or abolish the other."[71]

The question is, how did Kistiakovsky conceive of such a merging of the individual and society into a harmonious whole? In methodological terms, he was essentially advocating a reconciliation of the initially separated studies in the realms of *Sein* and *Sollen*. Though Kistiakovsky did avoid metaphysical obscurantism, he lived and worked at a time when the concept of the general will was in vogue. The revival of the idea of natural law and forms of general will was prevalent in both Western Europe and the Russian Empire at the turn of the century; it was part of the search for ideals to provide the positive laws with a standard of justice. Georgii Gurvich, the renowned sociologist of law, described the interplay of socialist individualism with the concept of the general will.[72] Kistiakovsky considered it possible for the autonomous wills of the individuals in society to function as constituent parts of the general will. That might have been implemented by invoking Kant's famous "categorical imperative": "Act so that the maxim of thy will may at times be valid as a principle of universal legislation." In effect, Kistiakovsky's idealized concept of potential social and political harmony allowed the empirical data—the positive—to gain a normative force that would permit "what is" to coalesce with "what ought to be." Though he objected to the application of Rousseau's theory of the general will if it was based on an absolute type of "natural law," he used the idealism of an empirically based neo-Rousseauistic position to resolve the problem of reconciling the norms and empirical data of his method for developing a legal system.[73]

Kistiakovsky's theory of social science and law served as the foundation for a projected sociologically based concept of law and potentially a form of general will that would provide the moral standards to guide society and its laws. His particular neo-Kantian method was distinct and controversial in German neo-Kantian circles precisely because of his belief in the possibility of discovering a unifying spirit and reuniting the positive and normative aspects of the study of society. This is a problematic area of Kistiakovsky's thought—by 1912 he was outspoken about his disagreements with the metaphysical idealists, while his own idea of a unifying spirit seemed close to the metaphysical.

Though other neo-Kantians, such as Max Weber and Emil Lask, looked for factors that interacted with both categories of *Sein* and *Sollen*, they did not believe that a reconciliation or reintegration was possible. They geared the study of society and law to developing a mode of perceiving reality rather than a means for ultimately formulating a system of ideals. Weber explained, " . . . it can never be the task of an empirical science to provide binding norms and ideals from which directives for immediate practical activity can be derived."[74] In the social-science methodology Weber constructed, the concept of the "ideal type" was formed on the basis of individual value judgments. Weber clearly separated those ideas from the empirical reality to be studied, for, as he stated, " . . . this quite naturally gives rise to the danger that the ideal type and reality will be confused with one another."[75] Emil Lask never made it clear when he considered law a means of fulfilling individual values and when—an embodiment of social values. However, for Lask the law could never be both; a community of persons freely and intuitively agreeing on the goals for the community remained an ideal.[76] As mentioned above, Hans Kelsen, the leader of the Marxist-influenced Vienna school of neo-Kantians, opposed any attempt at interrelating the social and juridical aspects of a study of law. He believed that jurisprudence was exclusively a normative science. In fact, Kelsen became the sharpest critic of Kistiakovsky's approach to social science and law. Kelsen, himself a neo-Kantian, agreed with the separation of the normative and empirical aspects of a study of law, but he argued that Kistiakovsky's attempt to directly connect the social sciences (*Sein*) with the law (*Sollen*) could never be accomplished in a concrete fashion.[77]

Kistiakovsky considered Kelsen's purely normative definition of the law by no means adequate as a mode of considering the possible legal forms for a society such as the Russian Empire, where the laws had been expressed in the form of absolutes imposed on the society from above. His own neo-Kantian method developed out of his early commitment to Marxism combined with scientific social analysis, individualism, and humanism. Individual citizens had to take responsibility for their history, instead of using it as an excuse for their fate. Much as the philosopher Vladimir Soloviev, Kistiakovsky emphasized absolute ethical standards as well as individual responsibility. However, he rejected the ideas of the ethical anarchists such as Leo Tolstoy, who disregarded existing social, political, and legal institutions.[78] For Kistiakovsky, law was a cultural phenomenon that, ideally, should become a moral force representing justice.

CHAPTER THREE

Human Rights: A Pre-Revolutionary Model

The major theoretical problem and practical task at the turn of the century, in Kistiakovsky's view, was to end the Russian autocracy and replace it with a governmental system that made human rights its focal point. He sought to establish a socialist, federally organized constitutional system in which human rights could be guaranteed and fully enjoyed by all citizens in the complicated fabric of the multinational empire. Kistiakovsky's personal experience with the denial of individual rights in his native Ukraine—his arrests, imprisonments, and expulsions from universities in the Russian Empire for his activities in the Ukrainian national movement—played a formative role in the development of his primary concern with the rights of the individual. Although he was a socialist influenced by Marx's writings, he was unwilling to leave the question of the role of the individual in a secondary position as did many Marxists. In Kistiakovsky's perception, the task facing the Russian constitutionalists entailed much more than abolishing the autocracy and granting rights to all peoples. The very concept of individual rights was unfamiliar in the Russian Empire, where neither peasant nor intellectual had the rights and duties of citizens. The prerequisite for the effective institutionalization of a constitutional regime in the empire required that the state's activities be based on law. The individual had to change his or her self-perception from a passive subject of the tsar to an active, self-determining citizen. This new individualism upheld by a new legal definition and a changed self-perception (or, self-definition) was Kistiakovsky's demanding formulation for the foundations of human rights.

Inhabitants of the Russian Empire were officially defined as "subjects" by the most progressive legal document of the tsarist era, the Basic Law of 1906. The autocracy dealt with the population according to certain rights and privileges granted on the basis of social and economic status. The tsar was the autocratic (*samoderzhavnyi*) and unlimited (*neogranichennyi*) monarch,"[1] and there was little hope of "contractual rights" between sovereign and subject. In fact, no prospect of the tsar's voluntary recognition of "natural" or "human" rights was expected to effectively lay the foundation for transforming subjects to citizens.

The legal status of all persons in the Russian Empire was determined by their social position as classified by legal estates in the *soslovie* system. The first estate was the nobility, then came the clergy, and then there were separate estates for town dwellers, peasants, and others in society. Each of the estates had its own legally defined rights and obligations.[2] Though class relations were changing, the state reacted to the increase in social and political unrest by trying to reinforce the status quo.[3] But new class groups, such as workers, professionals, and the intelligentsia, had no place in the antiquated *soslovie* system. The state recognized only an amorphous category called the *raznochintsy* (people of various origins who no longer belonged to a traditional group); thus, it became difficult to decipher the newly emerging groups in legal or social terms.

By the turn of the century, the social classifications of legal status were so ill-defined that some scholars have noted the existence of two distinct worlds in Russia. According to Frank Wcislo, for example, one world was the heritage of the collective *soslovie* system divided into the arbitrary autocracy, the landowning nobility, and the rural world, while the other "represented an underdeveloped but emerging civil society of classes, defended by a reformist bureaucracy willing to face a modern world that traditional Russia preferred to ignore."[4]

After the 1905 revolution, a clear opposition to the *soslovie* system was articulated during debates in the First and Second Dumas in 1906 and 1907. On June 2, 1907, the day before the arbitrary dissolution of the Duma by Petr Stolypin, the tsarist minister of interior,[5] a proposal for the abolition of the *soslovie* system stated:

> For the full development of the principle of legal equality and individual freedom in the state, it is necessary to abolish the *soslovie* system, that is, the division of the population into groups solely according to the principle of common origin, as a result of which members of *soslovie* corporations possess political and other rights

(established by law and transmitted by heredity), which are unequal for various groups.[6]

But for the tsarist regime, the very idea of formulating a legal system that would fully encompass the multifaceted worlds of the pre-revolutionary Russian Empire was an awesome, if not impossible, task. Besides, it would have meant that the autocrat's personal control over the constitutional monarchy would be curtailed. But if the government wanted to construct a viable stable legal order, then the disparate elements of the complex society had to be revealed and defined, and then integrated into one legal order that would hopefully make civil society cohesive. This process was complicated by the fact that the empire was an incongruous mixture of nationalities with large capital cities and a growing number of industrial complexes, all set against the vast backdrop of the overwhelming majority—the peasantry.

The idea of constructing a rule-of-law, constitutional government formed of elected representatives to replace an existing authoritarian or autocratic regime was associated with the West European concept of liberalism. But the liberal movement that formed in Russia was different from the liberal tradition in Western Europe. Russia was a less developed society whose liberal ideas were carried by the minority professional intelligentsia and *zemstvo* radicals rather than the substantial business middle class of Europe, which called for individual freedoms, a law-based state, a representative legislative assembly, and, in economics, a policy of *laissez-faire*. In Russia a vital socialist movement predated the growth of modern liberalism by nearly half a century. As Petr Struve explained:

> In all other countries socialism grew up on the soil already prepared by evolution of the regime of legality based on the principles of liberalism and democracy. It was not so in Russia where, after the Decembrists, who were not yet influenced by the ideas and yearnings of socialism, all the ensuing struggle for political reforms became closely intertwined with socialist tendencies and ideas.[7]

To replace the autocracy with a constitutional order based on individual rights, the rule of law, and a parliamentary system with elected representatives would only solve part of the problem in economically underdeveloped Russia. *Laissez-faire* liberalism was never a strong movement in Russia; on the contrary, the program of the Russian Liberation movement made a total commitment to democracy, bringing forward a demand for political, social, and economic equality. This meant a governmental system modeled on a welfare state rather than a *laissez-faire* one.

The Concept of Rights in the Union of Liberation and the Kadet Party

The goal of the journal *Osvobozhdenie* was to serve as the voice for a broad national movement for the liberation of Russia. In its first editorial, Struve wrote:

> The cultural and political liberation of Russia can be neither the monopoly nor the main burden of a single class, a single party, a single doctrine. It must be a national cause, one embracing all the people, one that will evoke a response from every heart able to distinguish between what is moral and what is amoral in politics, a heart, which for that reason is unwilling to come to terms with the violence and arbitrariness of a band of bureaucrats who administer a great people without being subjected to any controls and responsibility.[8]

Elaborate attempts to create a national coalition of *zemstvo* liberals, constitutionalists, and radicals failed during 1903 until Struve openly proclaimed the need for a liberal organization on the pages of *Osvobozhdenie* later that year.[9] The stormy discussions about the nature of the projected liberal organization were led by Pavel Miliukov, who wrote an article in *Osvobozhdenie* objecting to the lack of homogeneity and of a common, definite aim that would be accepted by the membership. Miliukov argued that the coalition Struve envisioned would include moderates and liberal Slavophiles, such as Mikhail Stakhovich and Nikolai Khomiakov, who were not yet constitutionalists.

> There is a definite need to think and care about a liberal organization. But because of the current mood of the *zemstvo* milieu, one must proceed very carefully: it would be more than enough at this stage if it were possible to organize a strong nucleus of the party made up of convinced constitutionalists. To win over at once a whole army of unreliable and partly suspicious elements around a vague slogan would be a great tactical error, weakening the energy of the movement and destroying its moral significance.[10]

Kistiakovsky's own opposition to the plan for a liberal party grew out of his fear of the radical forces in the coalition. In a letter to Struve in April 1903, Kistiakovsky warned that agitation for the purpose of forming an illegal political party "Liberation" was both premature and harmful because *Osvobozhdenie* was a publication designed precisely for people who would be reluctant to join an illegal party. Kistiakovsky feared that political radicals would become the predominant members of such an organization and subsequently destroy the liberal spirit of the journal and the liberal movement.[11] His letter was an emotional appeal to avoid using authoritarian measures in the course of organizing a political movement. Kistiakovsky felt that by organizing a political party, the radical elements would take over and start issuing ultimatums. Further, he feared the leadership, instead of being a natural outgrowth of the period of reforms, might transform into a central committee of the party issuing orders. Kistiakovsky ended his letter with a dramatic declaration to clarify his position: he did not want "to facilitate the replacement of the Romanovs' absolutism with the absolutism of Lenin in the name of the autocratic people."[12]

Although Kistiakovsky strongly objected to the formation of a party, he put his fears aside and, because of his commitment to the movement and to the establishment of a constitutional government, attended the first national conference of constitutionalists in Schaffhausen in August 1903. The secret meeting developed out of the provocative anti-autocracy articles in *Osvobozhdenie,* and the conference was organized clandestinely to prevent the Okhrana from finding out about it. To avoid the authorities, who were known to be spying on Struve in Germany, the conference days were spent in mountain towns near Schaffhausen— Singen, Hohentwyl, Radolfzell.[13]

The main agenda of the conference was the form the Liberation movement would take—a political party or a national front—and its program. Sharp differences of opinion among radical members of the movement caused numerous extended debates ranging from the name of the organization to the substance of the program. Concrete decision making was delayed by the conflicts among the delegates. The program for the new organization was not adopted formally until the first congress met six months later in St. Petersburg.

The initial congress of the Union of Liberation met in St. Petersburg in January 1904. The participants were fifty representatives of twenty local Unions of Liberation; they represented a broad spectrum of political views ranging from *zemstvo* constitutionalists to liberal academics, former legal Marxists, revisionist socialists, and Social Democrats.[14] At the St. Petersburg meeting, after a lengthy discussion, the participants agreed on the name "Union of Liberation" and voted on a program. The program, adopted at the congress, demanded the end of the autocracy and its replacement by a constitutional-democratic government that would be elected by the four-tail formula—universal, equal, and direct suffrage, and secret ballot.

> The first and main task of the Union of Liberation is the political liberation of Russia. Considering political liberty in even its most minimal form completely incompatible with the absolutist character of the Russian monarchy, the Union will struggle before all else for the abolition of autocracy and the establishment in Russia of a constitutional regime. In determining the concrete forms which the constitutional regime can assume in Russia, the Union of Liberation will make all efforts to have the political problem resolved in the spirit of extensive democracy. Above all, it recognizes as fundamentally essential that the principles of universal, equal, secret, and direct elections be made the foundation of the political reform.
>
> While placing the political demands in the forefront, the Union of Liberation recognizes as essential the definition of its attitude in principle to the socioeconomic problems created by life itself. In the realm of socioeconomic policy, the Union of Liberation will follow the same basic principle of democracy, making the same direct goal of its activity the defense of the interests of the laboring masses.[15]

The program of the Union of Liberation also supported the right to self-determination for non-Russian nationalities in the Russian state. In relation to Finland, the Union supported the demand for the restoration of the constitutional order which existed in that country prior to its violation during the present reign.[16]

The issue of *Osvobozhdenie* that contained the program of the Union of Liberation appeared not long after the events of Bloody Sunday in 1905. Thereafter, the censorship regulations were relaxed and *Osvobozhdenie* ceased to be one of the most important sources of information. The less stringent policy on press censorship made it possible to publish papers inside Russia, and the complicated and expensive process of smuggling *Osvobozhdenie* from abroad became unnecessary.[17]

Once the October Manifesto was proclaimed on October 17, 1905, the Constitutional Democratic Party (Kadets) was the largest political party to develop by organizing local groups throughout the country to participate in the first elections. The Kadet Party actually grew out of the foundations established by the Union of Liberation and the Union of *Zemstvo* Constitutionalists. At the First Party Congress (October 12–18, 1905), the Kadets adopted a program that essentially reproduced the March program of their predecessor, the Union of Liberation. It combined "constitutional" and "democratic" reforms that would unite the greatest number of nonrevolutionary intelligentsia.[18]

The Kadets' basic commitment was to the welfare of Russian society as a whole rather than to any particular class, estate, or socioeconomic group. For many Kadets, the nonclass, national character of their program was reflected in the advocacy of economic or equity rights for all social groups. In other words, they insisted on individual liberties and equality before the law of all citizens, including non-Russian nationalities, who were to have cultural self-determination as a basic right. Article 3 stated the demand for democratic local self-government as well as autonomy for Poland and the restoration of the Finnish constitution.[19]

In the economic realm, the Kadet program supported an eight-hour working day, organization of trade unions, compulsory government health and old-age insurance. The program included a provision for abolishing peasant redemption payments, the abolition of indirect taxes, and the gradual institution of a graduated income tax and other financial reforms. On the subject of land reform, Article 36 of the program proposed a substantial increase in land held by working peasants. This was to be achieved through the distribution of monastic and state territories as well as the "expropriation" of land held by private owners with fair compensation at "equitable (not market) prices."[20] The Kadets' view of a liberal constitutional order was that of a state based on social welfare and social justice—not a *laissez-faire* state.

Kistiakovsky, who was active in both the Union of Liberation and the early activities of the Kadet Party, was influenced by their dedication to social justice when he advocated both the political and economic rights of citizens. His unique contribution was to take the concept of human rights and combine it with a respect for legal concepts and institutions. He identified the foundation of a democratic system as the right to a dignified existence, which incorporated both economic and political rights. The concern with economic rights was nurtured by his awareness of inequalities in existing constitutional systems in the

West. They were not fully democratic because all enfranchised classes did not in fact exercise their right to vote and some systems, such as the French one, were overly centralized. To establish human rights in the Russian Empire, much more than the problems involved in instituting an equitable legal system, had to be solved. Superimposing a legal system would not make the new form effective if the citizens of the country did not comprehend the meaning of their rights and how to exercise them.

In Kistiakovsky's view, a representative constitutional government responsive to the complexities of the rapidly changing underdeveloped empire would have to do more than simply borrow the existing Western constitutional prototypes. He considered law as an expression of a social and political process: "No one, single idea of human freedom, of rule of law, of the constitutional state, is the same for all nations and all times, just as no social and economic organization, capitalist or otherwise, is the same in all countries. All legal ideas take on their own coloring and shading in the consciousness of each separate nation."[21] Drafting an appropriate and effective constitutional document for the Russian Empire required not only an examination of concepts of human rights, but also their reconsideration in the context of social, economic, and political conditions.

Political and Economic Rights

Kistiakovsky first addressed the practical aspects of defining, implementing, and guaranteeing the rights of the self-determining individual just before the Revolution of 1905 when he wrote the article "Prava cheloveka i grazhdanina" [The Rights of Man and the Citizen], in which he explained, " . . . it is where those freedoms are not recognized that the most burning and urgent demand of the society becomes the declaration and implementation of those rights."[22] However, merely borrowing forms of individual rights, such as those categorized in the French "Declaration of the Rights of Man and the Citizen" (1789) and the American "Declaration of Independence" (1776), could not be an effective solution for Kistiakovsky. He explained that:

> . . . it was not enough to declare the principles of individual and
> social liberties for them to become part of popular consciousness and
> be actually practiced in public life. The principles had been pro-

claimed repeatedly, but their implementation proceeded very slowly and often independently of declarations. The strength of the ideas in practice turned out to be less significant than those who first declared them imagined them to be.[23]

Individual political rights were merely nominal if imposed on a society without being reformulated to reflect the potential for exercising those rights in a particular social and economic structure. For instance, in a capitalist society with a democratic constitutional government, all citizens may enjoy freedom of expression according to the constitution guiding that government. However, there is no (automatic) mechanism guaranteeing an individual the opportunity to exercise these political rights publicly. In a society that encourages economic and political competition, a writer's chances of expressing opinions are determined by the economic market (demand) for the writer's work, the writer's ability to sell, or the acceptability of his or her ideas to those holding the largest share of economic and political power. In this way such political rights as the freedom of speech, association, and expression are not guaranteed equally for all members of society—as long as one class of citizens is able to dominate another by virtue of its economic power.[24] In sum, then, only when individuals in a society enjoy economic rights can there develop a guarantee that all citizens exercise their political rights equally. Conversely, only when individuals in a society enjoy political rights can there develop a guarantee that all citizens exercise their economic rights equally.

Political rights included governmental nonintervention in the individual's private life, the rights to privacy and freedom of association, as well as the right to participate in the guidance and governance of the state and all of its affairs. Economic rights were the individual's rights to share in the profits of the society's productive forces, to have access to such services from the state as social security, health care, and education, and to develop his or her talent.[25] These were corollaries to the right to work; theoretically, these economic rights provided the foundation for the formulation of socialist rights.

Socialist economic rights were first distinguished from political rights by the Austrian socialist and legal theorist Anton Menger (1841–1906). They included the right to the full product of one's labor, the right to work, and the right to a dignified existence.[26] Though Kistiakovsky commended Menger's contribution to the formulation of individual socialist rights, he considered the concept of the full product of one's labor described by Menger inadequate because it was conceived in a vacuum. Only in a communist society that had absolutely no net investment for economic growth could individuals earn the full product of their labor. Moreover, it might not be possible to exercise the rights Menger propounded in a technologically advanced industrial society where the individual's labor becomes increasingly alienated from the commodity being produced. A conception of socialist rights in isolation from the political social and economic arena in which they would be exercised, tested, and implemented would probably leave those "rights" in a purely formal, nominal role.

Kistiakovsky was as critical of those who formulated socialist rights in the abstract as he was of political and legal theorists who had borrowed Western codified forms of political rights without attempting to articulate them in an appropriate context. Laws expressing individual rights in the abstract would either remain ideals on paper or become the instrument of the group in political power.

Subjective Rights

Kistiakovsky, like the other legal theorists Georg Jellinek, Hans Kelsen, Karl Renner, and Emil Lask, objected to continental legal systems that had deceptive apolitical facades while containing a law divided into unequal private and public realms. It was precisely that distinction between public and private that established the arbitrary status of power under the special guise of public law and made the legal system an instrument of the state.[27] Karl Renner and Hans Kelsen, who both were members of the Marxist-influenced Vienna School of neo-Kantians, considered the distinction between private and public law a vehicle for the incorporation of capitalist political ideology into the legal system. Public law encompassed the relationship between the state, the public authorities, and the individual, while private law regulated the relations between individuals. One of Renner's major works, *The Institutions of Private Law and Their Social Functions,* described the means by which the private law could be manipulated by the public realm—by those in control of the political system.

Kistiakovsky argued that a legal system was one of the tools of the state, and the existing government perpetuated itself mainly in the public-law sphere, where it controlled the largest share of available political and economic resources in a particular society. The division of law into these two spheres revealed a relationship between those in the superior position, controlling the public law realm, and those in the inferior position, a part of the private law realm. Since the existing governmental order in such a society (which was presumably capitalist) chiefly looked to perpetuate its own primary position, the individual and his rights became secondary. To avoid limiting individual rights to objective, derivative rights, Kistiakovsky insisted that the self-determining individual be able to exercise subjective rights in both the public and private sectors of the society and its legal order.

He praised Georg Jellinek as " . . . the first legal theorist to classify both public and private rights as subjective rights," for Jellinek understood that the individual could exercise only objective rights if those rights were limited to the private realm.[28] But Kistiakovsky did not consider Jellinek's classification of individual rights as necessarily both private and public a satisfactory solution to defining subjective rights, the rights of the self-determining individual. Jellinek had a juridical orientation, and did not question the existing governmental and legal order; the individual possessed those subjective rights in the context of a specific state where each person had a definite legal status.[29] For individual rights to be subjective, the individual exercising those rights had to be expressing a choice. The individual would be voicing his or her will and thus be self-determining. As long as the inalienable rights of the individual were formulated as corollaries to the central concern of protecting the interests of the existing governmental order, they remained a limited area of permissible action, not the focal point, or priority, of the society. Kistiakovsky illustrated this derivative form of individual rights with the following legal example:

> When the tenant of the second floor placed a carpet on the public staircase, then the tenants of the third and fourth floors walk on it and attain the rights to walk on it; but they do not have a subjective right to the carpet which belongs to the tenant on the second floor. They use the carpet as an adjunct right or reflection of their rights to walk on the staircase.[30]

Kistiakovsky noted that Western constitutional regimes claimed to make individual rights their priority, but in practice, " . . . all individual and social freedoms or rights were not at all subjective rights but only

traces of known legal principles; all that was not forbidden was allowed. Expressed in legal terminology, individual and social freedoms
were not subjective rights, they were reflections of objective laws."[31]

Law and Social Change

Kistiakovsky was assessing legal questions from the standpoint of one
living in a society where the rights of the individual had never been
grounded in consistent legal codes that were the basis of a rule-of-law
state. Therefore, he looked for the political, social, and economic
changes in the society that would best facilitate the development of
subjective rights for all. He noted that for any person to be able to
exercise subjective rights fully, there were two basic prerequisites for a
just law not determined solely by ideology: (1) the social and political
inequalities incorporated into the organization of the legal system, such
as the distinction between the public and private realms of law, had to
be eliminated so that the legal system would become more than an
instrument of the state; (2) the purely theoretical and idealistic formulation of the rights of the individual had to be revived and revised to
become an integral part of the social fabric.

The legal system was considered by Kistiakovsky to be more than
the reflection of the social and economic organization of the society—
as the doctrinaire Marxists claimed it was. At the same time, he did not
perceive the legal system and laws as simple expressions of the values
of those individuals leading the society. For him, the interaction of
ideal legal forms of personal liberties with the real, social, political, and
economic world would yield the developmental process that could
guarantee political as well as economic socialist rights. These two
mutually interdependent types of individual rights, political and socialist (economic), would become human rights—but only when those
ideals were tested in the empirical realm and refashioned to function
effectively in a specific context, such as that of the Russian Empire.[32]

Nearly ninety years ago Kistiakovsky recognized the shortcomings
of abstract declarations taken out of legal, social, and economic context. To provide substance to human ideals and values, there must exist
a social framework capable of realizing them. Kistiakovsky asserted,
"Law cannot be ranked with such spiritual values as scientific truth,
moral perfection, and religious sanctity. It does not have the same

absolute significance, and its context is, in part, determined by change-able economic and social conditions."[33] Law is a cultural phenomenon created out of an interaction between social realities and human ideals and values. To realize his goal of the full and equal exercise of human rights by all citizens, Kistiakovsky insisted that the legal transforma-tion of the empire be accompanied by the simultaneous social and economic changes:

> For us [in the Russian Empire] it should now be clear that this question of human rights can only be properly solved when the social forces are organized more equally. Such a total organization of social forces which will lead to the real freedom of the individual can be actualized only in a government of the future or under a different social order.[34]

That social order had to be socialist; for Kistiakovsky, socialism was a social and political order generally based on principles of social justice. According to Kistiakovsky's definition, socialism would exist when all private property became public and class distinctions were eradicated. He equated socialism with social equality—social justice could not exist in a capitalist society, where one social class (or group) dominated the others.[35]

The institutionalization of individual liberties and of a constitution-based governmental system was the initial step toward the eventual development of human rights in an effectively functioning socialist society. Though some of the rights Kistiakovsky cited in his formula-tion of human rights had been included in the constitutions of some contemporary Western states, he pointed out that "existing constitu-tional governments did not fulfill them all, rather they fulfilled only an insignificant part of them."[36] Kistiakovsky found that every citizen could actively participate in the process of governing only in those countries that held *referenda* for specific issues (or all elections), such as North America or Switzerland.[37] However, none of these govern-ments guaranteed economic (socialist) rights.

Kistiakovsky was skeptical of the individual rights in Western con-stitutions because they did not represent self-determination of the citi-zens; rather, they were guaranteed by victors emerging from a revolu-tionary situation, such as in seventeenth-century England or eigh-teenth-century France. After the French Revolution, other European countries incorporated the ideas of individual liberties, although they were often not stated as the point of departure for the system. For instance, in the German states, the Bill of Rights stating that the rights of individuals were a part of the constitution of an individual state, was not incorporated into the Federal Constitution until 1900.

Kistiakovsky vigorously contradicted those socialists who argued that individual liberties and constitutional governments are necessarily bourgeois or liberal:

> A constitutional government is often called bourgeois as contrasted with socialist. It is clear that when a constitutional government is called bourgeois, this reflects the socioeconomic structure while in fact a constitutional government actually refers to the juridical character of the government. But many confuse the two, and the legal or juridical nature of a socialist government is neglected. Thus, though it is true that the socioeconomic aspects of a society are more important in understanding a socialist government, this does not justify ignoring the juridical aspect.[38]

The potential danger of state or collective dominance over the individual was as crucial and perplexing a problem in a socialist society as it was in a capitalist context. The secondary importance of law in socialist and Marxist-based thought was an outgrowth of the focus on the transformation of the socioeconomic base, the substructure of the society. Unlike orthodox Marxists and many socialists who had believed that the state would be entirely destroyed when the revolutionary change took place, Kistiakovsky feared that individual rights would be completely lost in such a revolutionary situation. He carefully outlined the political consequences of his theory on the role and force of law. He distinguished himself from both the liberals, who opposed socialism, and socialists, who overlooked the importance of individual liberties. Kistiakovsky recognized the practical problem of associating rapid changes in the social and economic fabric of Russian society with necessary changes in its frail constitutional system. Though he was consistent in his heterodox socialist convictions, the practical aspects of the process through which the social and political transformation would take place remained theoretical and he did not attempt to delineate the process.

It was clear, however, that the transformation to socialism did not mean that the private sector had to be forcibly nationalized. Kistiakovsky was consistent in his insistence on a society based on law and social justice. As if he were a participant in future debates on socialism and the welfare state, he disagreed with the claims that a socialist government would necessarily become the dominant force establishing policies in the name of the people and that, therefore, attention need not be paid to the rights of individuals:

> ... it is often claimed that a socialist state having been turned into the only and universal employer, will turn into a despotic state and that it would destroy individual freedom according to its needs as if it were not organized democratically. Some even call it a future slavery and think that it will turn a contemporary free society into some kind of a military settlement or a barracks.[39]

On the contrary, in a democratic socialist society, Kistiakovsky saw the possibility for increasing the forum for self-determination; once private property was abolished, the individual could participate directly in the government, take more initiative in the economic life, and contribute to the cultural life of the country. In this context, each would be an active self-determining individual, not oppressed by gross economic inequalities or subjected to rules proclaimed by those in power. Kistiakovsky was hopeful about such a development of human rights in the Russian Empire; he believed that the evolution of self-determining individuals could be established as a general rule of contemporary social and political movements. In his view, the foundations of a constitutional system, human rights, and " ... the participation of the people in the legislative process and governing of the country will be subsequently developed and broadened."[40]

> In the future state, the right to positive services from the state would be reformulated ... with the new view of the category of subjective public rights. These new aspects of law will actually flow from the conditions in which the means of production will be removed from the civil-legal realm and be turned into a general national property. It is clear that each person will be guaranteed the right to work, i.e., the right to use the land and other instruments of production on an equal level with others for the application of his labor and for the attainment of ... economic goals. From that point in the same way will flow the right of each person to develop all of his talents and to apply his work to that field which most closely corresponds to his talents; finally each will have the right to participate in implementing all material and cultural goals created by the contemporary culture. All these rights would be unified into one general subjective public right, namely the right to a dignified existence.[41]

This ideal is founded on the premise that citizens understand their rights and duties, which means that society must provide institutions and personnel to teach them what those rights are and what each person must do to be able to enjoy those rights. In cases of social conflict, individuals in the society must have not only the right to go to court or arbitration to fight for that right, but also the means to protect it—the money to pay for legal services, including both the legal talent and court time. Even the socialist ideal must be considered in terms of its social and economic context—for socialism cannot provide total social harmony.

Kistiakovsky hoped that individual rights for citizens of the Russian Empire would become not only subjective public rights, but, ultimately, human rights—both political and economic rights in a democratic socialist society. These would be the new and active natural rights of the man and the citizen.[42] That is, the rights of the individual would become inherent aspects of the person who could actively participate in determining his or her own fate through the legal process governing the society.

Kistiakovsky's conception of human rights was an outgrowth of his broader investigation into individual rights in a constitutional context and the ways those rights might be implemented in the Russian Empire. He viewed human rights not as abstract freedoms but as an integral part of a program for political and social transformation. Kistiakovsky's concept of human rights introduced the essential interconnection between the definition of rights and the social, economic, and political structure of a society.

CHAPTER FOUR

Constitutionalism and the Rule-of-Law State

From the time of Muscovy, the tsars established a governmental system designed to serve the will of the center. Law was identified with the head of state rather than with legal precepts. As Richard Wortman portrays those legal practices:

> The image of a patriarchal tsar dispensing a personal justice maintained its hold in the eighteenth and early nineteenth century and fed a distrust of formal institutions that might dilute the monarch's power to extend personal grace, benefits, and privilege. Personal connections, access to high individuals close to the tsar, gave the Russian nobility a way to avoid submitting themselves to the demeaning rule of petty officials.[1]

Although the failure to codify the law was recognized as a problem, the tsars drew back from permitting the establishment of an overarching theory of law. To acknowledge any principle of authority higher than the autocracy was unacceptable. Having refused to build a codified law based on a general theory of law (*pravo*), the autocracy resorted to the solution of issuing regulations (*zakony*) to deal with every problem.

The autocracy's situation was complicated in the first half of the nineteenth century with the growth of numbers of bureaucrats and the increase in numbers of people gaining legal education; officials trained in law gradually started to replace the noblemen who had controlled the legal system.[2] Their consciousness of law was based on the idea of creating a *Rechtstaat*, a state that would run in an orderly fashion through institutions and according to regular procedures and regulations—a concept that contradicted the idea of the personal rule of the tsar. The conflict between the tsarist rule and the rule of law led to political conflict and a fundamental ambivalence toward law.

Tsar Alexander I, whose reign extended from 1801 to 1825, had been educated in the spirit of the Enlightenment and recognized the lack of codified laws and legal procedures. During Alexander's reign, a talented rising star in government service, Mikhail Speranskii, became the deputy minister of justice. In that capacity, he headed a commission to codify Russian laws as well as improve Russia's institutions. The comprehensive plan drawn up by Speranskii was intended to transform the Russian autocracy from an absolute monarchy to a monarchy based on the rule of law. The proposed system left the tsar in the unquestioned executive position, but it specified a separation of powers between the legislative, the executive, and the judicial branches of the government. Speranskii's project never saw the light of day and most of Speranskii's proposed work was rejected by the tsar who did not accept the idea of limiting his authority.

The only part of Speranskii's plan that was implemented was the formation of a Council of State which was to function as a place where new legislation could be discussed before the tsar made his decisions; even this body lost its importance once the tsar attempted to reassert his power.[3] Though the council was supposed to review legislation proposed by the tsar or ministers, Alexander preferred to work with specific ministers and to maintain his personal control. In fact, the Russian government was not represented by an autonomous legal system or a constitutional form of government. Rather, there were a Senate, a State Council established in 1810, and a Council of Ministers that often performed overlapping duties. The tsars hoped for a well-organized government, but were too frightened to give up personal control to allow a government to operate on the basis of laws, or a constitution, they could not control. The result was that separate rules and regulations were made without any systematic overview.

By the middle of the nineteenth century, the system was not purely autocratic; it was a mixed system with some of the institutional grounding for a legally based order in place. As a result of new trends in legal education, two contradictory legal impulses developed in the Russian Empire[4]—the idea of the well-ordered police state and the concept of the rule-of-law government known as the *Rechtstaat*. One concept indicated the expansion of the tsar's authority; the other indicated the limitation of the tsar's powers through institutions, regular procedures, and laws. As Marc Raeff explains, the government of the nineteenth-century Russian Empire was neither a *Polizeistaat* nor a *Rechtstaat* in the original sense of these terms, but rather a *Reglamentstaat* consisting of a multitude of separate written regulations.[5] Some of the many specific rules, procedures, and institutions—formed to prevent individuals in the tsarist administration from acting as the personal agents of the tsar or using his authority to justify their own initiative—finally became a limitation on the tsar's personal power.[6]

Constructing a Legal System

Just after the emancipation of the serfs, the Legal Reforms of 1864 introduced an independent judiciary, jury trials, and a Bar (*advokatura*). The Reforms of 1864 established large judicial regions called ciruits (*okruzhnye sudy*), with a Judicial Chamber that served as a court of appeals for official and state crimes. The civil cassation department of the Senate was organized to be the highest court of appeal for civil cases and questions of law. Justices of the peace who presided over minor criminal and civil cases were elected by the *zemstvo,* the organ for local self-government that was created as part of the Great Reforms.

By the turn of the century judges were appointed for life and conducted public jury trials with substantial rights of appeal and attention to procedural rights for the defendants. Judges upheld the independent role of law even by abrogating executive administrative orders which they deemed illegal.[7]

The courts were opened in St. Petersburg in 1866, and functioned until they were closed in December 1917 by a decree of the People's Commissar of Justice that shut all judiciary institutions and abolished the Bar. Although there were many barriers to the effective practice of the law in the context of the tsarist autocracy, among legal practitioners and some of the intelligentsia there did exist a commitment to developing constitutional guarantees, the protection of individual rights, and the separation of state powers. For the liberal opponents to the autocracy, these elements were considered central to the stabilizion and gradual change of the society. During the period in which the courts operated, they represented a standard of legal ethics and practice that was comparable to the judicial courts in France, Germany, Britain, or America.[8]

The sophisticated legal system set up under the reforms of 1864 only applied to about 10 to 15 percent of the population. The rest were under the jurisdiction of the peasants' local customs. Thus, a peasant could essentially be charged with a crime under the judiciary, but the same peasant could usually find no protection through that court system. Sometimes the peasants' cases were heard by Justices of the Peace. The *volost'* courts also established at the time of the emancipation, were composed of elected members (judges) that were authorized to administer peasant customary law.

The *volost'* courts caused serious concern, because peasant judges were elected by peasants and no particular educational prerequites were required. Concerns about the capability of the judges were expressed in the *volost'* court reforms of 1889, which required a Land Captain (a noble) to confirm or reject the judge elected by the peasantry.[9] Recent studies of peasant society have shown that peasants did in fact have some forms of legal culture—they actively used the courts to address conflicts, insults, quarrels and property disputes using procedures set up by the state. Of course, the attempt to show peasant legal culture as totally logical and rational should not be overstated. As Cathy Frierson points out, some peasants resorted to traditional forms of justice such as arson, which " . . . should cause us to pause in our optimistic appraisal of the gains made in developing such a legal culture."[10]

With Tsar Alexander II's Reforms in 1861, the "emancipation" of the serfs was proclaimed, and the tsarist government effected a controlled change that would prevent a revolution from below. As Tsar Alexander himself explained to the Moscow nobles:

> . . . you yourselves are certainly aware that the existing order of serfdom cannot remain unchanged. It is better to abolish serfdom from above than to wait for the time when it will begin to abolish itself from below.[11]

However, land redemption payments and the position of the commune made the actual freedom of the serfs impossible until the debts they were burdened with were erased by official decree during the Stolypin era. At the same time, just as the reforms insured that redemption payments and taxes could be extracted from the peasantry, they also served to protect the peasants either from being reabsorbed into the world of the landowners or from becoming proletarianized.[12] The commune had its own method of settling disputes between peasants and between peasants and non-peasants. Essentially, the peasants were segregated into a separate estate within a realm in which they were allowed to live according to their specific customary law (*obychnoe pravo*) or popular law (*narodnoe pravo*).[13] The Great Reforms included an attempt to regulate the world of peasant customary law. Justices of the peace were to be elected by the *zemstvo* membership and were authorized to preside over minor criminal cases and some cases that involved the peasantry.

Much like other developing societies, the Russian Empire in the post-Reform era was a dual society: the majority of the populace consisted of the peasantry in their own cultural world or estate (*soslovie*), that was defined by village customs. In modern terms, peasant culture was turned into a giant South African-style "homeland"—a patriarchal, legal *apartheid* justified by the separate world of peasant laws.[14] Those unwritten rules were not always compatible with the realm of the written laws—laws for the upper classes, town dwellers, and educated society. The peasants thus were freed from their landlords' control, but then separated from the rest of society by their own laws and courts as well as by communal land tenure and the world of the commune.

The modernization of the legal system did not bring greater stability to Russia. Although the new legal profession impugned the tsar's claim that he was the source and protector of legality. In practice, the independent judiciary became another of the confrontational forces that the autocracy easily controlled.

For the tsarist regime, the very idea of formulating a legal system that would fully encompass the multi-faceted worlds of the pre-revolutionary Russian Empire was an awesome, if not impossible, task. The disparate elements had to be revealed and then defined as well as integrated into one legal artifice that would make up a cohesive civil society. This was complicated by the fact that the society was an incongruous mixture of impressive capital cities, and a growing number of industrial complexes all of which were set against the vast backdrop of the overwhelming majority—the peasantry, and a growing working class.

If legal institutions had been successfully established throughout the empire, a more powerful and resilient legal culture might have developed. However, the government intervened whenever it felt threatened by the independence of local authorities, the judges and juries. The *zemstva* were to have been an elected form of government representing all classes; the activities of the *zemstvo* were limited to maintaining roads, health, education and agriculture. They did not become model organizations in which all classes had proportional representation. The majority of elected representatives came from privileged or noble backgrounds. When the *zemstva* became too independent or liberal, they were often bullied by the local officals representing the central government.[15]

The courts had considerable autonomy in the area of political crimes until the Vera Zasulich case in 1878. Zasulich, a dedicated woman revolutionary in the populist camp, shot and wounded the Petersburg governor-general as a retaliatory gesture for his having beaten a revolutionary prisoner named Bogoliubov. When Zasulich was acquitted to cheers in the courtroom,[16] the regime intervened by taking many "political" trials out of the public realm of jury trials and remanding them to military courts martial. During the trials of the People's Will [*Narodnaia volia*] in the 1880s, forty-two of the seventy-three cases were heard by military courts and seven by special Senate session. Only the least significant were heard in a public jury trial.[17] In one year, 1906, about 1000 political prisoners were executed during field courts martial.

Citizens of the Russian Empire in the nineteenth and early twentieth centuries struggled to escape their authoritarian tsarist roots by establishing a democratic constitutional system. The term *pravovoe gosudarstvo,* a translation of the German *Rechtstaat* (a rule-of-law state), denoted a state based on a constitution, but that did not necessarily mean that the constitution would protect civil liberties and be established on popular sovereignty.

Kistiakovsky's conception of the transition from a monarchical to a constitutional state provides an example of his understanding of law as a cultural phenomenon simultaneously incorporating both empirical and normative facets (*Sein* and *Sollen*) that exist at the same time. In his portrayal of one form of state organization penetrating the other in the transitional period, Kistiakovsky's idea of the interaction of the normative and empirical realms conveys that he did not confuse the ideal with the real. The ideal form of a constitutional state was a statement of values, "what should be"—a model, as opposed to social and political reality. The state, in the abstract, embodied the legal relations of the society and government; it expressed the guiding ethical force which linked the political and social components of society. Furthermore, Kistiakovsky was by no means blind to the customary legal traditions of the peasantry. He grew up with the work of his father, which made him cognizant of the way in which legal traditions had penetrated into the everyday world of the peasantry.

Kistiakovsky envisioned two major ways in which human rights might be implemented in the Russian Empire: First, the formation of a truly representative constitutional government to replace the autocracy. Second, the establishment of federalism in the multinational empire. But federalism and constitutionalism would only be effective if they were established in a socialist context. Kistiakovsky's notion of social-ism combined with constitutionalism distinguished him from the liberal thinkers, such as Aleksei Chicherin, who believed private property was a prerequisite for a constitutional government to adequately replace the tsarist autocracy. Kistiakovsky's belief in philosophical idealism dis-tinguished him from the orthodox Marxists and socialists who believed that all change must come from the transformation of the social and economic base of the society and that political and constitutional ques-tions were secondary. For Kistiakovsky, ending the autocracy required the implementation of all three aspects of his socialist-based theory that embraced human rights, constitutionalism, and federalism.

Establishing a socialist constitutionalist regime to replace the autoc-racy became the basis for his activities in the liberation movement, even though his own ideas did not introduce a program of action. Kistiakovsky's commitment to the idea of a rule-of-law state led him into serious contradictions—between his radical liberal ideas and his desire to be an active participant in the movement to end the autocracy. Activists in the movement were often engaged in illegal activities that were violations of the existing laws, such as publishing oppositional materials and creating a political party before 1905. This dilemma was particularly difficult for such legal theorists as Kistiakovsky who wanted the laws of the society to become a fundamental part of Russia and its government.

Kistiakovsky's Reaction to the October Manifesto

Kistiakovsky was in Heidelberg in the fall of 1905, at the time when the October Manifesto was announced in Russia. He participated there in Russian émigré discussion groups which gathered to evaluate the sig-nificance of the liberal-sounding proclamation issued by the tsar on

October 17, 1905. It was in this manifesto that the tsar first announced the constitutional form of government through which he purported to share power by establishing an elected legislature, the State Duma. The manifesto granted civil liberties and rights and pledged electoral privileges to a broader sector of the population. On October 19, 1905, two days after the October Manifesto was proclaimed, the tsarist government declared that the State Council[18] would become an upper chamber of parliament and that the Council of Ministers[19] would become a cabinet to coordinate the policies and actions of the administration with the legislature and the tsar. The details of the new constitutional government were presented formally in the Fundamental Laws of April 23, 1906, which revealed some of the less democratic features of the tsarist constitutional formula. For instance, the State Council was, in fact, reorganized so as to limit powers originally granted to the Duma. Unlike the Duma, which was to be elected by three curiae—landed proprietors, urban citizens, and peasants, fifty percent of the State Council consisted of retired ministers and high ranking officials appointed by the tsar, while the other half were elected representatives of professional and upper-class organizations. The new government's Council of Ministers was also far from being a representative body, for the chairman as well as all of the ministers in the council were appointed by the tsar and were not accountable to the legislative body. In light of this "constitutional" formula, it is not surprising that the new constitution met with a mixed response both in the Russian Empire and the West.

Kistiakovsky, Max Weber, and the 1906 Constitution

Max Weber followed the dramatic events surrounding the Russian revolution of 1905 through his contacts with Kistiakovsky and the Russian students, exiles, and scholars who gathered at their traditional cultural center, the Heidelberg Russian *Lesehalle* (reading room).[20] The revolutionary events of 1905, naturally, reverberated among the members of the Russian colony in Heidelberg. The political leanings of the Russian students abroad were primarily with the Kadets, the Social Democrats, and the Social Revolutionaries. They as well as their European colleagues and professors struggled to get as much information as possible on the events surrounding the revolutionary era—the violent strikes and the initial steps to structuring a constitutional monarchy.

Max Weber enlisted Kistiakovsky's help, as the German sociologist exercised his extraordinary scholarly skills in producing two comprehensive, nearly encyclopedic articles about the Russian situation in 1905 and 1906. He had learned to read Russian well enough to follow the Russian daily press in just a few months. With the revolutionary developments in the unstable Russian Empire, the Russian crisis posed a threat to Europeans in general and Germany's international political situation in particular.

Both Weber and the young Russian students, including Kistiakovsky, were concerned with the problems of representative constitutionalism and individual liberties. Weber acknowledged the fact that he relied on Kistiakovsky for newspapers and monographs as well as his own opinions when Weber was working on his two 1906 book-length monographs on Russia—"On the Situation of Bourgeois Democracy in Russia" and "Russia's Transition to Pseudo-Constitutionalism." Kistiakovsky's role as advisor on reading materials helps to explain fundamental points of agreement between him and Weber. For example, Weber's understanding of the importance of the national question during the 1905 revolution and his reading of Drahomanov's works coincided with Kistiakovsky's editorial work on the collected works of Drahomanov and his commitment to publicizing the problems of non-Russian nationalities.

Kistiakovsky played an important role in helping Weber gather materials for his study of Russia.[21] As a member of the Union of Liberation, Kistiakovsky was a good source of information on the constitutional project developed by the Union of Liberation, which appeared in Russian in March 1905 and in French translation in August 1905.[22] In a letter of May 19 [O.S. May 6] 1906, Kistiakovsky responded to Weber's request for some books and a reading list on agrarian, worker, and self-government questions as well as for such works by the liberal intelligentsia as Struve's essays *Na raznye temy* [On Various Themes] and the collection *Problemy idealizma*. Weber inquired about Kistiakovsky's observations of the Russian events and the *Zeitgeist*. Kistiakovsky expressed his sense of the instability in the society:

> I cannot write about my impressions. I have seen a great deal including a visit to the State Duma. The Revolution is not yet ended. We

will probably still experience very bloody outbreaks. The world has
not yet seen such bloodshed, as there probably will be here. The
regime is guilty for that. It initiated the violence.[23]

The new governmental organization, the representatives to the Duma,
could not eliminate the social discontent imbedded in the society.

Weber's views on Russia differed from that of Kistiakovsky in part
because Weber wrote as a foreign observer and Kistiakovsky considered himself a participant. Weber analyzed the problems and potential
obstacles to the development of a functioning liberal movement and the
implementation of civil rights as well as the effective working of the
Russian constitution. Weber was doubtful that an effective constitutional state could be established in Russia because neither the industrial
bourgeoisie nor the leaders of the financial world had a material interest in a democratic, liberal order. Tsar Nicholas II's inflexibility and
fear of losing control made his role in a constitutional monarchy seem
impossible and left the new constitutional monarchy in the position of
"pseudoconstitutional" order.[24] But Weber's prediction that the bureaucracy would develop into a major political force in the Russian Empire
never became a reality.

Kistiakovsky considered the 1906 constitution an artificial system
arbitrarily imposed on society by the tsar and his ministers. He was
skeptical of a constitutional order "granted" to the Russian people by
the tsar, for to transform the existing order, it was necessary to wrest
power from the autocrat and decline his terms for the formation of the
new constitutional order.[25] The Russian government was a token form
of constitutionalism rather than a real representative system for the
following reasons: 1) the tsar and his ministers did not relinquish their
power, so the new government could not qualify as one representing
popular interests over all other interests; 2) the Russian constitution did
not give proportional voting rights to the groups and nationalities in the
empire. Kistiakovsky noted that a real representative constitutional
system could have been established through a popular constituent assembly in which the governmental forms would have been developed
"by all the Russian people."[26] This had not happened. The tsar retained
the title "autocrat," though the word "unlimited" was formally deleted
in the October Manifesto and the Fundamental Laws. Chapter 1(4) of
the Fundamental Law prescribed: "To the All-Russian Emperor belongs the Supreme Autocratic Power. To obey his power, not only by

reason of wrath, but also for conscience's sake, is commanded by God himself."[27] For Kistiakovsky, the fact that the autocrat still existed as the head of state was obviously contradictory to the very concept of a constitutional system. "In fact," he noted, "a granted constitution is not only a legislative act of an absolute monarchical power, but it is also the *last* law given by the autocratic monarch."[28]

However, Kistiakovsky felt that despite the shortcomings of the new order, the constitutional principles agreed to by the tsar signaled the potential end of the autocratic government. At least in theory, the monarch no longer had the power to make laws independently of the representative body, the State Duma.[29] In his 1906 article, "Gosudarstvennaia duma i osnovnye zakony" [The State Duma and the Fundamental Laws], Kistiakovsky vigorously supported the new constitution to counter those radicals who opposed it on the grounds that it was a temporary bourgeois constitution. He distinguished two viewpoints on the constitution—that of the professional revolutionaries who dismissed the importance of the document and that of its supporters, whom he called the holders of the juridical view. The revolutionaries considered the Fundamental Laws of the Duma as temporary laws that would change as the revolution that began with the 1905 outbreaks spread further and power shifted from the minority liberal forces to the masses. At that time, the radicals concluded a new constitution needed to be written to express the new interrelationship of social and economic forces.[30] The proponents of the juridical view maintained that " . . . the constitution grows out of the society's legal consciousness";[31] it was more than a "paper constitution" that failed to express the gross division between the educated elite and the majority of the population who worked on the land or labored in the growing numbers of factories. According to the juridical point of view, which Kistiakovsky advocated, the elements necessary for change were incorporated in the laws set down in the constitution. That is, the social and political transformation of the empire could and should take place in the context of the constitutional forms. And if the constitutional forms themselves had to be revised, the rules for such transactions were included in the document.

Irrespective of the autocracy's continuing arbitrary actions, such as the law of February 20, 1906 that confirmed the State Council as the upper chamber of the legislative branch of government (though the

Duma never voted on this ruling), Kistiakovsky still argued it was crucial that all segments of the society should lend their support to the Duma. He asserted, "In Russia now there is only one authoritative representative of the governmental power—the State Duma. Its authority is not only on paper, it is in the popular legal consciousness. The decisions of the Duma should be obligatory for the government; if the government should ignore the Duma's decisions, a permanent revolution will develop."[32] To avoid the anarchy that might accompany a violent popular revolution, Kistiakovsky called for the strengthening of the existing constitutional forms along with a concerted effort to build the lines of communication between the government and people. He perceived Russian economic backwardness as an advantage in developing popular opinion. For instance, he saw the lack of sharp class distinctions in Russia as beneficial to the building of a unified representative base for the constitutional experiment, when he wrote:

> In Russia the demand for total, equal voting rights is dictated by the democratic character and composition of our society. In our people there are no sharp social divisions, there is neither a feudal aristocracy nor a very strong and powerful bourgeoisie. Our intelligentsia always distinguished itself by its democratic qualities. For that reason we cannot have real constitutionalists who are not advocates of universal voting rights.[33]

For any viable and potentially powerful political movement to effectively express its interests in a representative system, it had to adequately represent the largest and most important interest group in Russian society—the peasantry. As Kistiakovsky noted, "In Russia the future belongs not to the agrarian nor the industrial bourgeoisie, but to the broad popular masses who are living by their own labor . . . The belief in the important role of the peasantry created a sense of unity between the intelligentsia and the popular masses and conveyed to them that moral and material strength which brought the autocratic order to ruin."[34] He felt that the peasantry was the main group that could provide support for the constitutional movement and he believed that the process of increasing peasant literacy and self-determination was already taking place in the development of the cooperative movement. In Kistiakovsky's view, that was a beginning for class alliances among the multinational peasantry.[35]

Kistiakovsky did not delve into the problem of enlisting peasant support and participation in the constitutional government other than through his involvement in popular education programs. Weber's view of the role of the peasantry was negative: as he grew more familiar with the Russian situation, he considered the task of integrating the peasantry into the system as an obstacle to the growth of liberal thought. Weber noted that this problem could only be solved by a fundamental transformation of the entire system.[36]

In particular, Kistiakovsky focused on constitutional and legal proposals that he hoped would bring about both the social and political transformation in the context of the democratic constitutional system. In contrast to Weber, Kistiakovsky used his criticism of the existing legislative forms as a point of departure for his proposals for the organization of a constitutional government.

Kistiakovsky's Concept of Constitutionalism

Kistiakovsky's devotion to a representative, democratic, and popular form of constitutionalism can be traced to his days as a left-wing Ukrainian activist when he had adopted the Ukrainian nationalist Drahomanov as his mentor. It was through the early influence of Drahomanov's political thought that he understood the primary importance of demanding a constitutional government in which there would be representation for all classes and nationalities based on universal suffrage[37] and a socialist economic and social system. Though he was not the only constitutionalist to support socialism in the empire at the turn of the century, what distinguished him from most other constitutionalists was his insistence on the development of both constitutionalism and socialism as necessary for the realization of his ideal—a socialist constitutional system. As discussed in the preceding chapter, Kistiakovsky believed that only a socialist state could facilitate attaining the goal of social justice and, ultimately, human rights, for social equality would remain impossible in a capitalist society in which one class or sector dominated the others. And a constitutional system was the only governmental order that would effectively and consistently protect the rights of the individual.

Kistiakovsky's definition of constitutionalism again emphasized the central place of the individual and the personal rights of the individual.

For example, when he described one of the main characteristics of a constitutional government, the limitation of powers, he wrote, "The limitation of power in a legally based government is founded on the recognition of the inalienable rights of the individual . . . For the first time, in a legal or constitutional government it is acknowledged that there is a certain sphere of self-determination . . . of the individual in which the government does not have the right to interfere."[38] In fact, he hoped that those rights would be established by the people themselves and not by the government, so that the constitutional form would be an expression of popular self-determination.[39] But this was a hope that he did not repeat after the June 3, 1907 *coup d'état* by Stolypin that led to a change in the electoral laws; thereafter, the tsar's intervention changed the political climate in the Duma, and the possibilities for representation were far less auspicious for left-wing and non-Russian activists in the Duma.

The only governmental system that could assure the exercise of human rights, as defined by Kistiakovsky, had to function on the principle of a written law—a constitution that was supported by the population. That ideal constitutional state conformed to the notion of a *Rechtsstaat*—a government established on stable and fundamental laws. Because social and political order were best guaranteed by a thoroughly legal order, Kistiakovsky maintained, " . . . the rule-of-law state is the most perfect type of state formation. It creates those conditions which allow for harmony between the whole of society and the person."[40] But Kistiakovsky's idea for a governmental system was more than just a legal order; it had to represent all people and classes and be based on the limitation and separation of powers, as well as the political and social equality that he considered inherent in a socialist system. Contrary to those who believed that the rights of the individual would be curtailed, if not eliminated under socialism, he envisioned that human rights would be developed most fully in a socialist constitutional system.[41] In a contemporary constitutional government, the one major social goal was the establishment of a completely just social order, based on the multiplicity of small and partial socioeconomic goals. The practical means found for the solution of these goals was included in various types of social and health insurance—medical insurance against illness and accidents, as well as for invalids and for the aged. All of these economic and social guarantees would have made it possible for citizens to live a dignified human existence.[42]

In sum, a constitutional state was the epitome of a *Rechtsstaat*, and constitutionalism and socialism were interdependent—that is, a socialist state could only reach its fullest form if governed by a constitutional government and a constitutional government could only be completely formed in a socialist system. In Kistiakovsky's words, that ideal system was:

> . . . a system of relationships in which all members of a given society possess the greatest freedom of actions and self-determination. But defined this way, a legal order cannot be contrasted to a socialist order. Quite the contrary, a more profound understanding of both leads to the conclusion that they are closely related and that from the juridical point of view a socialist order is simply a more rigorously implemented legal order. Conversely, a socialist order can only be brought into existence when all its institutions have been given a most precise legal definition.[43]

Kistiakovsky did not rule out a period of violence that could accompany a polarization between classes of people with different economic and political interests. In fact, he expected that a class struggle would probably take place, but he maintained that in a partially developed constitutional system (one that had constitutional forms) that struggle could be conducted through legal means in a legal forum: the class struggle would be interwoven into the organization of the contemporary constitutional and legal state. By means of their (political) parties, the separate classes would become the movers of the contemporary government in all its activities.[44]

Kistiakovsky focused his attention on the type of governmental form that would be created. For he wanted to avoid the chaos of revolution and hoped that the social and political transformation of the Russian Empire could indeed take place non-violently; that is to say, the class struggle would take place in a constitutional framework. He claimed that in its purest form a constitutional system would make it possible for the legal order to be democratic whether it was noble- or worker-dominated: "workers and peasants might also predominate in a constitutional state, . . . in fact, a constitutional state might be devoid of any specific class coloration in those cases in which there is an equilibrium between the classes and none has an unquestionable preponderance."[45] He emphasized that this would be true even in a less than perfect constitutional system: "In the contemporary constitutional state the acts of power will not be expressions of the opinions and wishes of the ruling class."[46] As a representative legal order, it would provide a formal context for working out compromise positions:

> Every reasonably important new law in a contemporary constitutional state is a compromise worked out by different parties that voice the demands of the social groups of the classes they represent. The contemporary state is itself based on a compromise, and the constitution of each individual state is a compromise of its most influential groups.[47]

Though Kistiakovsky hoped that a properly functioning constitutional system would provide a stable context within which decisions on social and political change could be made, he also assumed that the system itself would transform to reflect changes in the social, political, and economic structure of the society. In fact, his definition of a fully formed constitutional system—which, in his terms, was a socialist constitutional state—was an ideal type, or paradigm, by which to analyze the level of constitutional development at any one stage of its progress. For him, the formation of a representative constitutional system was a transitional process that could begin in the last stages of a monarchical state. In its last stages, an absolute monarchy was already permeated with some characteristics of a legal state. On the other side, a constitutional state was not completely free of the traits of the previous governmental order, so whole periods were transitional. Using the "ideal type" of constitutionalism such as Max Weber did, Kistiakovsky explained, "The contemporary constitutional state proclaims a certain principle as its motto and its goal, which it strives to realize, but it realizes it only partially and for a long time that state is not in a position to put it into practice fully."[48]

Kistiakovsky did not try to predict the precise way that political change would actually come about, but he did believe that radical changes would occur. He hoped that all facets of the political transformation would be intertwined and interactive—the class struggle would take place in the constitutional arena at the same time as the constitutional order was perfecting itself in a developing socialist context. Of course, he acknowledged the idealism inherent in his ideas as well as the complexities in the process. For instance, he underlined the importance of integrating conflicting opinions in a democratic system to provide the foundation for a set of shared social goals. He envisioned the shortest path to developing a harmonious popular voice through " . . . the shift from the representative phase to the phase of direct democracy . . . "[49] That might be implemented by forming *referenda,* such as those used in Switzerland and the United States, to encourage the expression of popular opinion and stimulate the responsiveness of the government to the people.[50] But Kistiakovsky did not feel bound to provide those answers and guidelines, for that social and political harmony (resembling a "general will") was part of an ideal type or form, a formulation of *Sollen,* "what should be," rather than *Sein,* "what is": "The idea of unity in a constitutional government is more a motto or ideal than a realizable fact, for this unity can only be realized fully in a socialist government."[51]

Because he regarded himself as a legal theorist of state law rather than a political activist, he concentrated on articulating social-science methods that could reveal the relationship of the empirical and the normative realms and ideal forms of constitutional government toward which the nascent movement should strive. He was an academic lawyer and not a political analyst of constitutionalism in the Russian Empire who concentrated on the day-to-day workings or snags in the system. Though he did make some political statements (for example, his public plea to grant amnesty to all political prisoners arrested during the revolution of 1905) and his skeptical comments on the nature of the "granted" constitutional order, the bulk of his writings were not activist expressions. He concentrated on constitutional forms, the establishment of human rights, and the role of the intelligentsia in the social and political transformation of the empire.

The erosion of the Fundamental Laws by the tsarist government's interventions combined with the growing atmosphere of Great Russian chauvinism reinforced Kistiakovsky's focus on civil liberties and individual rights. Arbitrary actions by Tsar Nicholas II had undermined the individual liberties incorporated into the constitutional monarchy created after the 1905 revolution. When the tsar disapproved of the political climate or acts of the Duma, he dismissed it. (Both the First and Second Dumas were dismissed.) With the proclamation of the new electoral laws in 1907, the tsar limited left-wing and minority nationality representation in the Duma.[52] After the restriction of non-Russian and left-wing representation in the Duma, Kistiakovsky's Ukrainian identity was fortified; he recognized his affinity with members of a non-Russian nationality more so than with members of the Russian intelligentsia. By 1909, in response to an upsurge of Great Russian nationalism, Kistiakovsky turned his attention more to questions of law and the defense of the rights of the nationalities—especially the Ukrainians. His profound conviction in individual liberties, social justice, and a rule-of-law state was strengthened rather than shaken by the growth of conservative forces. The belief that human rights had to be the basis of any viable constitutional order constituted a moral stance that was at the root of Kistiakovsky's thinking.

CHAPTER FIVE

The Role of the Intelligentsia

In the wake of the 1905 revolution, Kistiakovsky articulated his concern that the population of the Russian Empire gain an awareness of the role and function of law:

> From the point of view of pure governmental self-preservation, we have to raise the level of consciousness of law among the people and increase their feeling moral and legal responsibility for their conduct. It is necessary that the scornful attitude toward the law in our society ... be eradicated. Finally it is necessary to internalize a greater feeling of solidarity among the various elements making up our population. Only a firm feeling of solidarity among the people can guarantee the unity and safety of the government ... the main goal of the government is to satisfy and guarantee the interests of the people.[1]

Kistiakovsky contributed to improving popular understanding of law as an active member of the Committee for Popular Enlightenment founded in the 1890s. Like many liberal activists who wanted to perform public service, Kistiakovsky participated in producing the 1906 *Politicheskaia èntsiklopedia*, because the popular reference book was a step toward transforming the all-pervasive feeling of political helplessness into a potentially universal sense of self-determination.[2] In his introductory article for the encyclopedia, "Nashe politicheskoe obrazovanie," Kistiakovsky raised the major themes that he later elaborated in his *Vekhi* article. One such theme was the criticism of the abstract nature of political education and political consciousness. Kistiakovsky was critical of the faddish adoption of Western political and social theories in the Russian Empire: " ... the enthusiasm for ... Comte was replaced with enthusiasm for Spencer, and in the last place this position was yielded to enthusiasm for Marx and Marxism. In the era of the dominance of each of these thinkers, all political education was adopted schematically, worked out on the basis of theory, and did not go beyond the limits of the theory."[3]

Attempts to change the political situation in tsarist Russia had been met with repressive police-state measures, such as night visits, searches and arrests, censorship of organizations and professional unions, and exile; these activities on the part of the government did not nurture respect for law and civic consciousness among the empire's population. After all, Kistiakovsky noted ironically, the government was an absolute monarchy that could function better with a pacified population than with a politically active and aware population.[4]

The government's arbitrary actions, including the promulgation of the Stolypin electoral reforms in 1907 and the dismissal of the First and Second Dumas, caused Kistiakovsky and other liberal constitutionalists involved in popular education projects to realize the futility of their efforts in a context of lawlessness. The experience of living in a police state in Russia destroyed any individual social initiative for participation in government; Kistiakovsky wrote, "We Russians are well acquainted with police repression. We always have been subdued by the statement that the Leader will worry about it."[5] As subjects, the people traditionally waited to be directed and taken care of by their father tsar. Petrazhitskii wrote in his *Teoriia gosudarstva i prava* [Theory of State and Law] (1909) that ideally the law:

> . . . communicates the firmness and the confidence, the energy and initiative essential for life. A child brought up in an atmosphere of arbitrary caprice (however beneficent and gracious), with no definite assignment to him of a particular sphere of rights (although of a modest and childish character), will not be trained to construct and carry out the plans of life with assurance. In the economic field, particularly, he will lack confidence, boldness, and initiative: he will be apathetic, act at random, and procrastinate in the hope of favorable "chances," help from another, alms, gifts, and the like.[6]

For a constitutional system to function effectively, the individual had to become an active citizen who wanted to live in a society guided by and based on law. A fundamental disrespect for the law complicated attempts to establish a rule-of-law state. Aleksander Herzen explained that the Russian people had not learned respect for the law because there was no clear legal structure to regulate and mediate conflicts in their daily lives and to curb the corrupt ways of the government:

> Complete inequality before the law has killed any trace of respect for legality in the Russian people. The Russian, whatever his station, breaks the law wherever he can do so with impunity; the government acts in the same way.[7]

But Kistiakovsky did not accept the existing situation as a justification for the neglect of the role of law by the intelligentsia within the empire. Several years later, in 1909, he pointed out that the intelligentsia's negative attitude toward the law and a legal order was not just a result of the absence of legality in the empire; on the contrary, consciousness of legal problems and law constituted a social and cultural value that could be changed through the exercise of the will of the individual.[8] Kistiakovsky's sweeping critique in the controversial volume *Vekhi* [Landmarks] was directed against the intelligentsia's attitude toward the law and not against the complete lack of legality, legal institutions, and legal education. The gradual growth of legal consciousness and education among the government bureaucrats and the reforms of the nineteenth century should have made it natural for the intelligentsia to change its own attitude toward the role of law.

Vekhi

The political and intellectual world of society within the Russian Empire was in an uproar after the March 1909 publication of *Vekhi* in Moscow. The seven authors came together to condemn the violent revolutionary tradition of the intelligentsia and to convince its members of the need to end their customary alienation from the rest of society. This reaction was prompted by the trauma of the 1905 revolution and the subsequent failure to effect concrete changes through the newly established constitutional forms.[9] The *Vekhi* authors considered the intelligentsia a politically conscious sector of educated society within the empire that potentially could take an active part in creating change from within the governmental framework. *Vekhi* consisted of the following articles: Nikolai Berdiaev's "Philosophical Truth and the Intelligentsia's Truth"; Mikhail Gershenzon's "Creative Self-Consciousness"; A. S. Izgoev's "On the Intelligentsia's Youth"; Bogdan Kistiakovsky's "In Defense of Law: The Intelligentsia and Legal Consciousness"; Petr Struve's "The Intelligentsia and Revolution"; Semen

Frank's "The Ethics of Nihilism"; and Sergei Bulgakov's "Heroism and Asceticism."

Vekhi was comprised of sections that each of the authors wrote independently, without consultation with the others; only after the publication of the slim volume did they see the other articles, which were collected and prefaced with a general statement by the editor, Gershenzon.[10] In the introduction to *Vekhi*, Gershenzon attempted to create the connective tissue that would bind the articles into one entity:

> The platform common to all the authors is the recognition of the theoretical and practical primacy of the spiritual life over the outward forms of society in the sense that the life of the individual is the only creative force of human existence and that it, and not the self-sufficient elements of the political order, is the only solid basis for any social order.[11]

Gershenzon explained that the differences existing between the authors were not based on ideological positions, but on diverse approaches. As the editor, Gershenzon certainly hoped to emphasize the common points making the collection of essays a coherent whole.

The vagueness of the common platform and the lack of concrete solutions offered made these members of the intelligentsia, taken together, sound as socially impotent as the radical intelligentsia they criticized. Each of the seven contributors was a strong individualist who had come to *Vekhi* from his own distinct path of intellectual development and, in the same fashion, departed into his individualistic world both during and after the *Vekhi* debate.[12]

Struve became the editor of *Osvobozhdenie*, which later was the official Kadet journal. As mentioned earlier, Kistiakovsky had helped with the closing of the journal offices in Germany. The *Vekhi* authors had been active in the Union of Liberation and had joined the Constitutional Democratic Party after 1905. Only Berdiaev, who considered himself closer to the Social Democrats than to the "bourgeois liberals," did not join the Kadet Party.

After their move away from Orthodox Marxism in the early 1900s, Berdiaev, Bulgakov, and Frank became deeply involved with philosophical problems and eventually rejected political activism completely. Deeply influenced by the Russian philosopher Vladimir Soloviev, their attitude to ethical questions took on a clear religious character. Frank, Struve, Berdiaev, and Bulgakov had been members of the Religious-Philosophical Society, where problems of contemporary philosophy, religion, and society were discussed.[13] Involvement with religious and ethical questions led some of the former legal Marxists, including Bulgakov, Berdiaev, Frank, and Kistiakovsky, to contribute to the precursor of *Vekhi*, *Problemy idealizma* that ran counter to the convictions of the radical intelligentsia; it was critical of the positivist, populist, and materialist traditions of the intelligentsia and was a statement of the authors' break with Marxism.[14]

Vekhi was a less philosophical, more openly political appeal for the intelligentsia to work within the social system in order to transform it into one based on law and justice. Because of its broad sweeping critique of the intelligentsia, *Vekhi* created a sensation in all circles of Russian educated society. A controversy developed in the form of public meetings, lectures, collections of essays and articles.[15] Everyone from Lenin to Tolstoy commented on *Vekhi*. The Kadet party leader, Pavel N. Miliukov, traveled around Russia for party meetings organized to criticize the collection. In April 1909, a series of debates on *Vekhi* was held by the St. Petersburg Religious-Philosophical Society, whose leaders Dmitrii Merezhkovskii, Zinaida Gippius, and Dmitrii Filosofov were firmly opposed to *its principles*. In fact, every major political camp, with the exception of the extreme right, published a collection of essays in response to *Vekhi*.[16]

Comparatively few positive responses supporting the *Vekhi* authors appeared in Struve's journal, *Russkaia mysl'* [Russian Thought], and in the journal of the Trubetskoi brothers, *Moskovskii ezhenedel'nik* [The Moscow Weekly]. Some positive responses appeared in *Novoe vremia* [New Times], the symbolist journal *Vesy* [Scales], and the newspapers *Moskovskie vedomosti* [The Moscow Gazette] and *Slovo* [The Word].[17] More than two hundred responses to *Vekhi* appeared in newspapers, although the bibliography in the fourth edition of *Vekhi* included only about one hundred and sixty.[18]

The extreme right-wing welcomed *Vekhi*, for it saw the collection as an attack on the revolutionaries.[19] Lenin, on the opposite side, claimed that *Vekhi* was typical of the liberals, the Kadets, and that the publication of *Vekhi* signified the time when the liberals joined with the reactionaries.[20] Lenin described *Vekhi* as an "encyclopedia of liberal perfidy" in which the liberals were pretending to lash out against the intelligentsia, but in reality were attacking democracy.

> The formal themes of *Vekhi* were the sins of the Russian Intelligen-
> tsia; in reality its authors decided to form a court to judge the Russian
> Revolution, to defame it and to show the complete failure of the
> ideas, goals, and tradition of the Russian liberation movement.[21]

The Socialist Revolutionaries concurred with the Leninist accusa-
tion that the liberals had joined the ranks of the reactionaries. They
stigmatized *Vekhi* as the most reactionary volume to be published in
many years. As the title of the collection of Socialist Revolutionary
criticism, *Vekhi kak znamenie vremeni* [Landmarks as a Sign of the
Times], indicates, *Vekhi* was characteristic of the reactionary spirit of
the time following the Stolypin reforms and the autocracy's manipulation of the Duma. The long article by Ia. Bechev, "Pravovye idei v
russkoi literature" [Legal Ideas in Russian Literature], opens by distin-
guishing Kistiakovsky's article "V zashchitu prava" [In Defence of
Law] from the contributions of the other authors. Kistiakovsky did not
use religious imagery and phraseology, nor did he fear socialism when
combined with the rule of law. Bechev went so far as to describe
Kistiakovsky as alien to the historical heritage of the Russian intelligentsia.[22]

The Kadets' reply was published as a volume of essays, entitled
Intelligentsia v Rossii [The Intelligentsia in Russia], edited by Ivan
Petrunkevich. Though all the authors of *Vekhi* were Kadets, the party
quickly distanced itself from the book that criticized some of the hal-
lowed progressive traditions of Russia.[23] Pavel Miliukov's article was
an attack on the volume's attitude toward the revolutionary tradition
and potential in the Russian Empire. Miliukov exaggerated when he
criticized the *Vekhi* authors for welcoming the defeat of the revolution
and advocating a retreat to individual self-perfection.[24] Responding to
Kistiakovsky's contribution, Miliukov did not accept that the political
struggle to which he had been committed was " . . . creating obstacles
for the development of a 'sound legal consciousness' among Russians." Miliukov thought in political terms, and it did not occur to him
that his own party could be criticized for a lack of due respect for the
"spirit of law."[25] Vasilii Maklakov argued the same point, though his
criticism was of the Kadet Party. He wrote, "The Kadet leaders rejected
that which constituted the essence of liberalism: voluntary submission
to a legal order, work within the framework of the law, and respect for
the rights of others."[26] Kistiakovsky's article in *Vekhi* was a most

controversial part of the debate on the volume, because it was a hard-hitting critique that dared to attack even the liberal political parties in the Duma.

The Intelligentsia and Legal Consciousness

Kistiakovsky had clear philosophical as well as political differences with the other *Vekhi* authors. Of all the authors of the volume, Kistiakovsky emerged the least scathed by critics of the collection of essays. Both the Kadet Pavel Miliukov and the Socialist Revolutionary Viktor Chernov considered most of his points acceptable and useful. Unlike many of the other *Vekhi* authors who focused on the intelligentsia's spiritual renaissance—in some cases involving religion and national feelings—Kistiakovsky stressed the intelligentsia's self-awareness, education, and activities in the realm of law and government.[27] Some of the differences between Kistiakovsky and the other contributors (especially Struve) included the intelligentsia's failure to recognize the importance of the Ukrainian national struggle. But Kistiakovsky did agree with the other authors on the need for effective work within the framework of the Fundamental Laws of 1906.[28]

In his contribution to *Vekhi,* "V zashchitu prava. Intelligentsia i pravosoznanie," Kistiakovsky's concern with the self-determining role of the individual in society turned into an appeal—that the Russian intelligentsia play a guiding, vanguard role in establishing a constitutional form of government in the Russian Empire. The task of developing and defending the law devolved upon the intelligentsia because it was the only group within the Russian Empire with the capacity to understand the role of law and the need to educate society, build legal awareness, and change the governmental order. He called on the intelligentsia first to change its negative attitude toward a legal order and then to engage actively in the governmental processes to ensure the principles of freedom of speech, assembly, and universal suffrage. In that way, the intelligentsia would be able to press for reforms to guarantee that individual rights would not be lost during a (potential) social and political transformation.

Kistiakovsky was convinced that the change of the Imperial government from a "regime of force" to a "regime of law" had to be carried out in a constitutional system in which the powers were separated into the executive, legislative, and judicial branches. In such a governmental system, the function of intelligentsia was to utilize the existing legislative and judicial institutions and work from within them to institute change rather than simply to dismiss them as defective, turning to revolutionary goals and destroying the constitutional gains that had been made. He argued, " . . . if the intelligentsia continued to alienate itself from all the institutions set up after the reforms of the 1860s and the 1905 revolution, it would be overlooking strategic areas of applying its knowledge."[29] Because many radical members of the intelligentsia had refused to participate in the constitutional system, they were inadvertently contributing to the further destruction of the fragile and skeletal legal institutions that had been initiated in 1905. As discussed in the preceding chapter, Kistiakovsky believed that the October Manifesto and the Fundamental Laws of 1906 provided a framework for the development of a democratic constitutional system. However, he feared that the rights of individuals might never be guaranteed if the existing Russian system were allowed to perish, for then whoever took power would again subordinate individual rights to the needs of a particular governmental order.[30] Though the concepts of individual freedoms and the role of law in a constitutional government had been developed (at least theoretically) in Western European countries, Kistiakovsky explained that the process of implementing and internalizing those ideas would be different in the more primitive Russian context where the individual for centuries had been subject to the arbitrary will of the tsar:

> Borrowing is not enough—it is necessary to be seized by ideas at a certain moment in life. However old an idea may be, it is always new for the person experiencing it for the first time. It performs creative work in the consciousness as it is assimilated and transformed by the other elements present.[31]

Developing a sense of law and legal functions involved a complicated mental process that required a change in the intelligentsia's view of its own legal status. First, all individuals had to be classified as citizens who had inalienable rights as well as obligations and responsibilities to the proper functioning of the government and society.[32] At the same time, the individual had to change his perception of self from a passive subject to an active self-determining citizen.

Kistiakovsky's neo-Kantianism was an integral part of his view of the individual, the process of building awareness of law, and subsequently developing a governmental and legal order in the Russian Empire. He made it explicit in his earlier works that the individual had an inherent, absolute value and as such was a self-motivated agent in society that could interact with, or even counterbalance, the determining forces in the social and political context in question. The individual's actions in formulating laws or norms provided a forum for expressions of individual freedom.[33] Hence, legal consciousness was a cultural value formed mainly by the deliberate exercise of the will and the intellect.[34] In other words, the intelligentsia could decide to alter its own situation in society and end its disregard for the law. To begin changing its self-image, Kistiakovsky explained, " . . . the intelligentsia must withdraw to its own inner world and plunge deeply into it in order to refresh it and restore it to health. In the course of this inward labor, a genuine legal consciousness must finally awaken in the 'Russian intelligentsia.'"[35]

Unlike Marxists and other critics of Kistiakovsky's position who explained the intelligentsia's disregard for the law as a product of the lawless nature of Russian Imperial society and government, Kistiakovsky emphasized the positive creative view of the intelligentsia—its members could consciously change their perception of the law and, eventually, change the legal system. He added the following note to the second edition of *Vekhi*:

> It is unworthy of thinking people to say, we are corrupted and will be corrupted until the reasons for our corruption are removed. Every man is obliged to say, I must not be corrupted any longer, since I have understood what it is that is corrupting me and where the source of my corruption lies. We must now strain all the forces of our thought, feeling, and will to free our minds from the harmful effect of unfavorable circumstances. That is why the task of the time is to arouse the Russian intelligentsia's legal consciousness and summon it to life and action.[36]

Once the *intelligent* developed a legal consciousness, his new sense of self would have to be accompanied by behavior befitting a citizen. That is, the intelligentsia had to develop a sense of its role in a social organization—an awareness of what is correct and incorrect in a shared standard of social behavior. Otherwise, the intelligentsia and all members of society would remain the pawns of a system over which they had little or no control:

> Every social organization needs *legal* norms, i.e., not rules that regu-
> late the internal behavior of people, which is the objective of ethics,
> but rules that regulate their external behavior. Legal norms determin-
> ing external behavior, however, are not something external in them-
> selves, since they first exist in our consciousness and are internal
> elements of our spirits just as much as ethical norms. They only take
> on an external existence as well when they are expressed in the legal
> statutes or when applied in practice.[37]

In Kistiakovsky's view the intelligentsia overemphasized rules and discipline in its organizations; this was because the intelligentsia lacked a conscious sense of personal ethics to guide its behavior. He main-tained, "We need external discipline precisely because we have no internal discipline. In this area, too, we perceive law not as a legal conviction, but as a binding rule. And this is additional evidence of the low level of our legal consciousness."[37] The new political organiza-tions of the intelligentsia activists were hindered by problems of disci-plining their own members. Consequently, they engaged in endless discussions of binding rules for internal party discipline that ultimately diverted them from the goals of transforming the despotic society.[39]

The intelligentsia's principal failing in the nineteenth and early twentieth centuries lay in its larger concern with building a revolution-ary movement than with setting up a viable and democratic constitu-tional order to replace the old order. The intelligentsia's activists had concentrated on neither the practical nor the theoretical problems in-volved in the functioning of a democratic form of government. Thus, the intelligentsia had failed to produce any writings that would have practical value for the development of a codified form of common (customary) law or the importance of legal consciousness.[40] Legal writing within the empire tended to be technical, primarily for lawyers or members of the intelligentsia, and as such had little or no influence on the population as a whole. The Slavophiles of the 1840s and the populists of the 1870s did not concern themselves with legal questions or individual rights, for they felt that the absence of any legal order in the life of the Russian people only served to reaffirm their conception of the uniqueness of the Russian people and their situation.

Kistiakovsky's concern with making freedom and inviolability of person the cornerstone of a sound legal order, caused him to oppose those, especially among the populists, who declared freedom and individual rights . . . a *quantité négligeable* and defended the collective personality of the society.[41] For example, Nikolai Mikhailovskii held that the Western constitutional models were bourgeois systems in which the common person would be exploited by the upper classes of society: "Freedom is a great and tempting thing, but we do not want freedom if, as happened in Europe, it will only increase our age-long debt to the people."[42] Kistiakovsky's criticism of Mikhailovskii did not accurately convey Mikhailovskii's concern for individual rights, for the populist spokesman shared Kistiakovsky's goal of changing the individual's lamentable status in society. In fact, as N. I. Kareev, a major disciple of Mikhailovskii, pointed out, the theories of Kistiakovsky and Mikhailovskii have been characterized as similar in their conviction that society, law, and the state have a duty to protect the personal rights of all citizens.[43] In the second edition of *Vekhi*, Kistiakovsky added a note to acknowledge Mikhailovskii's sympathetic and supportive attitude toward the struggle for political liberties. But that acknowledgment did not eradicate the major point of difference between Kistiakovsky and Mikhailovskii—Kistiakovsky hoped to introduce the principles of individual rights into an imperfect constitutional system, while Mikhailovskii would object to working in a constitutional framework he characterized as bourgeois. As explained earlier, Kistiakovsky maintained that "bourgeois" was a term describing the socioeconomic structure while the legal guarantees for individual rights were part of a juridical form—a constitutional system. It was this distinction between bourgeois and constitutional that Kistiakovsky found lacking in Mikhailovskii's objection to a constitutional system for the Russian Empire.

For Kistiakovsky, any excuse for not supporting a constitutional form of government in the Russian Empire could potentially prolong continuing violations of the personal rights of individuals. The historian, liberal publicist, and lawyer Konstantin Kavelin (1818–1885) was one of the first scholars to note that, " . . . in the history of Russian legal institutions the individual has been overshadowed by the family, the commune, and the state, and has not received a legal status of his own . . . "[44] However, his position on constitutionalism did not reflect a comprehension of the importance of individual rights and the legal guarantees for them. Kistiakovsky explained that Kavelin rejected a

constitutional form of government for the empire because he felt that
the representative body would consist largely of nobles; hence, the
constitutional order would serve the interests of the privileged upper
class and not the majority—the peasantry. Kavelin explained:

> A constitution can only have some kind of sense when those who put
> it into effect and safeguard it consist of strongly organized rich
> classes, enjoying authority ... Many among us dream of a
> constitution ... and it is mostly those who hope with its help to seize
> power for themselves over the government, on the French Napole-
> onic model, to keep it in the hands of a few families, and exclude the
> people as a whole.[45]

Without examining the validity of Kavelin's contention that the social
structure was an inadequate foundation for a properly functioning representative system, Kistiakovsky commented, "For Kavelin, ... a truth
we consider indisputable—that freedom and inviolability of the individual can be realized only in a constitutional state—seems not to exist.
On the whole, the idea of struggling for individual liberties was at that
time totally foreign to him."[46] The point Kistiakovsky was making
might have been more convincing had he more carefully assessed
Kavelin's position. But he could not accept any position that might help
to delay the formal institutionalization of individual liberties.

Kistiakovsky explained that only with the influx of Western constitutional theories in the early 1890s, the intelligentsia began to understand that:

> ... political liberty was a prerequisite for a socialist system; that a
> constitutional state, despite bourgeois predominance, gave the work-
> ing class greater scope to struggle for its interests; that the primary
> needs of the working class were inviolability of person and freedoms
> of speech, strike, assembly, and organization; and that the struggle
> for political liberty was the first and most essential task or any
> socialist party ... [47]

However, Kistiakovsky held that the actions of the intelligentsia revealed that it still did not recognize the basic value of individual rights:

> ... during the liberation period (the revolution of 1905), the Russian
> intelligentsia could not even put the elementary rights of the indi-
> vidual—the freedom of speech and assembly into practice. Only
> speakers acceptable to the majority enjoyed free speech at our rallies;
> anyone who disagreed was drowned out by shouts, whistles, cries of
> "that's enough" and sometimes even physical coercion.[48]

> Now we have reached the point where complete and equal freedom of speech does not exist even in the Third Duma, since the dominant party and the opposition are not equally free to discuss the same questions. This is all the more sad because the popular representative body, whatever its composition, ought at least to reflect the entire nation's legal conscience, as the minimum expression of its ethical conscience.[49]

Legal principles based on the idea that the only element of absolute value in society is the individual and his or her rights had to be immutable even in a revolutionary situation. Nothing, including the idea of revolution, could be placed ahead of the legal statutes that could guarantee the human rights of all individuals. Kistiakovsky complained that even the progressive political parties such as the Social Democrats, the Socialist Revolutionaries, and the liberal Union of Liberation failed to consider the institutionalization of civil liberties and a constitutional legal order to be priorities:

> One would think that the statutes of a party composed of convinced republicans would guarantee its members of at least minimal guarantees of freedom of person and due process. But apparently, the representatives of our intelligentsia considered free self-determination of the individual and a republican system to be details unworthy of attention; at least, they deserved none when it was a question of putting those principles into daily practice rather than proclaiming them in programs.[50]

Civil liberties were denied the central and primary attention Kistiakovsky felt they should be given in the programs and practices of the political parties; furthermore, the political parties advocated revolutionary tactics that contradicted the fundamental fabric of human rights and a government based on law. For instance, the Social Democratic Party's most eminent theorist, Georgii Plekhanov, proudly stated that a popular revolutionary victory was the highest law of the land.[51] Kistiakovsky feared that using force or illegal tactics and imposing laws of war—a "state of siege"—would develop a self-perpetuating authoritarian system in which the individual would be arbitrarily controlled by the ruling elite.

The Role of the Courts in the Establishment of Law

Although the court system established in the Judicial Reforms of 1864 was based nominally on democratic principles, the executive and legislative branches of government were run autocratically.[52] Kistiakovsky advocated that the intelligentsia work on constructing a legal system by focusing on the courts. He recommended such an action in spite of his understanding that the development of popular legal consciousness had been hampered by the autocracy's reckless political repression of the court system.[53] Kistiakovsky believed that political manipulation of the court system only enhanced the popular attitude of indifference toward the legal system as a whole: "We . . . viewed trial by jury from just two perspectives, the political and the humanitarian; at best, we saw trial by jury as a court of conscience, an expression of passive humanitarianism rather than of an active legal consciousness."[54] But he maintained that "political conditions alone cannot be blamed for our bad courts; we, too, bear the responsibility. Under wholly analogous political conditions other nations have had bad courts that, nonetheless, upheld the law."[55] For, Kistiakovsky elucidated, "The court is the institution that plays the greatest role in stating and establishing the law. In all nations, before the legislative method had developed, the laws were clarified and sometimes even created by judicial decisions."[56] Kistiakovsky explained that in contemporary constitutional states, the courts had become mainly the custodians of existing laws, while the legislative activity of the state government took over the law-creating function. Unlike the Russian Empire in which written laws were not yet the basis for standard procedure of the courts, most European countries considered written law the predominant source of legal decisions applied in the courts. In describing the potential role of the Russian courts in those cases for which the written laws were nonexistent, he cited the example of the new Swiss legal code passed by both legislative chambers in 1907. This law prescribed that in cases that revealed the lack of an appropriate law, the judge would have the right to make his decision as if he were a legislator. For Kistiakovsky, this law emphasized the potential of the courts as custodians and executors of a country's legal system. In fact, he hoped that the Russian Empire might follow this progressive example set by "the most democratic and progressive European nation that recognized the judge as the spokesman for the people's legal consciousness as much as the deputy in the legislature."[57]

Kistiakovsky was frustrated that the Imperial legislature had failed to take any steps to give such a role to the courts. For example, he indicated his disappointment with the purely political rather than morally principled reactions of two Duma deputies to the emergency decree of August 1906, which instituted the use of courts-martial for civilians who committed blatant political crimes. He wrote, " . . . a representative of the extreme left in the Second Duma . . . asserted that this court is the most terrible of all, while a representative of the extreme right justified the courts martial as preferable to 'people's mob law.'"[59]

Nevertheless, Kistiakovsky remained optimistic that the courts could be made an effective forum for the building of a functional legal system for the Russian Empire. While there was still an autocratic rule, he limited his hopes for the future role of exercising law to the civil courts as opposed to the criminal courts: " . . . our civil courts are relatively independent, and if their activities were controlled and administered by the intelligentsia, they might have an enormous impact on the consolidation and development of our legal system."[59] It is precisely those "relatively independent" civil courts that became important forces in addressing issues of individual freedom and the role of law in the realm of marriage, divorce, and the family. As William G. Wagner demonstrates in his important study, *Marriage, Property and the Law in late Imperial Russia,* which focuses on the civil courts and the Civil-Cassation Department of the Senate, public efforts to change existing imperial marriage and divorce law led to public debates that eventually influenced state officials. Wagner shows that " . . . the boundary between state and society was much more porous and interactive than depicted conventionally."[60]

This sociological approach to the formation of legal changes and legal consciousness in society was comensurate with Kistiakovsky's concept of law as a social phenomenon. The interpenetration of legal ideas and practice were always fundamental to his notion of forming a viable legal system. Civil (private) law dealt with everyday problems of social, commercial, and family life, so Kistiakovsky felt that these largely uncodified areas of the law could become influential if the intelligentsia began to formulate laws based on the common practices of the population.

Contrary to the Slavophiles and, later, the populists, who considered "juridical principles" alien to the communally oriented Russian peasantry, Kistiakovsky argued that the common law tradition of the peasantry was an important source from which to begin formulating a legal system that would correspond to the specific social and economic conditions of the country:

> The Russian people as a whole do not lack organizational talents; undoubtedly, they even have an innate inclination for particularly intensive forms of organization. Their agrarian communes, their *arteli*, and so on, provide evidence on this point . . . This predominantly inner quality of the Russian people's legal consciousness was responsible for the erroneous view of their attitude toward the law.[61]

The downfall of the populist intelligentsia lay in its failure to work toward a formulation of the intuitive forms of common laws practiced by the masses into the written body of laws.[62] The common laws of the peasant masses could in fact have created the foundation for a well-defined legal system; "[o]nly then could the populists have carried out the task they set for themselves—of helping to consolidate and develop communal principles; at the same time it would have become possible to transform the communes into higher forms of social life that would have approximated socialism."[63] However, Kistiakovsky noted, " . . . the courts cannot occupy the lofty position intended for them if the public is not completely aware of their real functions, and there is exhaustive evidence that our intelligentsia itself lacks this awareness."[64]

Though he perceived the court system as deeply flawed, he hoped that judges and lawyers would maintain legal standards in their work with the system. He demanded that such legal experts make their behavior conform to the standard procedure of an objective legal system; they should refrain from manipulating that system to achieve what he considered personal and limited political goals that could jeopardize the methodical development of a codified legal system. For example, he criticized those radical attorneys of the turn of the century who used the courts as a political arena for expressing their objections to the existing regime:[65]

> We did and do have eminent criminal and political defense lawyers, among them some ardent proponents of a humane attitude toward

criminals. But most of them fought only for a particular idea, for a 'new law' . . . rather than for 'law' in the apolitical, strict sense of the word.[66]

The Role of the Intelligentsia after 1913

After 1906, having witnessed the growth of illegal actions of the tsar and the bureaucracy along with the increase of terrorism and assassinations, Kistiakovsky's appeal for guidance from the intelligentsia became more focused and urgent in the journal of the Moscow Juridical Society, *Iuridicheskii vestnik,* which he began to edit in 1912. By 1913, he identified the intelligentsia lawyers as those responsible for rescuing the damaged principles of the October Manifesto and the Fundamental Laws.[67] Since the laws establishing the State Duma and State Council were supposed to guarantee that "no new law could be instituted without the sanction or the approval of the State Council and the State Duma," Kistiakovsky noted that the government should also be expected to follow those rules. But the Fundamental Laws did not do more than create a " . . . boundary between the laws on the one hand, and the government edicts and administrative orders on the other . . . the principle of the supremacy of law was introduced into our legislature so that the edicts would be promulgated 'in accordance with laws.'"[68]

Kistiakovsky observed, however, that in practice, the authority of laws had declined in contemporary life within the empire. Though the October Manifesto had formulated the rights of the individual into law, these rights were not guaranteed; in fact, " . . . statistics show that in this period crimes against the individual have increased significantly."[69] The individual was still being treated as an inferior part of the system instead of the center of it. For example, Stolypin's agrarian legislation of 1906–1907 purportedly granted certain rights to the peasantry, while in fact those reforms actually embodied the imposition of the government's control on the largest sector of the society. That legislation was established to eliminate the peasant commune by turning the peasants into private landowners. Because of the peasant uprisings of 1902–1903 and 1905–1906, the government was convinced that the peasants in the communes presented a serious threat to the existing political and social order.[70] The officials who implemented Stolypin's

land policy hoped that the large class of small freeholders in the villages would give the regime a broader base; that is, they would divert
the attention of the peasants from future confiscations of private lands
by allowing them to become private owners. Though the new agrarian
legislation appeared to be a way to change the lot of the peasantry, the
policy was introduced on political grounds rather than considerations
of economic or legal rights.[71] As Kistiakovsky noted, "The general
impression from the new agrarian legislation is that the person of the
peasant serves as an object for experiments, but the actual rights of the
person are not guaranteed nor protected in this superimposed legal
order."[72] At that time, the law served state or administrative purposes
and was not recognized for its independent role in society within the
Russian Empire.[73] But Kistiakovsky insisted that the status of law had
to change:

> The law must have force wholly independent of the political trends
> which prevail in the country and in the government. Law, by its very
> essence, stands above all parties . . . and therefore to put it in a subor-
> dinate relationship to one or another party would be to distort its
> nature.[74]

Kistiakovsky considered it the duty of legal experts to introduce as
many juridical criteria as possible into the discussion of whether one or
another reform might be desirable.[75] Ideological and political standards
were not to be used to judge the validity of the law. He hoped that the
intelligentsia in the legal profession would use the techniques of his
social-science method in order to formulate the legal norms of the
society. Those norms would be derived through an analysis of social
conditions and necessities. At the same time, social conditions also
would provide the context for interpreting the norms. In the terms of his
neo-Kantian methodology, the laws would have an organic relationship
to the specific society rather than provide abstract juridical statements
of "what should be." In fact, the legal experts could participate in the
process of social change by formulating the morally conscious and
active role of the law. Kistiakovsky most clearly articulated his goals
for the legally trained intelligentsia when he wrote:

> The Councils of Moscow and Petersburg Juridical Societies, united
> around *Iuridicheskii vestnik,* consider the basis of their goal—to
> facilitate the recognition of the independent and autonomous mean-
> ing of law in our lives. This grew out of the conviction that only when

law will be considered a means for the achievement of various goals as well as a goal in itself, then we will have a stable and sensible legal order in Russia.[76]

In 1915, in a short introductory article to an edition of *Iuridicheskii vestnik*, Kistiakovsky reemphasized the important role of the intelligentsia lawyers in the process of social change. In that article, "Politicheskoe i iuridicheskoe znachenie manifesta 17 oktiabria 1905 goda" [The Political and Juridical Meaning of the Manifesto of 17 October, 1905], Kistiakovsky pointed out that even though all facets of the manifesto had not been put into effect, the document was still a law in the formal sense of the word.[77] The problem was with the failure to implement properly and guarantee the provisions in the manifesto, and it was the intelligentsia's role to take note of those laws and make sure that the process of social change takes place in the existing legal framework. This article was Kistiakovsky's last appeal in behalf of a legal rather than a potentially destructive revolutionary solution to the problems seething within the empire.

His faith in the possibility of accomplishing social transformation and political change through legal, constitutional forms proved not to be a viable alternative in light of the erosion and degradation of the principles of the October Manifesto and the Fundamental Laws of 1906. Nevertheless, as late as 1915, Kistiakovsky did not compromise his idealistic position on using constitutional forms. His notion of the role of the law and the legally trained intelligentsia remained a utopian ideal for a future attempt at social transformation in a constitutional framework.

The intelligentsia was to act as the leading force in remodeling society by its own example of showing respect for law. Its members were to gain an understanding of the ongoing changes in the society and contribute to giving direction to that process of social transformation. Instead of relying on the spontaneous course of events in terms of social and economic development, the intelligentsia trained in law was expected to inculcate the ideas of self-worth (the inherent value of the individual) and civic consciousness in the citizens of the empire and to formulate the direction of the state; both the state and the individual were to play an active role in the transformational process.

Kistiakovsky emphasized that the intelligentsia's struggle to establish and guarantee individual rights and a *Rechtsstaat* could be carried out simultaneously on several fronts; that is, developing its own legal awareness from within, participating in the parliament, and working in those parts of the court system that were not completely controlled by the autocracy—the civil courts. He boldly articulated each of these areas as central for the development of a viable legal system, though his process of change could only begin when the intelligentsia developed a legal consciousness. Kistiakovsky took a most unorthodox position, which explains why his article stimulated so much response. For him, the movement to create a democratic society was inseparable from the challenge of establishing a system of constitutional law in a society based on principles of social justice.

CHAPTER SIX

The Ukrainian Movement within the Multinational Russian Empire

The multinational nature of the Russian Empire complicated the process of developing plans for the transition from autocracy to a form of democracy. To facilitate an end to the dominant administrative role of the Russians (known then as "Great Russians," *Velikorusy*) the largely illiterate peoples of the empire had to be inculcated with the ideas of national self-determination and constitutionalism. This meant reaching people from more than two hundred ethnic and linguistic groups inhabiting the territories of the Russian Empire.

At the end of the nineteenth century, the Russian population nearly equaled the combined number of the other nationalities. Those who were grappling with the nationalities question had to face not only the disproportionate gap in the economic and cultural development between the various nationalities, but their numerical inequality as well. Moreover, some nationalities lived in defined areas, while others lived in areas inhabited by other nationalities. The peoples of the Caucasus, for example, Armenians, Georgians, Caucasian mountain peoples, and other European and indigenous peoples, created a nationality problem in parts of the Russian Empire that resembled the situation in the Hapsburg Empire.[1] Even the Ukrainian territories were mixed, containing, in addition to the dominant Ukrainian element, Russians, Jews, and other minority nationalities. How could the principle of national self-determination be put into practice? Was it possible to devise such a principle that would preclude the eventual domination of a larger and more powerful national group over a smaller one? Building an anti-autocratic public opinion among the national populations of the Russian Empire involved emphasizing the development of the cultural life of the various nationalities and, gradually, the transmission of the principle of individual rights and constitutional government to the peoples of the empire.

Kistiakovsky as a Ukrainophile

Kistiakovsky's Ukrainophile stance placed him in a conflicting position between his roots in the Ukrainian movement and his political allegiance to the Russian oppositional movement. His views on the national question remained unchanged during his initial period of student activism until 1905, when he worked with the Union of Liberation. He was wary of the developing Russophobia among Ukrainian nationalists and made clear his opposition to any national separatism, be it Ukrainian or another non-Russian nationality.[3] In 1905 he chided Ukrainian nationalists for attacking Russians participating in the liberation movement for their indifference to the nationality problem. By attacking Russian liberals and radicals who did not stress the national rights of the Ukrainians, he pointed out, the Ukrainian nationalists were losing sight of the enemy that Ukrainians shared with Russians and other non-Russians—the autocracy.[2]

Kistiakovsky encouraged Ukrainian activists to stop blaming others for their inferior state and, instead, to join the Union of Liberation and at the same time organize their own national movement: " . . . the Ukrainians could only become an equal part of the revolutionary movement if and when they organized themselves nationally."[3] Furthermore, he pointed out, the Ukrainian movement had failed to effectively demand that the cultural rights of other non-Russian nationalities become an integral part of the plans for building a democratic constitutional system. He explained, "I observe Ukrainian affairs . . . and I do not like the narrow nationalist position of the movement. In the Ukrainian movement now, there is no place for Drahomanovites—that is, for a cultured, broad, all-European orientation. All that exists is the stale Russian (nationalist) view in reverse."[4]

Kistiakovsky considered that out of all Slavic cultures, only Russian could potentially become a world culture on the scale of Greek, Roman, German, and French culture. Still, Kistiakovsky did not view the development of the Ukrainian culture and language as secondary—Ukrainian connections with the more powerful Russian nation would help in building and protecting the Ukrainian national culture. The

Russophobia of Ukrainian nationalists was, in his opinion, self-defeating in the empire-wide drive to eliminate the autocracy. He saw no contradiction between Ukrainians joining the predominantly Russian Union of Liberation and, at the same time, pressing their own national demands.[5]

Kistiakovsky was careful to remind Ukrainian activists that the Ukrainian national question was not ignored by all Russian political parties. In its party program, the Union of Liberation, the precursor of the Constitutional Democratic Party (Kadets), had advocated federal organization of national regions and the strengthening of local self-rule within each region. In his view, the only hope of success for the 1905 movement was to end the autocracy and Russian hegemony in the formation of a coalition of activists of all nationalities in the empire. He understood that a purely chauvinistic (nationalist) program would in all likelihood result in a divided multinational empire with the Russians again dominating all other nationalities.[6]

Kistiakovsky conceived of developing Russian Ukraine on economic and cultural levels that would form the basis of a Ukrainian national consciousness—only then the active participation of the Ukrainian people in a federation of nationalities would be possible. The largely peasant Ukrainian population would not exercise their autonomy in daily lives unless they could use their local customs and language.[7] The rapid growth of the peasant cooperative movement signified for Kistiakovsky the beginning of such a local Ukrainian national movement.

The period following 1905 witnessed a great surge in the development of cooperatives in Russian Ukraine. By 1910 there were more than two thousand cooperatives, and by 1914 there were 6,510 cooperatives, of which half were rural and half urban.[8] Kyiv became the center of the cooperative movement and when a cooperative congress was held there in 1908, the transactions were conducted in the still officially illegal Ukrainian language.[9] At another conference of Russian and Ukrainian cooperatives held in St. Petersburg, the Ukrainian representatives played a leading role: "At this meeting it became clear that the cooperative movement in Russia can only develop if the cooperatives are organized into a non-centralized federal system with representatives of autonomous regions."[10]

While the cooperative movement in Western European countries developed to cope with the needs of industrial workers, the Russian and Ukrainian cooperative movements emerged at the end of the 1860s as a response to the needs of the recently emancipated peasants, artisans, and laborers in towns.[11] In Ukraine, the cooperative movement had been started by the Ukrainian intelligentsia, primarily Ukrainian Social Democrats, as a type of social and economic self-defense and became an important part of the Ukrainian movement. In fact, the self-governing economic associations became schools for popular civic responsibility and leadership.[12]

Liberals, socialists, and Ukrainophiles considered the cooperatives to be a possible way to escape the horrors of capitalist development and to encourage socialist ideals and values. Others believed the cooperative movement important to be an independent economic force; the cooperatives provided a way to reach the rural world of villages and simultaneously promote the growth of Ukrainian national consciousness.[13] Kistiakovsky's concept of a federal structure of peasant cooperatives would serve two purposes: first, it would enable separate local economies to function effectively, and second, link them into the economies of the other nationalities of the Russian Empire. Though he recognized the need for the economic development of Ukrainian territories, he perceived that development in limited terms of specific local economic initiatives, such as the cooperative movement. The economic aspect of cultural life was a vehicle for the development of national consciousness. Cultural autonomy was not something that could be imposed on the Ukrainian-speaking peasantry by the largely Russified educated national activists. Rather, a real cultural autonomy could develop among the Ukrainians only through their free use of local language and customs. The burgeoning new cooperative movement would form a federation of peasant organizations. That federation would provide the foundation for Ukrainian cultural autonomy and would become part of a powerful and self-determining multinational peasant class. Kistiakovsky thought that the exercise of national customs and rights and local economic initiative were complementary rather than conflicting with the drive against the autocracy throughout the empire. The increasing class distinctions did not contradict the idea of solidarity among the proletariat—although solidarity is based on class, it is supposed to turn into a national phenomenon that leads to common goals between nations or national collectivities. After all, Marx and Engels were speaking of international solidarity when they wrote, "Proletariat of all lands [nations], unite."[14]

Kistiakovsky's conception of national rights as a part of individual rights in a socialist context is remarkably akin to those of his two contemporaries—the Austrian Social Democratic theoreticians Otto Bauer (1881–1938) and Karl Renner (1870–1950), who had to face the complicated nationalities problem in the Hapsburg Empire.[15] As socialists, Renner and Bauer were unusual, for they tried to understand and solve the dilemma of nationalities in the Hapsburg Empire, instead of minimizing it in the name of the more important goal of building socialism. This also made their approach attractive to socialist parties of non-Russians, such as the Jewish socialist party, the Bund, which adopted Renner and Bauer's "Austrian Project" in its program.[16] The idea that national cultural autonomy for citizens of multinational states (or, *Nationalitätenstaaten*) constituted a part of individual rights was analogous to Kistiakovsky's conception for the Russian Empire. The controversial "Austrian Project" for national cultural autonomy, which classified national rights as civil rights, was formed from Karl Renner's legal expertise and Otto Bauer's social and political acumen and differed from traditional nineteenth-century socialist treatments of the national question.[17] Generally, socialists were not concerned with the national questions of multinational territories—they even tried to avoid them, for national problems complicated the development of class solidarity that could lead to social and economic as well as political change.

Until 1912, the Bolshevik and Menshevik factions of the Social Democratic Party opposed federalism, because they conceived of building socialism in the context of a large centralized state rather than on a local level and along national or ethnic lines. Though there was a period of Menshevik concessions to the demands of the Jewish Bund in 1903, the early anti-federalist position of both Social Democratic factions was firm:

> Social Democracy . . . has as its fundamental and principal task to assist the self-determination, not of peoples or of nations, but of the proletariat of every nationality. We must always and unconditionally strive toward the closest unification of the proletariat of all nationalities, and only in individual, exceptional cases can we advance and

actively support demands for the creation of a new class state, or the
replacement of a state's full political unity by the weaker federal
bond.

The growth of Great Russian chauvinism after 1907 forced the Bolsheviks and Mensheviks to change their positions on the national question.
Under increasing pressure from non-Russians in the Social Democratic
Party, such as the Caucasian Mensheviks, the Ukrainians, and the Jews,
the Bolsheviks and Mensheviks were forced to recognize the plight of
non-Russian nationalities in the empire.

Kistiakovsky shared with Renner and Bauer the basic notion that
national autonomy should not interfere with the political unity of the
state. The two major alternatives to the problem of nationalities in
multinational states were the territorial or extra-territorial organization
of nationalities. Territorial organization entailed the fragmentation of
the empire into provinces that would correspond as closely as possible
with the ethnographic boundaries of each nationality. Extra-territorial
organization meant that every national group was to have self-rule in
cultural and linguistic matters, irrespective of its geographic distribution.[18] In the extra-territorial case, the state would be divided adminis-
tratively rather than by nationally defined territories. This, of course,
was a solution more suitable to those areas in which the population was
too mixed to allow for national territorial divisions.[19]

Renner and Bauer's extra-territorial organization of nationalities
presupposes that people of the same nationalities organized themselves
into unions or cooperatives within a geographic area.[20] Since there
were more serious problems with the areas of mixed nationalities than
those of one predominant nationality in the Hapsburg Empire, the
extra-territorial solution was the only rational one to be applied as an
organizational principle. In contrast, Kistiakovsky's orientation for
Russian Ukraine was territorial, though he shared with Renner and
Bauer the conviction that a multinational empire would be organized
most effectively when the national or ethnic units were subordinate to
the supranational state government and when state government served
to administer and coordinate the military, economic, and social affairs
of all the national units.[21]

Kistiakovsky and his Austrian counterparts were determined to prevent the national question from becoming a stumbling block to the
development of democratic socialism in their respective multinational

empires. Hence, they limited their demands for national autonomy to cultural autonomy to ensure that the drive for national rights should not hinder or complicate the movement against monarchical government, nor the development of class alliance leading to economic and social transformation.[22]

Defending the Ukrainian Movement after 1907

In the First and Second State Duma, the majority of deputies were liberal Constitutional Democrats (Kadets) and peasant *Trudoviki*; both groups took the problem of nationalities seriously. In their address to the throne at the opening of the First Duma in 1906, the Kadets stressed the importance of establishing a federal system to give all nationalities some local autonomy and ultimately equal rights.[23] However, the dissolution of the Second Duma by the tsar in 1907 and the new electoral laws marked the end of the brief period of liberalism in the realm of minority nationality rights.

The crisis of the constitutional experiment was clearly revealed when Stolypin, the minister of interior, promulgated his controversial electoral laws of June 3, 1907, which reduced the representation of non-Russian nationalities,[24] and declared that the new Third Duma would be "Russian in spirit." In the face of burgeoning Russian pressures against minority nationalities, during the Third and Fourth Dumas, Ukrainian political parties were forced to curtail their activities.[25] Given that only 43 percent of the population of the empire was Russian according to the 1897 census, the cutback of non-Russian representatives made it clear that the Duma system failed to provide adequate representation for the non-Russian nationalities.[26] The revival of Russian chauvinism manifested itself in the legislative chambers during the Third and Fourth Dumas, when most of the predominantly conservative deputies took a strong stand against any proposal to grant other nationalities equal rights with the Russians. To make matters worse for non-Russians, a growing similarity between the pro-Russian, anti-minority-nationalities positions of both the liberal and conservative Duma representatives led to the increasing number of nationalistic decisions adopted during these sessions. In the Third Duma even the Kadets (the party to which Kistiakovsky was closest) betrayed their former federalist position and revealed their unwillingness to deal with the plight of the Ukrainians.[27]

The intensification of Russian nationalism from 1909 to 1910 was directly related to Stolypin's campaign to extend elective local government institutions (*zemstva*) to western areas of Russia; Alexander II had not created *zemstva* in the western provinces, because he was afraid that the Polish landlords, who made up only four percent of the population, would control the provinces and prevent representation for the majority of Great Russian citizens in the area. The Western Zemstvo Bill was intended to strengthen the position of the Russian inhabitants at the expense of the Poles, Jews, and Ukrainian peasants. Tensions among the nationalities grew after the Western Zemstvo campaign, the attack on Finnish autonomy, and the drive against the use of native languages in the schools of the non-Russian nationalities. Stolypin ignored the Ukrainian issue because he considered the Ukrainians and Belarusians to be "Russians" in so far as they were Orthodox believers, and he assumed that they would be receptive to the Russian nationalist program for the western part of the empire.[28]

The international situation exacerbated the problems for the Ukrainian movement. Relations between the Austro-Hungarian Empire and the Russian government became strained after the Austrian annexation of Bosnia-Herzegovina in October 1908 and the Bulgarian Declaration of Independence, both of which served to dash Russian nationalists' Pan-Slavic hopes for active support by all Slavs. The problems raised by the Ukrainian movement concerning the rights of the Ukrainian population in the Russian Empire were viewed with suspicion in Russian circles. The Russian government and Russian nationalists considered Ukrainian demands to be a part of an Austrian-Polish-German conspiracy against the Russians that could affect the security and boundaries of the Russian Empire.[29]

One of the issues at the forefront of Ukrainian concerns involved the struggle for the rights of the Ukrainian population during the discussions over the separation of Chełm (Kholm). The Russian government, afraid that the Polish landlords in the region would take control of the region through the *zemstva*, had proposed anti-Polish *zemstva* in Lithuania, Belorussia, and Right-Bank Ukraine as well as the creation of a new "Russian" province, Kholmskaia guberniia, located in the eastern borderland of the Congress Kingdom of Poland, an area inhabited mostly by Ukrainians and Poles. The formation of this new "Russian" province was actively supported by Russian nationalists and the

Russian Orthodox Church, believing that the new province would make it possible to protect the local "Russian" population from Polish and Catholic influence.[30] The problems of the Ukrainian population in the Chełm area were secondary to the struggle against Polish control of the region. In fact, the Ukrainians in Chełm were largely ignored by the Russian liberal leaders despite the efforts to enlighten the Russian public by Ukrainian intellectuals, including Kistiakovsky. In a long article entitled "Kholmshchina i Ukraina" [The Kholm Region and Ukraine], published in *Moskovskii ezhenedel'nik* [The Moscow Weekly], Kistiakovsky tried to bring the problem to the attention of Russian society as well as the Council of Ministers at the time the bill for the Duma was being prepared. But all the efforts were to no avail, and in the Duma debates of 1909, Ukrainian interests were ignored. The Ukrainian community felt betrayed by the Russian liberals—the position of the Ukrainian population was not considered as significant as the Polish threat in the region.[31] Kistiakovsky later commented that the Russians and Poles had acted as though they were deciding on whether they should Russify or Polonize the Ukrainians; consequently, those that fought for the autonomy of Ukrainian culture interfered with the plundering of the Russifiers and Polonizers.[32]

Defenders of national rights, such as Kistiakovsky, were faced with a special problem, for they shared the Russian goal of replacing the autocracy, but were at odds with supporters of Russification. The continuing repression of national cultures in the empire, in Kistiakovsky's view, was a violation of individual rights: "Those among Russian progressive people who advocate an ideological struggle against the Ukrainian popular movement should know that there are no devices with which they can relieve themselves of the moral responsibility for that violence to the human spirit which is inherent in compulsory Russification."[33] Kistiakovsky argued that the very existence of a Russification policy contradicted the ideas basic to a constitutional movement striving to insure individual rights and potentially human rights for all citizens; the establishment of a federal organization for the multinational empire was the only feasible and democratic solution to the problem of minority nationalities.

A Course on the Ukrainian Movement for Russians

Kistiakovsky had not taken part in the daily activities of the Ukrainian national movement since his student years in Germany. However, when the Russian attacks on Ukrainian cultural and political activities increased, he resumed his position as a spokesman for the Ukrainian cause in a series of articles he published in the Russian-language journals *Ukrainskaia zhizn'* [Ukrainian Life] and *Russkaia mysl'* [Russian Thought] in 1911–1912.[34] He intended to make educated Russian society aware that it was neglecting the effects of the Russian domination over the Ukrainian people and their culture.[35] In addition to describing the abuses that accompanied Russification, the articles also provided the Russian reader with a history of the concept of federalism in Russian and Ukrainian thought. In his role as spokesman for the Ukrainian national movement, Kistiakovsky attempted to raise Russian political consciousness about the Ukrainians and to build support for a possible collaboration between Russians and Ukrainians (as well as other non-Russian nationalities) in the building of a federation of nationalities for the Russian Empire.

To present the Russian audience with historical perspectives on supporters of federalism for the Russian Empire, Kistiakovsky noted Aleksandr Herzen's perceptive writings on the Ukrainian national question in the article, "Gertsen i Ukraina" [Herzen and Ukraine]. He considered Herzen's comments particularly noteworthy in view of the fact that he was a Russian.[36] Unlike most Russian political activists and journalists of Kistiakovsky's time, Herzen had been deeply involved with the fate of the non-Russian peoples in the empire. In the wake of the Polish revolution of 1830–1831 and the romantic nationalist movements of the 1840s in Western Europe, Herzen, the Westernizing revolutionary, had called for the guarantee of the civil rights of speech, conscience, and creed, and for the end of the oppression of nationalities by the Great Russians. At approximately the same time that the secret Ukrainian society—the Cyril and Methodius Brotherhood—voiced its national demands and was silenced, Herzen left for London. There, in 1847, he founded the journal *Kolokol* [The Bell] and contributed articles to *Poliarnaia zvezda* [The Polar Star] to continue propagating his ideas for the decentralizing and dismantling of the tsarist government. In 1851 he wrote:

Centralization is contrary to the Slav genius; federalism, on the other hand, is its natural form of expression. Once the Slav world has become unified, and knit together into an association of free autonomous peoples, it will at last be able to enter on its true historical existence . . .

. . . the majority of the Slav peoples have never been subjugated by a conquering race. For them submission has, on the whole, been confined to the recognition of an overlord and to the payment of some form of tribute. Such, for instance, was the Mongol rule in Russia. As a result, the Slavs have managed to preserve for some hundreds of years their nationality, their way of life, and their language.[37]

In the articles with the common title "Rossiia i Pol'sha" [Russia and Poland], which Herzen published in *Kolokol* in 1859–1860, he openly demanded self-determination for Ukraine. Herzen wrote, "Now tell me, what kind of heirs to the Congress of Vienna are we if we assign where a strip of land should belong without asking the people who live there what they want . . . In my opinion, the question is answered simply: Ukraine should be recognized as a free and independent country . . ."[38] Herzen's advocacy for Ukrainian independence was predicated on the idea that the Ukrainian people should only become a part of a Slavic federation if they elected to do so. In that way, the Ukrainian people would be self-determining. Herzen passionately proclaimed:

Untie their hands, unleash their tongues; Let their speech flow completely freely, and then let them speak their mind on whether they will join us (Russia) . . . or you (Poland), . . . or, if they are clever, extend both of their hands to a brotherly union and remain independent of both powers. That is why I value federalism so highly. In such a system, federal parts are connected by a common goal and no one belongs—not Geneva to Bern, nor Bern to Geneva.[39]

Kistiakovsky's hope for joint Ukrainian and Russian efforts in eliminating Russian control over non-Russians in his own time was evident in his systematic emphasis on all signs of such cooperation in his presentation of the Ukrainian movement's history. He recorded such a moment of alliance between representatives of the Russian and Ukrainian movements: in 1860 the Ukrainian historian Mykola Kostomarov, one of the founders of the Cyril and Methodius Brotherhood, responded to Herzen's comments on the Ukrainian question in a letter to Herzen.[40] Kistiakovsky reported that Herzen was sufficiently impressed by the letter to publish it in full. Moreover, Herzen announced that Kostomarov's letter would represent *Kolokol*'s position on the

Ukrainian national problem.[41] Kostomarov's letter articulated a non-separatist Ukrainian nationalist position; that is, Ukrainian national autonomy did not require that Ukraine sever all relations with the rest of the Slavic peoples. Kostomarov wrote:

> The solution to the problem is simple: the disputed lands do not belong to this or that land—they belong to the people who have always inhabited them, inhabit them now and cultivate them . . . We do not demand for ourselves anything which is independent of the general desires of all of Russia. No one of us thinks of tearing Southern Russia from connections with the rest of Russia. On the contrary, we would wish that all other Slavs would join into one union with us even under the scepter of the Russian government, if this government is made up of free peoples . . . [42]

Though Herzen was a great advocate of a constitutional system of government, he failed to put the freedom of person on the same level as the freedom of peasants from serfdom. Kistiakovsky maintained that unless individual freedoms were placed in the focal position during the construction of a constitutional order, the people would participate in the running of the country without guaranteeing clear limitations on the power of the state.

Drahomanov and Kistiakovsky

Kistiakovsky's constitutionalist, federalist, and anti-separatist stance was influenced by the liberal socialist ideas of Mykhailo Drahomanov, his intellectual mentor. Their liberalism placed the individual in the center of any social-political system. The state was to be organized to serve the needs of the people. As mentioned earlier, Kistiakovsky made a lifelong commitment to making Drahomanov's ideas known in Russia and the West and had convinced Peter Struve to publish Drahomanov's political writings, using Struve's "Osvobozhdenie" press in Paris. Struve served as editor for the first volume, and the second volume was completed by Kistiakovsky in 1906. These publications appeared just around the 1905 revolution, when there was an increased interest in Drahomanov's concepts of political freedom and constitutionalism.

Kistiakovsky identified with Drahomanov's maverick position in the world of Russian revolutionaries. By writing about Drahomanov, Kistiakovsky clarified his own position as a supporter of cultural autonomy and attempted to win Russian support for the Ukrainian cause.

In his 1912 article on his mentor "M. P. Dragomanov i vopros o samostoiatel'noi ukrainskoi kul'ture" [M. P. Drahomanov and the Question of an Independent Ukrainian Culture], he described Drahomanov's anti-separatist view of Ukrainian autonomy and federalism.

The political evolution of Drahomanov can serve as a prototype for Kistiakovsky's development from radical Marxism to reform socialism. In the late 1870s, when Drahomanov was publishing *Hromada* at his Ukrainian press in Geneva, he was a radical revolutionary socialist. However, by the early 1880s, when he collaborated with the Zemstvo Union, he had become an outspoken advocate of reform socialism.[43] The failure of the populist and terrorist attempts of the 1870s stimulated Drahomanov's decisive change to evolutionary reform, socialism, and constitutionalism. He asserted that "social reforms should be prepared from above, and what is most important—from below."[44] The ideals of constitutionalism and federalism would not become natural parts of the population's consciousness unless these principles were injected from above to accompany social and economic change from below.

From 1881 to 1883 Drahomanov embarked on a cooperative venture with the Russian constitutionalists of the Zemstvo Union. The Zemstvo Union's goal was to establish a constitutional regime based on the political liberty of the peoples of Russia. This group was designed to eliminate revolutionary terrorism and ensure that a constitutional system would be instituted in the empire and that it would have a moderate leaning. Drahomanov's reputation was severely tarnished by charges that he had been duped by tsarist representatives who had co-opted the constitutionalist Zemstvo Union and its journal, *Vol'noe slovo* [The Free Word], which Drahomanov edited for a short time in 1883. The allegation that Drahomanov was working with an organization controlled by the "enemy" tsarist forces appeared in V. Ia. Bogucharskii's 1912 book, *Iz istorii politicheskoi bor'by v 70kh i 80kh gg. XX veka* [On the History of the Political Struggle of the 1870s and 1880s].[45]

In response to Bogucharskii's book, Kistiakovsky initiated a polemic in 1912 to protect the reputation of the great Ukrainian patriot and to demonstrate the falsity of incrimination. In doing so he adopted the pattern established by nineteenth-century Ukrainian historians, such as his former professor, Volodymyr Antonovych,[46] who devoted much of their writing to contrasting the inherently democratic nature of the Ukrainian people with the dominant stance of their Polish or Russian conquerors. In that tradition, Kistiakovsky's refutation of Bogucharskii in *Stranitsy proshlogo* [Pages of the Past] emphasized the liberal-democratic orientation of the Ukrainian activist Drahomanov, while denying the accusations that there were connections between the Zemstvo Union and the Holy Brotherhood, the anti-revolutionary clique of courtiers.[47]

Kistiakovsky construed the allegations concerning Drahomanov as yet another Russian attack on the Ukrainian movement.[48] He maintained that even if there was some infiltration by anti-revolutionary elements, the Zemstvo Union was nevertheless largely a group of constitutionalists. Hence, the organization and its goals should be judged by the programs and articles in the journal *Vol'noe slovo*.[49] Drahomanov's role as editor of the journal in 1883 was far from a waste of effort. After all, it was Drahomanov who had injected consciousness of the nationality problem and the goal of federalism into the program of the Zemstvo Union:

> . . . in the beginning of the seventies and eighties of the last century, the Russian constitutionalists did not produce one major political writer who, having become an émigré, could voice their aspirations in the foreign press. In the end, as we have seen, they could only turn to a Ukrainian, M. P. Drahomanov. But while for Drahomanov the cause of the Russian constitution was his own, for the Russian constitutionalists, his Ukrainian cause was altogether foreign. Besides, Drahomanov, as he himself admitted, through his energetic work brought out in the Russian constitutional movement elements that were closer to the Ukrainian cause and de-emphasized the things that were far from that cause. Indeed, of all Russian constitutional programs, the political program of the Zemstvo Union included the largest number of federalist elements.[50]

Kistiakovsky's undaunted defense of Drahomanov and of his role in the Russian constitutional movement was partly a justification and an explanation of his own views on the Ukrainian national question and federalism. Like Drahomanov, Kistiakovsky considered an empirewide state government essential as a protective mechanism enabling the free development of national cultures. He also conceived of a number of locally self-governing ethnic or national units as the foundation of a federal government and state structure in a multinational empire. These ethnic or national units would elect representatives to a proposed two chamber national parliament.

However, Kistiakovsky lived in another era and his views differed from Drahomanov's in several ways. First, Kistiakovsky focused more on the internal cultural-political and socioeconomic factors fundamental to establishing national identity within the boundaries of the Russian Empire. For Kistiakovsky, the Polish annexationist tendencies were much less of a threat than they were for Drahomanov. Drahomanov was twenty-two years old in 1863, the year of the Polish revolution, while Kistiakovsky was born only five years later. Thus, it is understandable that the Polish nationalist threat of annexation of Ukrainian lands was much less important to Kistiakovsky's thinking in the last decade of the nineteenth century and the early part of the twentieth century, when he wrote on the national question and federalism. In fact, Drahomanov criticized Kistiakovsky for his excessive involvement with the Polish language and students in his student days at Dorpat University. Drahomanov's criticism was based on the fact that many Ukrainians left their own movement for other causes, while Polish and other non-Russian national groups ignored the Ukrainian cause.[51] Consequently, it was more effective for the movement to focus its activities in Galicia, for there were greater rights for Ukrainians as well as other nationalities in the Austrian Empire. Only after the Russian autocracy was overthrown would Drahomanov support Ukrainian national activities in the Russian Empire.[52]

Kistiakovsky's Synthesis

Kistiakovsky did advocate close cooperation between the Ukrainians who resided in the Russian Empire and those in the Hapsburg Empire, but his approach was essentially confined to the existing boundaries of the empires; he never advocated the political unification of the Ukrainians. His first priority was the establishment and implementation of principles of equality for nationalities in general and the Ukrainians in particular. The exercise of national cultural rights was, in his view, basic to a popular government in any multinational empire.

Kistiakovsky could not escape the ambiguities inherent in a federal system in a multinational state, which simultaneously sought to perpetuate the movement for centralization and to foster the independent development of national groups in the empire. Clearly, the interests of the Russians pressing for centralization would clash with the movements among the nationalities. The Russians did see the growing impulses for national rights as a threat to the building of a powerful and unified Russian state—the policies of the Russians toward nationalities grew even more oppressive in the era following the October Manifesto of 1905. For non-Russian nationalities, on the other hand, the movement for national rights could not expect a peaceful reception from Russian majority. At best, a negotiated agreement might yield a nominal national autonomy, while the economic and social life of each nation would still be controlled completely by the Russians.

In summary, Kistiakovsky held an opinion that the only way the nationalities could effectively gain their rights was through a struggle on two levels: a socioeconomic one based on cross-national class alliances and, simultaneously, a political one to overthrow the autocracy and to replace it with a constitutional form of government representing all the peoples. A constitutional government in the multinational empire had to be a federation of the many national and ethnic groups rather than highly centralized Russian government. A federal system denoted an organization of political institutions with two centers of power—central and regional. In that type of a system, Kistiakovsky believed, the peoples of the empire would enjoy some local autonomy—at least, cultural autonomy. All nationalities would be equal and, at the same time, part of an effectively governed state.

CHAPTER SEVEN

The Debate on the Ukrainian National Question: Kistiakovsky vs. Struve

In *Imagined Communities*, Benedict Anderson argues that nationalism "was born in an age in which Enlightenment and Revolution were destroying the legitimacy of the divinely ordained, hierarchical dynastic realm."[1] As cultural and political nationalist movements developed among the peoples of the Hapsburg and Russian empires in the nineteenth century, nationalism started to evoke conflicting images. For minority nationalities in multinational states, it represented the liberal ideas of human rights, self-determination, freedom of religion, freedom of conscience, and expression in one's native language. For the dominant nationalities, however, nationalism meant proselytizing the dominant national identity in the name of the freedom and power of the imperial "nation-state." Liberal nationalist movements concentrated on defining a national identity for a social and cultural entity that shared language, customs, religion, and a belief in a common history and origins; this search for identity became the focal point for diverse nationalities that had been politically subsumed within the national framework of an empire. In their quest for national cultural self-determination, vocal non-Russian peoples, such as Ukrainians and Jews, fostered a broad decentralizing force that challenged the more traditional nationalism represented by the tsarist Russian Orthodox model for a unified Russian Empire.

The historical memories of Ukrainians, Jews, and other non-Russian nationalities had been shaped by the harsh tsarist national policies. The tsarist government tried to eliminate the Ukrainian, Belarusian, and other national problems through Russification. Non-Christian inhabitants of the empire, including Jews and nomadic peoples, were legally classified as "outsiders" (*inorodtsy*) and were subject to special laws, distinct from the laws governing the territories in which they lived. The

Jews were restricted to live in the confines of the Pale of Settlement in the western borderlands of the empire.

The constitutional era between 1905 and 1917 allowed the troublesome issues involving non-Russian nationalities to come into the public eye and enter the debates on the floor of the Duma. As government restrictions that previously prohibited and silenced open discussion of the nationalities problem were lifted after the 1905 revolution, the Ukrainian question emerged as the focal point for a passionate debate on the pages of major liberal journals. The brief period of liberalization resulted in a lapse of the harsh provisions of the Ems Ukaz that stopped the publication of Ukrainian newspapers, journals, and books, though teaching in Ukrainian language was still not allowed in elementary schools. In the First and Second Imperial Dumas between forty and fifty deputies formed a Ukrainian caucus.

But liberal hopes for Ukrainian rights ended with the redrafting of the electoral law put into effect by the imperial decree in 1907. This new electoral law changed the composition of the legislature so that representation was weighted in favor of the upper classes, which for Ukraine meant Russian or Russified.[2] In addition, Prime Minister (after July, 1906) Petr Stolypin allied himself with vocal Russian nationalists, such as the Black Hundreds [Chernye sotni] and the Club of Russian Nationalists [Klub russkikh nationalistov] in Kyiv, which spread anti-Ukrainian and anti-Semitic propaganda.[3] Liberal and radical colleagues, such as Kistiakovsky and Struve, who had worked side-by-side in the struggle to replace the monarchy, turned into enemies, as the public at large and the government became increasingly preoccupied with foreign policy concerns and grew more conservative on questions involving minority national rights. For the many non-Russian peoples of the empire, individual freedoms had to include national rights.

Nationalism on the Rise

Russia's astounding defeat in the Russo-Japanese War in 1905 along with the destruction of the Russian navy led political activists from nationalists to Kadets to address the problem of the responsible conduct of foreign policy and the national reputation of Russia. In fact, two types of nationalism developed after 1905: one was the nationalism of the autocracy, while another was developing among some of the constitutionalists.[4]

It was in Petr Struve's controversial and surprisingly conservative article "A Great Russia," that he provided one of the clearest statements in support of the reconciliation and alliance of the liberal factions with the Russian State.[5] As a reaction to the humiliation of the 1905 debacle, which marked the first defeat of a major European power by an Asian one, Struve formulated a curious combination of Pan-Slavism and romantic nationalism in which the state was defined in Darwinian terms, as an organism with its own laws of existence. Although Struve had advocated a government based on law and individual rights during his days as a leading figure in the Union of Liberation, he now believed that there were times when the state had the right to go beyond the laws of society. Struve's liberal convictions were corrupted by the fear that Russia would lose its prestigious place in the world arena, and that bowing to the pressures of national movements was destructive to the need for a strong national image. In a bizarre departure from the liberal democratic ideals he espoused just a few years earlier, Struve became a Great Power broker: "A state has to be revolutionary when the maintenance of its power demands it. A state cannot be revolutionary when revolution could undermine its power. This is the law which governs dynasties and democracies alike. It overthrows monarchs and governments, and kills revolutions."[6] Unlike Kistiakovsky, who emphasized the individual rights and a balance between the interests of the individual and the legally based state, Struve noted that the state's goals sometimes had to transcend the interests of the individual in society: "From the painful experience of the last five years, the Russian people have learned to understand that the State is a collective personality and stands above any individual will."[7] Struve felt that the domestic and foreign threats to the survival of the Russian state had to be met and dispelled, before one could focus on the question of individual rights in the country. Only a strong national culture that would actively bind together the regional differences with its Russian cultural force could create the stable and strong state that Struve envisioned.[8]

Struve was one of the most articulate members of the intelligentsia to clarify the importance of setting new priorities, particularly in the field of foreign policy. In "A Great Russia," he pointed out that the goal of setting up a viable constitutional order needed to be fulfilled at the same time as Russia worked to re-establish its reputation as a world power. The Far East policy had proved to be disastrous and unwelcoming to the Russian cultural influences. Struve wanted foreign policy interests to shift to the Black Sea basin, where Russian interests could successfully be realized and Russian culture would be closer to other Slavic peoples and home.[9]

But the national problems in the Black Sea region had to be dealt with in a conciliatory fashion. After all, some of the national groups, such as the Jews, were important for their remarkable entrepreneurial talents and could make valuable contributions to Russian economic life. Struve advocated the removal of all legal constraints placed on the substantial Jewish population, which in 1912 constituted 32.25 percent of the total population in Odesa.[10] His hope was not that the Jews would have the possibility to exercise their cultural autonomy, but, instead, that the Jews would become assimilated into the Russian population.[11] As he later noted,

> The Russian intelligentsia has always considered the Jews to be their own . . . the conscious attempt to reject Russian culture was not the goal of the Russian intelligentsia, but of the Jewish movement known as Zionism. Even if we say that it is created by the juridical conditions of the Jews in Russia, it is still a fact. I do not sympathize with Zionism at all, but I realize that the problem of "Jewish" nationality is a reality and that, unfortunately, it is now a growing problem.[12]

Struve, wary of the growing liberation movements among the non-Russian nationalities, considered the government's main task to be the elimination of all factors that did not contribute to the unification and strengthening of the Russian state. In 1905, Struve had already made clear his opposition to the idea of self-rule for Ukraine, as it had been expressed in the program of the Union of Liberation. Struve would not accept self-rule for any nationalities other than the ones inhabiting Finland and the Kingdom of Poland—which were fully formed nations with constitutional forms of government.[13]

In his March 1909 article, "Intelligentsia i natsional'noe litso" [The Intelligentsia and the National Face], Struve criticized the intelligentsia for having divested itself of its national ties and thereby concealed its "national face."[14] He claimed, "The national idea of present-day Russia is in the reconciliation of the Government with a people awakened to a consciousness and initiative, a people that is becoming a nation. State and nation must become one . . . "[15] But the national identity he conceived of was to be formed out of a creative cultural nationalism, not

passive nationalism. Creative nationalism, according to Struve's definition, was free and could lead to the formation of an organic Russian
state through the merging of state and nation.[16] The other form of
nationalism, the passive one, would culminate in a nationality which
would fear all the other nationalities.[17] Struve repeated his proposed
solution: Russia, the Great Power, was to assimilate all the non-Russian
nationalities, with the exception of the Poles and the Finns who would
retain their identities and some self-government while remaining
within the Russian Empire.

The increasing pressures of Russian nationalism posed a major
threat for those cosmopolitans who considered themselves part of
the Russian intelligentsia, representatives of non-Russian national cultures, and were deeply involved in European intellectual life. Two of
the most articulate respondents to the rising trend toward Russian
national chauvinism characterized by Struve's concept of "Great Russia" were Bogdan Kistiakovsky and the Zionist leader Vladimir
Jabotinsky (1880–1940), who became a vocal supporter of the Ukrainian movement.[18]

The Debate

In January 1911, Struve started a new series of articles in *Russkaia
mysl'*, called "Letters on the Nationalities and Regions," in response to
the numerous articles concerning the national question and his own
clear commitment to combating the rise of nationalism among non-
Russians. The purpose of the series was to provide a forum for a broad
spectrum of views expressing ideas on the national question, particularly the views of non-Russian authors. The editors of *Russkaia mysl'*
would be respondents to the articles on the national question.

The first article in the series on the nationalities and regions was
Jabotinsky's article "Evreistvo i ego nastroenie" [Jewry and its Mood],
which was a survey of the organizations and political and social trends
in the Jewish community in the post-1905 era. His article was in part a
refutation of Struve's proposal that the Jews should become assimilated
into Russian society. Jabotinsky pointed out that the issue of Jewish
assimilation depended on the future of Russian policy; would Russia
become a nation-state or a multinational state? If the state was primarily unilingual, then minorities scattered across the country would as-

similate sooner or later. But if the state was multinational, then a minority would be able to retain its cultural identity amidst other nationalities speaking many languages. Jabotinsky was in favor of the multinational variant and argued that the Russian government cannot ever be a national government. Russian dominance over other nationalities could only be construed as national arrogance, considering that the Russians comprised only 43 percent of the population.[19]

Jabotinsky came to the Ukrainian movement through his life experience in the rich and stimulating multinational, multiethnic world of Odesa, one of the most cosmopolitan areas of the Russian Empire. According to Jabotinsky's description:

> Even if it was a city in Russia and in my time very russified in language, Odessa was not really a Russian city. Nor was it a Jewish city, though Jews were probably the largest ethnic community, particularly when one takes into account that half of the so-called Russians were actually Ukrainians, people just as different from the Russians as Americans from Britons, or Englishmen from Irishmen. At least four great peoples—three ancient ones and the fourth a young one—united to build the city: first the Greeks and Italians, a little later came the Jews, and only in the 1840's did the actual Russian influence begin to grow. The city was also full of Poles, Armenians, Caucasians, Tatars, Moldavians, and a half dozen other peoples. Yet it did not look like Constantinople, where the Levantines were foreigners and lived apart from any Turkish influence, nor like New York, where people are divided into natives and immigrants. In Odessa, everybody was Odessan and everyone who was literate read the same newspapers and thought about the same Russian problems.[20]

Jabotinsky was an active, dedicated Zionist who strove to prevent the assimilation of the Jewish population. From 1907 to 1908 he spent a year in Vienna where he set himself the goal of understanding the complexities of national relations and conflicts in Austria-Hungary. It was during his studies in Eastern Europe and visits to Galicia that Jabotinsky came into contact with the dynamic Ukrainian movement and started to appreciate it. When Jabotinsky returned to Russia in 1908, he was convinced that an alliance of Jewish and Ukrainian national movements would contribute to the growing democratization of the political structure, the development of national cultures, and the initiation of a form of self-rule.[21] Ukrainian and Jewish activists looked at the Austro-Hungarian Empire as a blueprint for a multinational state, for nationalities had both freedoms and representation there. Though Jabotinsky knew the history of antagonism between the Jews and Ukrainians in Galicia and parts of Russia, he overlooked pogroms and other manifestations of anti-Semitism and explained them as being largely a creation of the social and political system. In fact, he ignored some of the realities of the sentiments among the popular masses and found a common language with other non-Russian compatriot *intelligenty* with whom he faced a common foe. In her incisive article on Jabotinsky, Olga Andriewsky concludes, " . . . Jabotinsky had come to believe the fate of all the non-Russian nations, and the Jewish nation in particular, rested with the ability of the Ukrainians to resist assimilation."[22] As Jabotinsky's stated in "Evreistvo i ego nastroenie":

> We, non-Russians (*inorodtsy*), foresee only one of two possibilities: either there will never be freedom and justice in Russia, or else each of us will consciously exercise this freedom and justice, first of all, for the development of our own unique national identity and for [our own] emancipation from foreign culture. Either Russia will go the way of national decentralization or else every one of the foundations of democracy, starting with universal voting rights, will be unthinkable. For Russia, progress and the *Nationalitätenstaat* [multinational state] are synonymous, and every effort to disregard this fact, to introduce order against the will and consciousness of 60 percent of the population, will end in failure . . . [23]

In "Na raznye temy—Chto zhe takoe Rossiia?" [On Different Topics—What is Russia], which was Struve's response to Jabotinsky that appeared in the same issue of *Russkaia mysl'*, he argued that the minorities should have the right to use their own languages and customs, but that for any person in the empire to be a truly "cultured person," he or she must know Russian.[24] The Slavic peoples of the empire, "the 'Little Russian' or 'Belarusian' nations had the same relationship to the 'Great Russian,' as the Czechs to the Germans or the Austrian 'Ukrainians' to the Poles."[25] In fact, the Russians, according to his calculations, constituted not 43 percent, but 60 percent of the population, because he incorporated the Belarusian and Ukrainian populations in the Russian category. The Slavic nationalities were not separate political and cultural entities. He conceived of Russia as a gradually developing American-style melting pot:

> Placing the ethnographic terms "Great Russian," "Little Russian," "Belorussian" on one plane, the author [Jabotinsky] forgot that there

> is in each case the term "Russian," and that Russian is not an abstrac-
> tion amidst these three "terms" (with the prefixes "great," "small,"
> and "white"), but rather it is a living cultural force, a great develop-
> ing, and growing national element, a nation in the making, as the
> Americans say of themselves.[26]

The ongoing cultural integration led Struve to the conclusion that Russia
was not a multinational empire comparable to Austria-Hungary, but it
was a national state like the United States or Great Britain.[27] He believed
that Russia's national unity should be defined by cultural rather than
ethnic factors; therefore, the idea of Ukrainian cultural separatism was
even more threatening than the idea of political separatism.

Furthermore, Struve pointed out that Jabotinsky himself provided
evidence for a tendency toward the development of one general Great
Russian culture for the empire, when he wrote that assimilated Jews
adopted the language and culture of the Great Russian nation rather
than that of the Ukrainian or Belarusian nationalities. The major goal of
unifying and strengthening the Russian state could be achieved by
encouraging the spreading of the Great Russian language and culture to
all parts of the empire. Attempting to establish the position of other
cultures on the same level with the Russian culture would require
tremendous means and energy; for Struve, national cultural autonomy
would lead to "the nationalistic multiplication of cultures" instead of
the development of a single culture that would strengthen the empire.[28]

In January 1911, Kistiakovsky actively joined the ongoing debate on
the national question on the pages of *Russkaia mysl'*. He and Struve
took opposite sides, though they had been Marxists who embraced
neo-Kantian idealism and collaborated on the journal *Osvobozhdenie*
as well as the constitutional organization, the Union of Liberation.
Until 1905, Struve had maintained close ties with Kistiakovsky and
other representatives of non-Russian nationalities. Kistiakovsky actively contributed his articles to Struve's various editorial ventures
after 1905, which included *Poliarnaia zvezda* [The Polar Star],
Svoboda i kul'tura [Freedom and Culture], *Duma*, and, finally,
Russkaia mysl' [Russian Thought], which Struve began to edit early in
1907. In addition, they both were contributors to the above-mentioned
controversial collection of essays about the Russian intelligentsia,
Vekhi, in 1909. Their paths had already begun to diverge before the
publication of *Vekhi,* when Struve's nationalistic articles about build-

ing a Great Russian state started to appear. Just about that time, Kistiakovsky reasserted himself as a spokesman for the Ukrainian national movement. The long-term friendship between the two constitutionalists became strained, and Struve revealed his right-wing stance within the Kadet camp—his Russian nationalist position on non-Russian nationalities.

Kistiakovsky submitted to the editor of *Russkaia mysl'* a letter, entitled "K voprosu o samostoiatel'noi ukrainskoi kul'ture" [On the Question of an Independent Ukrainian Culture], under the pseudonym "Ukrainets" [the Ukrainian]. He began by reminding Struve, to whom he addressed his letter, that he never was a proponent of separatism. In fact, his 1905 article for *Osvobozhdenie,* in which he criticized Ukrainian activists for their antagonism toward the Russian Liberation movement, led to a series of journalistic attacks in a number of publications, including the Vienna-based *Ruthenische Revue* and the liberal German newspaper *Frankfurter Zeitung*. His purely cultural leaning, he pointed out, proved that separatist views were alien to him, and that position elicited sharp attacks from Ukrainian nationalists.[29]

Nevertheless, in his extensive response to Struve, Kistiakovsky expressed his anger at the continuation and intensification of repressive acts by the Russian government against the Ukrainians:

> The facts which I have observed during the last five years have forced me to change completely my opinion about the attitude of Russian society toward the Ukrainian movement. Earlier I rationalized most things using censorship or the significance of the moment [to explain]. Now I must admit that the point that characterizes the attitude of Russian society towards the Ukrainian movement is a sharply expressed egoism.[30]

The times had changed and the issue of Ukrainian rights could no longer be placed on a back burner. There had been a proliferation of conservative anti-Ukrainian organizations in Galicia, Moscow, and Kyiv. The anti-Ukrainian mood had also spread in the press as conducted on the pages of *Kievlianin* [The Kyivan], *Novoe vremia* [New Times], and other publications. To Kistiakovsky's horror, neither progressive representatives of Russian society nor the Russian press had reacted to the attacks against Ukrainian rights. Kistiakovsky's tone became more and more alarmed as he described the renewed Great Russian national pressures against Ukrainian activists that developed after 1907[31]—Russian nationalist organizations in Galicia and the Russian Ukraine Slavic organizations, such as the Society of Slavic Reciprocity and the Neo-Slav Movement, were formed in support of Great Russian nationalism. They were organized to fight the "Ukrainian danger," which was considered a growing reality in both Austria-Hungarian Galicia and Russian Ukraine where Ukrainian nationalism increased in the critical period preceding World War I. The supporters of the Russian nationalist organizations feared that the growing Ukrainian movement would become a Mazepa-like uprising to unify all the Ukrainian inhabited lands.[32] "In reality . . . Ukrainianism is considered the 'Ukrainian danger'; that concept was unknown before 1905, but it is now extremely characteristic . . . that the strivings of certain sectors of the Ukrainian people to resurrect and establish its culture are perceived as a danger for Russia and the great Russian people."[33] The threat of Ukrainian separatism and disloyalty to the Russian autocracy in time of possible war was, in Kistiakovsky's view, used as an excuse for ignoring the rights of minority nationalities in the empire.[34]

Struve's justification of Russian dominance was based on his perception of the historical destiny of Russia and its culture, according to which "Little Russia" was relegated to the mission of enhancing the greatness of Russia; the Little Russian masses were looked upon as if they were part of the raw material for the creation of Great Russian culture. On the contrary, Kistiakovsky pointed out, the long historical tradition of imposed Russification had established the dominant position of Russian culture. Already in the eighteenth century, ecclesiastical and liturgical texts printed in Ukrainian were forcibly replaced by the Holy Synod's version.[35] Once restrictions against the use of Ukrainian were lifted after 1905, Kistiakovsky continued, it became obvious that the dominant role of Russian culture was not at all natural. Ukrainian language started to be used in public events as well as publications; in the short space of one year, the Holy Synod distributed 100,000 copies of the Gospel of St. Matthew published in Ukrainian.[36]

These actions against the Ukrainian movement and the Ukrainian people jeopardized the very principles of individual liberties that the October Manifesto had heralded in 1905. To counter Struve's point that it was a waste of mental energy to teach in Ukrainian, he proposed that the schools in Ukraine teach in the residents' native language and that Ukrainian be made the legal basis of the developing culture and society of that region.[37] Kistiakovsky exclaimed, "Finally, look at the 'Russian' intelligentsia in Little Russia.[38] You know half of it speaks in some gobbledygook (*Volapük*)[39] of 'Russian' and 'Little Russian,' because both the 'Russian' and 'Little Russian' language are equally alien to them, and this is one of the most horrible examples of wasted mental energy."[40]

One of the most reprehensible anti-Ukrainian gestures was the amendment issued by the Duma that prohibited teachers from using Ukrainian language in Ukrainian elementary schools. Kistiakovsky angrily explained, "In this way, the State Duma made it impossible for the Little Russian population to study seriously even the Russian (Great Russian) language and condemned a significant part of it, that is, all the less able, to illiteracy."[41] As for the peasantry, if they could get an education, it was in Russian; and, it was not unusual that they learned neither Russian nor Ukrainian well. To be responsible citizens, the Ukrainians as well as other minority nationalities had to be able to represent their own interests. Otherwise, they would become passive residents who would eventually be absorbed into the Russified empire. Russification of the minority nationalities would not form a literate, potentially self-determining population.

In response to Struve's chauvinistic claim that a truly cultured person must speak Russian, Kistiakovsky responded:

> As for myself, I was born in one of the biggest and, therefore, Russified Ukrainian cities; the family into which I was born was highly educated and, therefore, to a large degree, Russified. I know not only Russian and Polish, but also foreign languages, I can even write in them; and until now I have not stopped cursing my fate of not being educated in a native [Ukrainian] school; I curse it because as a child I rarely heard the songs and melodies of my country, because my imagination was not being molded by native folk-tales, because my first encounter with literature was not in my native language, in essence, because I was alien to the people among whom I lived, alien to my own nation. Only as an adolescent did I begin a serious study of the Ukrainian language, become acquainted with Ukrainian songs, literature, and poetry, come to love Ukrainian theater; and I have always thought, and continue to think that only then did I begin to be an educated and cultured man. The emotional experiences of that part of my life greatly broadened my perceptions. Only then did I become deeply responsive to the irresistible force of Russian and European lyrical poetry, only then did I suddenly penetrate the essence of dramaturgy and elaborate a completely new view of literature. You

believe that Ukrainian culture does not yet exist; perhaps you are right; but is it not strange that the elements from which this culture is to be composed or already is being composed, made me an educated and cultured man? This paradox has been created by life itself.[42]

Kistiakovsky, who spent his youth in and out of prisons as an activist for the Ukrainian national cause, could not accept the negation of any nationality—the right to cultural freedom was a "a manifestation of the divine spirit in man . . . and to violate it is a sin."[43] The non-Russians, he asserted, had to develop their identities to become culturally autonomous—capable of equal participation in a federal constitutional government. That meant, the representatives of the various national groups to the empire-wide legislative bodies should also be able to speak Russian, the common language for all nationalities in the empire.

Even when Kistiakovsky's tone became militant in favor of ending Russian repression of Ukrainian national rights, he stressed that he still did not revert to a separatist or chauvinist position.

I am deeply convinced that historical fate has connected the Ukrainian people with the Great Russian people forever, and at the same time, separated them from their other neighbors, mainly the Polish people. For that reason, the future growth of the Ukrainian people is only possible in solidarity with the Great Russian people . . . I maintain the belief that of all the Slavic cultures, only the Great Russian culture can attain world significance.[44]

Furthermore, he never considered this anti-separatist stance in contradiction with his position on the national rights of the Ukrainians and other non-Russian nationalities:

At the same time the most important goal for the Ukrainian people is . . . [to] develop their own culture. I do not consider it possible to predetermine the limits of that development: that question can only be decided by history. In any case, there is nothing inconceivable about the fact that the Ukrainians will eventually have both their own *gimnazii* and universities.[45]

He concluded with the conciliatory assertion that he was trying to take an objective view of the problem. He hoped that Struve and other members of the Russian intelligentsia would stop being blinded by their egotism and try to take a fresh look at the national question.[46]

Struve responded to "Ukrainets" with an article entitled "Obshcherusskaia kul'tura i ukrainskii partikuliarizm" [All-Russian Culture and

Ukrainian Particularism], which presented his most complete articulation of the national question. Struve wrote the article to prove that Ukrainian should be a regional language rather than a national one. While Kistiakovsky was primarily concerned with the realization of a cultural identity for minorities in the multinational Russian Empire, Struve was most interested in the status of the empire among the major powers. The latter wanted any forces that might threaten the strength of the empire eliminated. He stated:

> I personally suggest that in dealing with the Ukrainophiles . . . in the future, Russian progressive social opinion should energetically and without hesitation . . . enter into an ideological struggle with "Ukrainianism" as with a trend to weaken or even in part abolish the great achievement of our history—an all-Russian culture.[47]

History, Struve pointed out, had proved that the Russian language was the most widely used language in the empire. One would have to alter the entire course of Russian history in order to change the status of the Little Russian language. He stressed that his goal was not to eliminate Little Russian culture or language, but he maintained his belief in the prominent and dominant role of the Great Russian culture. Struve characterized his concept of the relationship of Russian and Ukrainian cultures by citing the example of the unification of Germany in which regional particularities were preserved while the German nation became one unified state. Struve hoped that the relationship of the regional German language (*Plattdeutsch*) to High German (*Hochdeutsch*), the official language of Germany, could be the prototype for the Ukrainian language's role with respect to Russian. Just as *Plattdeutsch* was a spoken dialect in Germany, so Struve hoped Ukrainian, too, would be a spoken rather than a written literary language in the Russian Empire. To Struve, the German intelligentsia's support for the formation of a unified national language, culture, and state was a deep act of patriotism. He maintained, "With this they rendered their people a great political and cultural service that contributed to the development of the country as a whole."[48] Following the same pattern of development, Struve hoped the Russian intelligentsia would make minority languages, such as Ukrainian, officially local or regional (*oblastnye*).[49]

To reinforce his argument, Struve asserted there were clear economic reasons for not elevating non-Russian languages to the level of

Russian in the empire. There would be unnecessary complications if several languages were used in conducting the economic business in the empire; he argued:

> Capitalism will not speak Ukrainian, it will speak Russian . . . This economic process will be interesting to study precisely from the cultural perspective, as a struggle of particularlism with the unification tendencies, which are deeply rooted in all aspects of our economic and social development.[50]

Struve considered the growth of capitalism a universalizing force that would eliminate pockets of regional particularism and counteract movements for independence. In fact, the mixture of Russian and Ukrainian that Kistiakovsky had given the derogatory name *Volapük* was for Struve a positive sign that the cities of Kyiv and Odesa among others were becoming integrated into the Russian culture. But Struve did not take into consideration the developing war against the Ukrainian movement, particularly when the Kyiv Club of Russian Nationalists was formed in 1908 and turned itself into a powerful lobbying group against Ukrainian, Jewish, and other national movements.

Kistiakovsky had a very different vision, which derived from the pre-revolutionary Ukrainian tradition of federalism most clearly expressed in Mykhailo Drahomanov's works. Individual rights could never be placed in a secondary position in a law-based constitutional state. Furthermore, national rights were an integral part of such political rights as freedom of speech, freedom of conscience, and freedom of religion. The importance of Ukrainian language for the largely peasant population as well as for the intelligentsia was a critical aspect of the development of a federal government made of locally self-determining parts, such as Ukraine. Kistiakovsky perceived federalism through the prism of economic initiatives, particularly through peasant cooperatives in which local national languages were fundamental to forming the cross-national network of exchange.

With the increasing international strains associated with the outbreak of World War I, the tensions between Struve and Ukrainian nationalists built up. Struve, along with many Russian nationalists, considered the Ukrainian movement synonymous with Ukrainian separatism. They believed Ukrainian national strivings were used by the Austrians and Germans to ultimately weaken the Russian Empire. As the Russian offensive went deep into Galicia during the war, annexing a sacred territory many Russians considered part of the Kyivan-Rus′ heritage became a possibility.[51] But the Russian tendency to overlook Ukrainian interests and demands led to a further straining of relations between Russians and Ukrainians.

The positions of Struve and Kistiakovsky on the national question grew even more polarized. Struve rejected even the moderate nationalist stance of the Moscow-based journal *Ukrainskaia zhizn′,* which stressed cultural independence rather than political and economic national autonomy, or separatism.[52] Struve's statements on the Ukrainian national question became more openly anti-Ukrainian and his comments grew so aggressive that his liberal colleagues on the Central Committee of the Kadet Party were embarrassed and tried to disassociate themselves from him. They simply could not reconcile their liberal stance with the nationalist and imperialist ideas Struve asserted in "A Great Russia." Struve argued, "Russian liberalism will always doom itself to impotence until such time as it acknowledges itself to be Russian and national." It was his conviction that liberalism and socialism were gradually merging with nationalism. Nationalism was no longer exclusively advocated by right-wing movements.[53]

Around Christmas 1914, Struve went to Galicia to see the areas the Russian troops conquered. He stayed in L′viv and concluded that Ukrainian culture was fundamentally a secular political ploy used by the local Uniate (Ukrainian Greek Catholic) population as a weapon against Polish domination. After the Russians had occupied the area, there was no more need for Ukrainian culture except as a regional idea. Struve concluded that a broad Russification program for Galicia was essential and unavoidable.[54]

Struve's position on the question of Ukrainian culture finally led to his resignation from the Kadet Party's Central Committee, which had rejected his position. He was isolated, and in June 1915, at a conference of the Kadet Party, a formal resolution condemning Struve's position on the Ukrainian issue was passed.[55] Struve's departure from the Central Committee of the party marked the end of his active work with the Kadets. Although the Kadet Party had not actively championed Ukrainian issues in the Duma debates on Ukrainian-language use in the schools, they would not support a Russian chauvinist position that violated basic liberal principles.

Nationality Problems

After the Russian entry into World War I, the need for national cohesiveness to marshal economic, social, and political resources was essential for winning the war against outside enemies. Opposition to the demands for national rights among the minorities grew more intense at the same time as the peoples of the borderlands suffered the hardships of war, death, exile, and homelessness. As lives were torn asunder, the issues of national autonomy, unity, and identity became even more important than they had been before the war. Kistiakovsky joined with representatives of nationalities to publish the journal *Natsional'nye problemy* [Nationality Problems]. The fundamental principles of the publication were national-cultural self-determination and the guarantee of the rights for national minorities. On questions of international relations—Polish-Belarusian, Polish-Lithuanian, Polish-Ukrainian, Polish-Jewish, Armenian-Georgian, and Armenian-Tatar—*Natsional'nye problemy* took the position that guaranteeing the rights of national minorities was mandatory for a viable government that would not be torn apart by national and ethnic conflicts. "The journal will strive to broadly and deeply familiarize Russian society with the life and intellectual trends among each of them." The editors worked to collect materials on the nationalities question and embarked on the publication of the new journal. They were aware of their responsibility to the non-Russian peoples and hoped their effort would gain support among the intelligentsia.[56]

In the journal, first published in May 1915, Kistiakovsky became a militant spokesman for the minority nationalities and their rights in the face of their common enemies: the warring European powers and the threat of Russification. The first issue of the short-lived publication (it eluded the tsarist censorship for only five months before it was forcibly closed after the September 1915 issue appeared) was introduced by Kistiakovsky's essay, "Chto takoe natsionalizm?" [What is Nationalism?]. In the essay, he refuted Struve's distinction between a passive nationalism and a creative "aggressive" nationalism that would build an all-Russian culture for the empire. He pointed out the stark distinction between the progressive and reactionary forms of nationalism— the terms Kistiakovsky used to counter Struve's concepts of active and passive forms of nationalism. The nationalism of the people in power had most often became a force opposing the movement for the national rights of the oppressed minority peoples;[57] reactionary nationalism was propelled by a messianic idea in the process of trying to establish a dominant Russian national culture and personality. The other, progressive form of nationalism that Kistiakovsky professed, involved an attempt to understand popular interests and needs in order to discern what would be good for the people as a whole.[58] The nationalism of those in power most often turned into a tendency to suppress the rights of others, while the nationalism of the minorities could be a progressive social and political force that was a part of a national self-determination movement.[59] The Russian Empire could not become a Russian Orthodox haven without suppressing the cultural and religious rights of minorities holding other beliefs, such as Moslems, Buddhists, Ukrainian Greek Catholics, Roman Catholics, and Jews.

Kistiakovsky sounded a warning against the enemy—Russian nationalists, such as Struve, who proposed a national campaign against Ukrainian activities. He hoped that the end of World War I would free the energies of representatives of non-Russian nationalities and direct them against the internal foe, the dominant Russians: "Now we are liberating ourselves from the external Germans, but the 'internal German' is still strong among us."[60] The "internal Germans" obviously were the Russian chauvinists who tried to dominate other nationalities, and Kistiakovsky made no effort to conceal the fact that he considered Struve one of the leading "internal Germans." The merging of nation and state could be the least democratic goal for the diverse peoples of the empire. As a Russian nation-state, the empire would become a messianic force nourished and driven by the Great Russian culture and religion. Kistiakovsky added:

> We should recognize that any nationalism that comes from a state as a totality, which alludes to the state as a personality, will always . . . lead to the renunciation in other nations of rights that it defends for itself. Only the nationalism that fights for the needs of the popular masses is not able to change its principles of equal rights and freedom for all. Only that type of nationalism will always insure democracy and progress.[61]

The norms guiding a democratic state should be an expression of the will of the masses. The state envisioned by Struve would be served by the Russified peoples, who would always be secondary to the needs of the national state. Kistiakovsky considered Russification tantamount to violence against the non-Russian peoples of Russia, for national identity was an integral part of human rights—to cultural freedom in a multinational federal context.

The only effective replacement for the existing constitutional monarchy was a constitutional government that would proportionately represent all the nationalities in the empire, organized as a federation of many national and ethnic groups. Individual and national rights were central to Kistiakovsky, whose position was based on his major concern—human rights. To make the exercise of human rights possible, he considered it mandatory that the nationalities be culturally autonomous. Progressive nationalism of the non-Russian nationalities and of the subjugated sector of the Russian population would join forces to combat national oppression at the same time as they struggled to replace the autocracy with a truly representative constitutional system. Within that system, the non-Russian nationalities would have the freedom to exercise their national and religious rights. Only in a representative system could they hope to be protected against the dominant, imperialistic type of nationalism, which Struve advocated more vehemently as the war dragged on and revolution threatened his ideas of a Great Russia.

Conclusion

Legal theorists in nineteenth- and early twentieth-century Russia struggled with the idea of setting up a rule-of-law state, *pravovoe gosudarstvo*. The definition of this concept, however, varied depending on the theorist using the term. For liberal lawyers at the turn of the century, the term, "rule-of-law state" meant a state based on a constitution (*Rechtstaat*). It did not necessarily mean that the constitution would protect civil liberties and be based on popular sovereignty. For others such as Kistiakovsky, the rule of law state meant a constitutional form based on the inalienable rights of the individual, universal suffrage, and democratic principles. To make matters more complex, the difficult debates on the need for a legally based state took place in the Russian Empire, where law and legal practice was undermined by the interventions of the autocratic state officials and the tsar himself. It was precisely that weak sense of legality that Kistiakovsky hoped to replace with a legally based state.

Although a liberal constitutional state never became a reality in Kistiakovsky's lifetime, his work still speaks to societies trying to develop an appropriate framework on which to construct legal guarantees for the individual and a constitutional order. Kistiakovsky's universal intellectual, legal, and political principles focused on the struggle for social justice for underprivileged estates and for national groups who had been deprived of their political and cultural rights within the Russian Empire. His commitment to human rights was nurtured by his harsh experience with the Russian autocracy's suppression of Ukrainian language and culture, especially when the tsar proclaimed the Ems Ukaz in 1876. He was an outsider who informed Russian society on Ukrainian issues and history, and simultaneously participated in the debates of the Russian intelligentsia who were trying to transform the autocracy into a constitutional form of government. Through his writings and the debates on human rights, constitutionalism, and federalism at the beginning of the twentieth century, one becomes acutely aware that the roots of a sophisticated legal culture were severed at the time of the revolution in 1917. In the wake of the collapse of the Soviet Union there has been a revival of interest in a rule-of-law state. During the past twelve years, historians and legal scholars as well as politicians in Russia and Ukraine have been examining pre-revolutionary ideas about a constitutional system based on the legally guaranteed rights of the individual.[1]

It is questionable whether commonly understood conceptions of human rights and citizenship were central to the opponents of the Tsarist autocracy in the nineteenth and early-twentieth centuries. These concepts expressed in Western terms were foreign to the majority of the population, the peasants, in the Empire's vast domain. Citizenship was defined by regional, national, and social factors within the multilayered society that was organized according to an outmoded *soslovie* (estate) system. What is emerging from the increasingly sophisticated analyses of social historians is that Russian subjects did not conceive of themselves as citizens of the empire. Rather, their social identities were based on their place in the fragmented world of the Russian Empire—their estate, nationality, or region determined the individual's relationship to his or her particular social sector and the rest of society.

The attempt to create a nation-wide unified legal system was based on the assumption that the peasant courts (*volost'* courts) would be integrated into a court system that was modern (Western) in its form, but actually only served a small fraction of the Empire's subjects.[2] The reliance on customary law in the *volost'* courts reinforced the peasantry's tendency to live in their own world. "For most peasants the bureaucracy was an intrusive and disruptive element in their lives offering few if any services in return for ever-increasing obligations . . . they sought land and liberty and nothing beyond that but to be left alone."[3] As the son of a leading legal Ukrainian scholar immersed in recording and analyzing the world of peasant customary laws, Kistiakovsky was well aware of the overwhelming obstacles facing those involved in developing and integrating the legal world of the peasants. He was convinced that the customary law traditions of the peasantry were essential, since they would correspond to the specific social and economic conditions of the various regions in the Russian Empire. As Kistiakovsky perceived the problem, legal culture was not law formulated and imposed on society from above, but the legal practices functioning in the various levels of society. Law was a cultural phenomenon rather than a series of norms.

Kistiakovsky's social science method was based on his attempts to find a formula for a legal system based on sociological, anthropological, legal and philosophical studies. He argued that the legal concepts used had to be grounded in research on all levels of the multifaceted societies and nationalities in the Russian Empire. As if he were reinforcing Kistiakovsky's perceptive approach to studying the complex society, the prominent historian Alfred Rieber proposed a decade ago the following approach to research on the vast fragmented Russian society:

> If social historians are bold enough to cross boundaries into institutional and legal history they should also march in the opposite direction toward culture defined in its broadest anthropological sense to include institutional norms and materials artifacts as well as values, belief systems and attitudes. The social historian has two objectives here, the first is to analyze the ideology of the specific reference group, i.e. class, estate, elite and so on and the second is to identify those common elements of a national culture that transcend social divisions and provide a network of shared social values.[4]

The basic theme of Kistiakovsky's life and work, in Ukraine, Germany, and Russia, was how to establish a social, economic, and political order in which the individual could be self-determining and eventually enjoy human rights—the combination of political and economic rights. Self-determination could only become a reality in the underdeveloped Russian Empire when the individual had not only gained the inalienable rights of a citizen, but also had undergone a psychological transformation which would allow him or her to be an active participant in, as opposed to a passive object of, a system of government.

The Marxism which he embraced as a young Ukrainian activist did not provide an adequate framework for such a redefinition of the individual and the individual's role. As long as the individual's role remained secondary or unclear, as it did in Marxist or positivist analyses of society, the individual could not perform a self-determining and morally conscious role in guiding the formulation of laws and the government. When his interest in individualism developed, Kistiakovsky modified his earlier Marxist approach with the German neo-Kantian view that scientific social analysis demanded the inclusion of human value judgments. In the Russian context, members of the intelligentsia had to become analysts and actors who were motivated by a sense of social justice.

On the eve of the First World War and the 1917 Revolution, the rifts developing within the ranks of the Russian intelligentsia undermined the leadership of the liberal oppositional movement. Despite Kistiakovsky's position as a member of the empire-wide drive against autocracy and his commitment to a law based state, it was ultimately his national identity as a Ukrainian that caused him to break with the Russian intelligentsia as he struggled against the Russian chauvinism that erupted with the First World War. The reaction of Kistiakovsky and other representatives of minority nationalities to Russian dominance elucidated the struggle for human rights within ethnic communities as well as the threat to such rights by chauvinistic nationalism. While facing the problem of building a democratic constitutional state in a multinational context, the Russian and non-Russian opponents of the autocracy increasingly articulated the two contradictory impulses that came back to life at the end of the twentieth century: how to respect the demands of the non-Russian nationalities while simultaneously combatting the potential break-up of a unitary state.

The problem of national rights which was considered solved by the tsarist policy of Russification proved a serious problem in the Revolutionary era (1917–1921) when nationalist and separatist movements were burgeoning. The Soviet regime wanted to establish a multinational federal system, but setting up a system based on ethnically based republics laid the groundwork for severe national problems. Once the Soviet regime started to disintegrate, the issue of national rights re-emerged as a series of rifts that had grown deeper than most analysts had anticipated.

Since Kistiakovsky was aware of the turmoil building in the Russian Empire, he sought a way to develop a legal system that could function effectively in a time of radical change. The legal system he envisaged, based on his social science method, would respond to the social and economic processes in question. Ideally that system would allow change to take place through the legal forms in that system, and at the same time play a guiding role in the process of change with the self-determining individual in the guiding position.

Kistiakovsky's constitutionalist solution to the goal of forming a government to replace the Russian autocracy was distinguished by his commitment to national cultural autonomy and his consistent focus on the individual and his or her inalienable rights. Kistiakovsky's background as an upperclass Russified Ukrainian who had to learn Ukrainian as a foreign, and then illegal, language, raised his awareness of Russian oppression of national rights and the divisive role that social and economic distinctions played within all the nationalities in the empire. It was through a constitutional and federal organization that he foresaw the possibility of gaining representation for the oppressed minority nationalities and the exploited groups of all nationalities. To reach the ideal of a fully representative form of socialist government, the constitutional forms had to be both resilient, yet structured enough to bear the stress of a virtual class struggle within it. He consistently sought to assure that violent revolution be avoided and that fundamental changes in the society be effected without denying any political party, group, or individuals their basic inalienable liberties. Violent means would allow a dominant group to impose its program in as despotic a manner as the autocracy which it was replacing. The only way effectively to institutionalize human rights, according to Kistiakovsky, was through a constitutionalism and federalism that would be based on an egalitarian social and economic system.

Bogdan Kistiakovsky was the consummate idealist. He posited that the individual and society would become equally important elements when, through the " . . . final merging of the individual and society into one harmonious whole, whereby each of them, as an end in itself, would complement the other, and not suppress or abolish it."[5] Perhaps it is most accurate and useful to consider his search for social and political harmony as a part of the revival of the idea of natural law and forms of the "General Will" which were in vogue in both Western Europe and the Russian Empire at the turn of the century. Kistiakovsky's search for evidence of the expression of the individual's goals in the government and, conversely, evidence of the government's goals in the individual and society is part of a quest for what Alfred Rieber referred to as "shared social values."

Kistiakovsky hoped to allow both the individual and society to exercise freedom. In addition he wanted to let both national minorities and the majority nationality have their rights. His focus was not on delineating the practical ways of coping with dissent and social discord, such as compromise and trade-offs based on negotiations. Nevertheless, his ideal system is and was most instructive for the liberal constitutionalists of developing societies in which an adequate governmental and legal system must function in place of autocratic forms. Kistiakovsky was a systematic thinker living at a time when disorder and chaos were commonplace. He did not leave a consistent body of work that would provide coherent answers or a blueprint for social and legal development. Rather, he left a sophisticated social science methodology and a profound moral vision.

Notes

Notes to the Introduction

* The Ukrainian form of his name is Bohdan Oleksandrovych Kistiakivs'kyi and the Russian is Bogdan Aleksandrovich Kistiakovskii. Transliteration and usage for names is explained on p. viii.

1 Susan Heuman, "A Socialist Conception of Human Rights: A Model from Prerevolutionary Russia," in *Human Rights: Cultural and Ideological Perspectives*, ed. Adamantia Pollis and Peter Schwab (New York, 1979), pp. 49–50.

2 S. L. Frank, *Biografiia P. B. Struve* (New York, 1956), p. 97.

3 Isaiah Berlin's title was inspired by Immanuel Kant's statement, "Aus so krummen Holze als woraus der Mensch gemacht ist, kann nichts ganz Gerades gezimmert werden" [Out of timber so crooked as that from which man is made nothing entirely straight can be built]. Translated by Isaiah Berlin. Immanuel Kant, "Idee zu einer allgemeinen Geschichte in weltbürgerlicher Absicht," 1874. Isaiah Berlin, *The Crooked Timber of Humanity* (New York, 1991), p. xi.

4 Ibid., p. 40.

5 A. V. Poliakov and I. Iu. Kozlikhin, ed., *Vlast' i pravo, iz istorii russkoi pravovoi mysli* (Leningrad, 1990).

6 B. A. Kistiakovsk y, "V zashchitu prava. Intelligentsiia i pravosoznanie," in *Vekhi, Sbornik statei o russkoi intelligentsii*, ed. M. O. Gershenzon (Moscow, 1909), pp 125–55. Most recently, see Laura Engelstein's reference to Kistiakovsky's liberal vision in "Combined Underdevelopment: Discipline and the Law in Imperial and Soviet Russia," *American Historical Review* 98(2) April 1993: 346; William Wagner, "Civil Law, Individual Rights, and Judicial Activism in Late Imperial Russia," in *Reforming Justice in Russia, 1864–1996,* ed. Peter H. Solomon, Jr. (Armonk, 1997), pp. 22–43.

7 Alexander Vucinich, *Social Thought in Tsarist Russia: The Quest for a General Science of Society, 1861–1917* (Chicago, 1976), pp. 125–52.

8 Andrzej Walicki, *Legal Philosophies of Russian Liberalism* (Oxford, 1987), pp. 342–403.

9 Max Weber, *Zur Russischen Revolution von 1905*, ed. Wolfgang J. Mommsen and Dittmar Dahlmann (Tübingen, 1989), pp. 6–76 [= *Max Weber Gesamtausgabe,* 10].

10 He was a student of the constitutional and federal ideas of Mykhailo Drahomanov (1841–1895) who is now being rediscovered as a Ukrainian

national hero. A conference entitled "Mykhailo Drahomanov i problemy suspil'no-politychnoho i natsional'no-kul'turnoho rozvitku na Ukraïni i v Ievropi" and dedicated to Drahomanov in honor of his 150th birthday, was held in Kyiv, Ukraine on September 9–11, 1991.

[11] Larysa Depenchuk, *Bohdan Kistiakivs'kyi* (Kyiv, 1995); B. A. Kistiakovsky, "V zashchitu prava. Intelligentsiia i pravosoznanie," with an introduction by Aleksandr Iakovlev, *Nashe Nasledie* 4(16) 1990:1–12. Kistiakovsky's works are to be republished in Moscow.

Notes to Chapter 1

[1]   Vladimir Kistiakovsky [Volodymyr Oleksandrovych Kistiakivs'kyi; Vladimir Aleksandrovich Kistiakovskii], born in 1865, was a reknowned chemist. Igor Kistiakovsky [Ihor Oleksandrovych Kisitakivs'kyi; Igor' Aleksandrovich Kistiakovskii], born in 1876, was a prominent Moscow and Kyivan lawyer and jurist. For biographical information on the family, see the three entries on the Kistiakovskys in Brokgaus Efron, *Entsiklopedicheskii slovar'*; Mykola Vasylenko [Nikolai Vasilenko], "Akademik Bohdan Oleksandrovych Kistiakivs'kyi," in *Zapysky sotsial'no-ekonomichnoho viddilu, Ukraïns'ka Akademiia nauk*, vol. 1 (Kyiv, 1923), p. lx; and *Encyclopedia of Ukraine*, volume 2, ed. Volodymyr Kubijovyč (Toronto, 1984–1985), pp. 562–63.

[2]   Alexander Kistiakovsky [Oleksander Fedorovych Kistiakivs'kyi; Aleksandr Fedorovich Kistiakovskii] was an expert on the death penalty in the Russian Empire; *Issledovanie o smertnoi kazni* (Kyiv, 1867) was his dissertation. The 1896 edition was introduced and edited by B. A. Kistiakovsky. O. F. Skakun, *Politicheskaia i pravovaia mysl' na Ukraine (1861–1917)* (Kharkiv, 1987), pp. 113–27, contains an extensive discussion of the legal and criminological work of Alexander Kistiakovsky.

[3]   Zenon Kohut, *Russian Centralism and Ukrainian Autonomy: Imperial Absorption of the Hetmanate, 1760s–1830s* (Cambridge, Mass. 1988), pp. 54–55.

[4]   Alexander Kistiakovsky [Aleksandr Fedorovich Kistiakovskii], *Prava, po kotorym suditsia malorossiiskii narod* (Kyiv, 1879); Kohut, *Russian Centralism*, p. 55.

[5]   Ivan L. Rudnytsky, *Essays in Modern Ukrainian History*, ed. Peter L. Rudnytsky (Edmonton, 1987), pp. 128–32; M. S. Hrushevs'kyi [Grushevskii], "Istoriia ukrainskogo naroda," in *Ukrainskii narod v ego proshlom i nastoiashchem*, ed. Volkov et al. (St. Petersburg, 1914), pp. 326–34; W. E. D. Allen, *The Ukraine* (Cambridge, 1940), pp. 245–47.

[6]   As a result of the Polish rebellion, Poland once again lost its autonomous position that had been granted in 1862 by Alexander II.

[7]   It was this organization that established the first Ukrainian publication in the Russian Empire, *Osnova*. See *Encyclopedia of Ukraine*, vol. 2, pp. 244–

47; Hrushevs'kyi, "Istoriia ukrainskogo naroda," p. 343; Vasylenko, "Akademik Kistiakivs'kyi," p. xi; P. L. Tuchaps'kyi [Tuchapskii], *Iz perezhitogo, devianostie godi* (Odesa, 1923), pp. 13–15.

[8] Volodymyr Antonovych was descended from the Polonized Ukrainian nobles who felt a social debt and guilt toward the traditionally exploited peasantry and headed a group called the *khlopomany* (lovers of peasantry). At the time of the Polish revolt of 1863, the *khlopomany* severed connection with Poland and joined the Kyiv *Hromada* to contribute to its popular enlightenment projects.

[9] Hrushevs'kyi, "Istoriia ukrainskogo naroda," p. 341; cf. B. A. Kistiakovsky, "M. P. Dragomanov i vopros o samostoiatel'noi ukrainskoi kulture," *Ukrainskaia zhizn'* 6 (June, 1912): 10–35.

[10] For a review of the awakening of national consciousness in Ukraine, see Subtelny, pp. 221–42; Vasylenko, "Akademik Kistiakivs'kyi," p. x; Martha Bohachevsky-Chomiak, *Feminists Despite Themselves: Women in Ukrainian Community Life* (Edmonton, Canada, 1988), p. 35.

[11] Vasylenko, "Akademik Kistiakivs'kyi," pp. ix–x.

[12] Hrushevs'kyi, "Istoriia ukrainskogo naroda," p. 343; Vasylenko, "Akademik Kistiakivs'kyi," p. ix; Tuchaps'kyi, *Iz perezhitogo*, pp. 13–15.

[13] M. P. Drahomanov, "Introduction to *Hromada*," as cited in Ivan L. Rudnytsky, "Drahomanov as a Political Theorist," in *Mykhailo Drahomanov. A Symposium and Selected Writings*, ed. Ivan L. Rudnytsky (New York, 1952), p. 73.

[14] M. P. Drahomanov, "Istoricheskaia Pol'sha," cited in ibid., p. 75.

[15] Ivan L. Rudnytsky, "Drahomanov as a Political Theorist," p. 74.

[16] Drahomanov, *Lysty do Ivana Franka i ynshykh*, vol. 1 (L'viv, 1906), pp. 138–39.

[17] B. A. Kistiakovsky, "M. P. Dragomanov i vopros o samostoiatel'noi ukrainskoi kulture," p. 10.

[18] Dragomanov's letter to George Kennan, *Documents for the Study of Literature and Ideological Trends 1857–1933*, vol. 3 (New York, 1992), pp. 57–58.

[19] M. P. Drahomanov [Dragomanov], "K voprosu o natsional'nostiakh v Rossii," in *Sobranie politicheskikh sochinenii M. P. Dragomanova,* ed. B. A. Kistiakovsky, 2 vols. (Paris, 1905), 1: 864–70; M. P. Dragomanov, *Istoricheskaia Pol'sha i Velikorusskaia demokratiia* (Geneva, 1882), which was later published as volume 1 of the collected works of Dragomanov edited by Kistiakovsky (cited above); Georg von Rauch, *Russland: Staatliche Einheit und nationale Vielfalt* (München, 1953), pp. 132–33.

[20] John-Paul Himka, *Socialism in Galicia* (Cambridge, Mass., 1983), pp. 3–8.

[21] Olga Andriewsky, "The Politics of National Identity: The Ukrainian Question in Russia, 1904–1912," Ph.D. dissertation, Harvard University, 1991, pp. iix–xi.

[22] Himka, *Socialism,* pp. 4–8.

[23] Prior to 1772, when it was annexed by Austria, Galicia had been a part of the Polish-Lithuanian Commonwealth. At that time, Galicia included the eastern and western territories now divided between Poland and Ukraine.

[24] Tuchaps'kyi, *Iz perezhitogo,* p. 31; Kistiakovsky's letters reveal little political insight into his activities in the Ukrainian movement.

[25] From time to time contraband books in Ukrainian were smuggled into Kyiv from L'viv and the political activists there raised money for the movement in Galicia. L'viv became the center of the Ukrainian national movement after 1876. See Tuchaps'kyi, *Iz perezhitogo,* pp. 25–32; Hrushevs'kyi, "Istoriia ukrainskogo naroda," pp. 352–54.

[26] For brief biographies of Pavlyk and Franko, see Himka, *Socialism,* pp. 56–59, and *Encyclopedia of Ukraine,* vols. 1 and 2.

[27] Himka, *Socialism,* pp. 164–65; see V. I. Kalynovych, *Politychni protsesy Ivana Franka ta ioho tovaryshiv* (L'viv, 1967), pp. 120–34.

[28] Tsentral'nyi derzhavnyi istorychnyi arkhiv Ukraïny (TsDIA), Kyiv, fond 263, opys 1, ed. kh. 56. Vasylenko, "Akademik Kistiakivs'kyi," p. xii. For a report on this adventure, see V. I. Kalynovych, *Politychni protsesy Ivana Franka ta ioho tovaryshiv* (L'viv, 1967), and "Vypysky z sudovykh aktiv u spravi Pavlyka Mykhaila i Ammy," TsDIA, L'viv, fond 663, opys 1, ob. zb. 125, 15–23.

[29] Vasylenko, "Akademik Kistiakivs'kyi," p. xii, as quoted from the *Arkhiv Kievskogo gubernskogo zhandarmskogo upravleniia.*

[30] Ibid.; HH, Informationasburo, 2248, 2591–93, 2607.

[31] Vasylenko, "Akademik Kistiakivs'kyi," pp. xiii–xiv.

[32] Ibid., pp. xv–xvi. Dorpat University was centrally located for students from the Baltic *gubernii*—Rizhskaia, Revel'skaia, and Kurlandskaia. Unlike most universities in the empire, Dorpat University had a self-governing University Senate Corporation; this corporation was mandated by Tsar Alexander I in 1802. The student body was comprised of various nationalities and social classes. Until the 1850s, students could exercise freedom of choice in courses of study and the corporation could invite and elect members of the faculty. In 1852 the autonomy of the university was curtailed when the Russian government ended the teaching of European public law and increased surveillance over the university community. The pressures of Russification intensified in the 1860s and 1870s, when the threat of a revolutionary movement among the students grew. By 1889, many of the German professors left the university and were replaced by Russians who fulfilled the requirement that lectures be given in Russian. "Iur'evskii Universitet," *Entsiklopedicheskii slovar',* Brokgaus

Efron, vol. 81 (St. Petersburg, 1904), p. 437; see also R. Wittram, *Geschichte der baltischen Deutschen* (Stuttgart, 1938); Georg von Rauch, *Russland,* pp. 87–88.

[33] Stanisław Stempowski, *Spohady* (Warsaw, 1932), p. 126 [=Pratsi Ukraïns'koho naukovoho institutu, 8].

[34] Ibid., p. 127.

[35] Ibid., p. 128.

[36] Vasylenko, "Akademik Kistiakivs'kyi," p. xvi.

[37] *The Erfurt Program,* written by Eduard Bernstein and Karl Kautskii, was the official party program of the German Social Democratic Party (adopted in 1891).

[38] Vasylenko, "Akademik Kistiakivs'kyi," p. xvi.

[39] Dorpat University was renamed Iur'ev University in 1893.

[40] Tuchaps'kyi, *Iz perezhitogo,* p. 49. The Liberation of Labor, also known as the Emancipation of Labor, was an independent Marxist group founded in 1883 by Plekhanov, Aksel'rod, and Vera Zasulich. It had developed in response to disillusionment with the terrorist wing of the populist movement as well as the general failure of populism. Cf. Leopold H. Haimson, *The Russian Marxists and the Origins of Bolshevism* (Cambridge, Mass., 1955), pp. 43–48.

[41] Tuchaps'kyi, *Iz perezhitogo,* pp. 45–50.

[42] Stempowski, *Spohady,* p. 128.

[43] Ibid.

[44] Ibid., p. 129.

[45] Kistiakovsky did not reveal his contacts and tore up the letter he carried. The pieces of paper were collected and put together by passersby, one of whom pieced the papers together to give the police the information they needed. Stempowski, *Spohady,* p. 128.

[46] Ibid., p. 129.

[47] Vasylenko, "Akademik Kistiakivs'kyi," pp. xvii–xviii.

[48] Ibid. p. xv.

[49] To show respect for his father, Kistiakovsky remained the anonymous author of the forty-page introduction, signing it "T.S."—the initials for *tvoi syn* (your son); A. F. Kistiakovsky, *Issledovanie o smertnoi kazni,* pp. v–xlv.

[50] Kistiakovsky's mother to Panteleev, 25 October 1905; TsDIA, Kyiv, fond 264, opys 1, ed.kh. 50.

[51] Of the small group of legal Marxists, Petr Struve and Nikolai Berdiaev, who was born in 1874, were the most reknowned. Kistiakovsky collaborated with them in several publications, including the famous *Vekhi.*

[52] B. A. Kistiakovsky, "Iuvileinaia vystavka Beklina v Bazele," *Novoe slovo* 3(2) November, 1897: 88. Arnold Böcklin was most well known for his paintings on mythical themes, but Kistiakovsky limited his article to the artist's landscape paintings. The second article was a lengthy report on the condition and politics of the agricultural sector in Germany. Idem, "Agrarii v Germanii," *Novoe slovo* 6 and 7(2) July-August, 1897.

[53] The revival of neo-Kantianism in Germany began sometime in 1871 with the publication of Hermann Cohen's *Kant's Theory of Experience,* which proved to be a revolutionary work in philosophy. Cohen's goal was to emphasize Kant's view that the mind plays an active role in knowledge, a "constitutive" role. Philip Swoboda, "The Philosophical Thought of S. L. Frank, 1902–1915: A Study of the Metaphysical Impulse in Early Twentieth Century Russia," Ph.D. Dissertation, Columbia University (1992), pp. 59–60; Richard Kindersley, *The First Russian Revisionists: A Study of "Legal Marxism" in Russia* (Oxford, 1962), pp. 110–20.

[54] B. A. Kistiakovsky [Dr. T. Kistiakowski], *Gesellschaft und Einzelwesen* (Berlin: Verlag von Otto Liebmann, 1899).

[55] Ibid., pp. 67–74.

[56] *Gesellschaft und Einzelwesen* was reviewed in *Kantstudien* 5 (1900): 252–55; A.Vierkandt wrote the review for *Zeitschrift für Sozialwissenschaft* 3 (1900): 748–49; Dr. Gottfried Koch reviewed it in *Archiv für öffentliches Recht* 16 (1) 1901; Paul Ernst summarized it in "Zur Methodologischer Soziologie" in *Beilage zur Allgemeinen Zeitung* 73 (March 29, 1900); and Karl Diehl reviewed it in *Jahrbucher für Nationalökonomie und Statistik* 3 (Band 22) 1901: 878–79.

Georg Jellinek cited it in his *Allgemeine Staatslehre,* second edition (Berlin, 1914), pp. 150, 161, noting Kistiakovsky's contribution to the concept of the sociological foundations of the state; Emil Lask commented on Kistiakovsky's conception of neo-Kantianism in "Rechtsphilosophie" in *Die Philosophie im Beginn des 20 Jahrhunderts,* ed. Wilhelm Windelband (Heidelberg, 1905) pp. 34–35; Hans Kelsen emerged as Kistiakovsky's most severe critic in his book *Der Soziologische und der Juristiche Staatsbegriff* (Tübingen, 1928); Kistiakovsky's position within the realm of neo-Kantian legal theory will be discussed in the following chapter.

Kistiakovsky was also commented on enthusiastically by the American sociologist R. E. Park who was then studying in Berlin. See L. A. Coser, *Masters of Sociological Thought,* second edition (New York, 1977), pp. 368, 374–75.

[57] For reviews of the life and work of Novgorodtsev and Petrazhitskii see Andrzej Walicki, *Legal Philosphies of Russian Liberalism* (Oxford, 1987), chapters 4 and 5.

[58] TsDIA, Kyiv, fond 263, opys 1, ed. kh. 51; Vasylenko, "Akademik Kistiakivs'kyi," p. xxiii.

[59] Walicki, *Legal Philosophies*, p. 346.

[60] Petrazhiitskii was trying to convince Kistiakovsky to take a teaching position at Demidov Lyceum in Iaroslavl'. TsDIA, Kyiv fond 263, opys 1, ed. kh. 52.

[61] Kistiakovsky described his contact with Jellinek and the Heidelberg seminars in B. A. Kistiakovsky, "Georg Jellinek kak myslitel' i chelovek," *Russkaia mysl'* (May 1911); he wrote this article just after Jellinek's death. Vasylenko, "Akademik Kistiakivs'kyi," p. xiii.

Max Weber cited Kistiakovsky's article for *Problemy idealizma* in "Critical Studies in the Logic of the Cultural Sciences." This appeared in *The Methodology of the Social Sciences*, trans. and ed. Edward A. Shils and Henry A. Finch (New York, 1949), pp. 128, 166, 188. See also Max Weber, *Zur Russischen Revolution von 1905*, ed. Wolfgang J. Mommsen and Dittmar Dahlmann (Tübingen, 1989), pp. 5–7 [= *Max Weber Gesamtausgabe,* 10]. pp. 5–7. Kistiakovsky's collaboration with Weber on the latter's articles about the Russian constitutional experiment will be discussed in the section pertaining to Kistiakovsky after the 1905 Revolution.

[62] Sergei V. Svatikov, "Piat'desiat let nazad. Osnovanie russkoi chital'ny v Geidel'berge v 1862 godu. (Liudi i epocha)," Speech held on 15 December 1912 for the fiftieth anniversary of the Lecture Hall in Heidelberg, Columbia University Library, Bakhmeteff Archives, Svatikov Papers, Box 74, p. 14.

[63] P. I. Novgorodtsev, ed., *Problemy idealizma* (Moscow, 1903).

[64] The transition from legal populism to legal Marxism and subsequently to Marxism in the lives of Struve, Berdiaev, and Bulgakov is discussed in Arthur Mendel, *Dilemmas of Progress in Tsarist Russia* (Cambridge, Massachusetts, 1961), pp. 165–227; and Kindersley, Chapter 2, 3, and 4. See also Leonard Schapiro, "The *Vekhi* Group and the Mystique of Revolution," *The Slavonic and East European Review* 34 (December 1955/1956): 58–59; V. V. Zenkovskii, ed., *Sbornik pamiati Semiona Ludvigovicha Franka* (Munich, 1954), p. 11.

[65] "Russkaia sotsiologicheskaia shkola i kategoriia vozmozhnosti pri reshenii sotsial'no-eticheskikh problem," in B. A. Kistiakovsky, *Sotsial'nye nauki i pravo* (Moscow, 1916), p. 31. This article was first published in *Problemy idealizma*, pp. 295–391.

[66] Mikhailovskii was a central target for such attacks because of his prominence as a prolific writer and the editor of *Russkoe bogatstvo* [Wealth of Russia] from 1892 until his death. Mikhailovskii's debates with Struve, Vorontsov, and Plekhanov are the most famous examples of the controversy surrounding his populist theory. Thomas G. Masaryk, *The Spirit of Russia*, trans. E. and C. Paul, vol. 2 (New York, 1955), pp. 136–90; Mendel, pp. 1–37; Kindersley, pp. 109–120. See also James Billington, *Mikhailovsky and Russian Populism* (London, 1958).

[67] See Petr Struve, *Kriticheskie zametki k voprosu ob èkonomicheskom razvitii Rossii* (St. Petersburg, 1894) and Kistiakovsky, *Gesellschaft und Einzelwesen*; Kindersley, pp. 144–45; Mendel, pp. 188–93.

[68] Kistiakovsky argued that there was no contradiction between necessity and duty, since duty had the idea of necessity it and both ideas were opposed to subjectivism. Thus, he concluded that populist "subjective sociology" was founded on the idea that human knowledge could not be objective and neutral—the concept that led to a type of sociological relativism. Subjective sociology was not then an attempt to cope with the cultural crisis of positivism, it was part of the crisis. B. A. Kistiakovsky, *Sotsial'nye nauki i pravo*, pp. 73, 117–19.

[69] George Gurvitch, "Bogdan Alexandrovich Kistiakovsky," in *Encyclopedia of Social Sciences* 1932 (3): 575; Vladimir Starosolskyj, "Bogdan Kistiakovskyj und das Russische soziologische Denken," *Sonderabdruck aus Abhandlungen des Ukrainisch-Wissenschaftlichen Institutes* (Berlin, 1929), p. 118; Klaus von Beyme, *Politische Soziologie im zaristischen Russland* (Wiesbaden, 1965), pp. 42–46, 96–98, makes some inaccurate statements, for example, that Kistiakovsky never went through a Marxist period, p. 42. See also Gisela Oberländer, *Die Vechi-Diskussion* (Köln, 1965), pp. 40–42. Alexander Vucinich, *Social Thought in Tsarist Russia. The Quest for a General Science of Society, 1861–1917* (Chicago, 1976), devotes an entire chapter to Kistiakovsky. B. A. Chagin, ed., *Sotsiologicheskaia mysl' v Rossii: Ocherki nemarksistskoi sotsiologii poslednei treti XIX–nachala XX veka* (Leningrad, 1978), pp. 260–64.

[70] "Ukraïns'ki hurtky v Kyievi druhoï polovyny 1880-ykh ta pochatku 1890-ykh rokiv," *Za sto lit*, vol. 3 (Kyiv, 1928), pp. 206–225.

[71] Maria Berenshtam Kistiakovsky's [Mariia Berenshtam Kistiakivs'ka/ Kistiakovskaia] memoirs have not been available. See Bohachevsky-Chomiak, *Feminists Despite Themselves*, pp. 33–38. In her recent book, *Bohdan Kistiakivs'kyi*, Larysa Depenchuk (pp. 101–102) describes the progressive kindergarten that Maria Berenshtam Kistiakovsky organized in Moscow in 1900 under the auspices of the "Commission for National Schools."

[72] TsDIA, Kyiv, fond 263, opys 1, ed. kh. 57. See also Bohachevsky-Chomiak, *Feminists Despite Themselves*, pp. 33-43, 327.

[73] Ibid., pp. xxi–xxiii.

[74] Correspondence between Kistiakovsky and Jellinek, Nachlass Georg Jellinek, BA Koblenz, n. 13.

[75] Drahomanov's dedication to the Ukrainian movement and the problems of non-Russian peoples were evident in his demand for a constitution, a parliament and civil liberties, as well as in the liberal constitutionalist program of the journal *Free Word* which focused on political decentralization, autonomy, and rights for non-Russian nationalities more than *Liberation*. Struve, "Otkuda

i kuda?" in *Osvobozhdenie: Kniga Vtoraia* (Paris, 1904), p. 15; Richard Pipes, *Struve, Liberal on the Left* (Cambridge, Mass., 1970), p. 310.

[76] The activities of the Zemstvo Union formed in 1879 by the chairmen of several provincial *zemstva* had been cut short by the assassination of Alexander II in 1881 and the repression that followed it. D. I. Shakhovskoi, "Politicheskie techeniia v russkom zemstve," *Iubileinyi zemskii sbornik, 1864–1914* (St. Petersburg, 1914), pp. 453–62.

[77] Ivan I. Petrunkevich, *Iz zapisok obshchestvennogo deiatelia. Arkhiv russkoi revolutsii* (Prague, 1934), pp. 329–39; S. L. Frank, *Biografiia P. B. Struve* (New York, 1956), pp. 37–38; George Fischer, *Russian Liberalism* (Cambridge, Mass., 1969), pp. 83–117; Gregory L. Freeze, "A National Liberation Movement and the Shift in Russian Liberalism, 1901–1903," *Slavic Review* 28(1) March 1969: 81; Shmuel Galai, *The Liberation Movement in Russia, 1900–1905* (Cambridge, 1973), pp. 177–96; Richard Pipes, *Peter Struve, Liberal on the Left* (Cambridge, 1970), pp. 332–33; Victor Leontovitsch, *Geschichte des Liberalismus in Russland* (Frankfurt am Main, 1957), pp. 277–86.

[78] Kistiakovsky's initial contacts with Russian students in Germany dating back to his arrival in 1895 continued to develop each time he was in Germany doing research and working with the neo-Kantians. By 1902, his connections with the Russians in Germany developed into a working relationship, when he began editing and writing for *Osvobozhdenie* in Stuttgart. Petr Struve, Kistiakovsky's first Russian friend in Germany, and his staff, including Kistiakovsky, decided to move the offices of the journal to Heidelberg after the Stuttgart offices were forcibly closed by the German authorities. Vasylenko, "Akademik Kistiakivs'kyi," pp. xxiii–xxiv.

[79] Kistiakovsky and his wife together with Vasilii Vasil'evich Vodovozov, Sergei Nikolaevich Bulgakov, Nikolai Aleksandrovich Berdiaev, U. N. Vagner, V. I. Zheleznev, and Mykola Vasylenko were the members of the Kyiv *Osvobozhdenie* group that organized the banquet. Vasylenko, "Akademik Kistiakivs'kyi," pp. xxiv–xxv. See also Leonard Schapiro, "The Vekhi Group and the Mystique of Revolution," *The Slavonic and East European Review* 34 (1955–1956): 57–76; Jeffrey Brooks,"Vekhi and the Vekhi Dispute," *Survey* 86 (1973): 21–50; and Terence Emmons, *The Formation of Political Parties and the First National Elections in Russia* (Cambridge, Mass., 1983).

[80] "Predislovie," in B. A. Kistiakovsky, ed., *Sobranie politicheskikh sochinenii M. P. Dragomanova,* vol. 2 (Paris, 1906); Vasylenko, "Akademik Kistiakivs'kyi," pp. xxiv–xxv; Depenchuk, *Bohdan Kistiakivs'kyi,* pp. 93–94 points out that the first volume did not sell well, which may explain why it took several years to bring out the other volumes.

[81] "M. P. Dragomanov. Ego politicheskie vzgliady, literaturnaia deiatel'nost' i zhizn," in B. A. Kistiakovsky, *Politicheskie sochineniia M. P. Dragomanova,* ed. I. Grevs and B. Kistiakovsky (Moscow, 1908), pp. ix–lxxvii.

[82] Marianne Weber, *Max Weber—Ein Lebensbild* (Tübingen, 1926), p. 342.

[83] In the first of these two monographs, Weber thanked "Dr. Theodor [i.e., Bogdan] Kistiakowski" for sharing his knowledge of research materials and personal experiences. Max Weber, "Zur Lage der bürgerlichnen Demokratie in Russland," 1906, *Beilage, Archiv für Sozialwissenschaft und Sozialpolitik*, Band 22, p. 234. Both essays have been republished in Max Weber, *Zur Russischen Revolution.* Max Weber, "Russlands Übergang zum Schein-konstitutionalismus," ibid., Band 23. Marianne Weber, p. 342; Richard Pipes, "Max Weber and Russia," *World Politics* 7 (1955): 380; Wolfgang J. Mommsen, *Max Weber und die deutsche Politik, 1890–1920* (Tübingen, 1959), pp 64–65.

Weber's ability to read Russian enabled him to cite Kistiakovsky's 1902 article in *Problemy idealizma* in Max Weber, "Critical Studies in the Logic of the Cultural Sciences," pp. 128, 166, 188. For an edited English version of Weber's monographs, see Max Weber, *The Russian Revolutions*, trans. and ed. Gordon C. Wells and Peter Baehr (Ithaca, 1995).

[84] B. A. Kistiakovsky, "Gosudarstvennaia duma i osnovnye zakony," in *Duma* 2 (April 28, 1906); Vasylenko, "Akademik Kistiakivs'kyi," pp. xxv–xxvi.

[85] Vasylenko, "Akademik Kistiakivs'kyi," p. xxvii.

[86] Ibid. *Vysshie zhenskie kursy* were the first courses in higher education for women in Europe. K. Shokhol', "K voprosu o razvitii vysshego zhenskogo obrazovaniia v Rossii," in *Zhurnal ministerstva narodnogo prosveshcheniia* 40 (August 1912): 1–58. The last part of this article focuses on the twentieth century. By 1906, since thousands of women enrolled in *Vysshie zhenskie kursy*, the courses were no longer considered the dissident cause they had been regarded as at their inception in 1878. See also Cynthia H. Whittaker, "The Woman's Movement During the Reign of Alexander II: A Case Study in Russian Liberalism," *The Journal of Modern History* 48(2) June 1976: 35–70.

[87] TsDIA, Kyiv, 1909, fond 263, opys 1.

[88] He felt there were many younger people ahead of him; Kotliarevskii and Kokoshkin were two such qualified people looking for positions. TsDIA, Kyiv, 19 December 1909, fond 263, opys 1.

[89] Ibid. B. A. Kistiakovsky, "Konstitutsiia darovannaia i konstitutsiia zavoievannaia," *Poliarnaia zvezda* 11 (26 February 1906): 747–48; idem, "Kabinet ministrov," I and II, *Svoboda i kul'tura* 2-3 (10 April 1906; 16 April 1906); 95–105, 139–58; idem, "Tret'e zasedanie gosudarstvennoi dumy i amnistiia," *Duma* 1 (27 April 1906); idem, "Nashe politicheskoe obrazovanie," *Svoboda i kultura*, 6 (7 May 1906): 415–22; idem, "Gosudarstvennaia duma i osnovnye zakony," *Duma* 2 (28 April/ 11 May 1906).

Poliarnaia zvezda was edited by P. B. Struve every week from December 1905 to March 1906; *Svoboda i kultura* was edited by P. B. Struve and S. L.

Frank trimonthly from April 1906 to May 1906; *Duma* was edited by P. B. Struve from 27 April to 11 June 1907.

[90] Kistiakovsky was an active member of the *Komissiia po organizatsii domashnego chteniia*. For this organization he developed a program for the study of the theory of state and state law that appeared as a forty-five-pages-long brochure with the following words on its title page: "Programma dlia samoobrazovania. 1. Obschchaia teoriia gosudarstva. II. Obshchee gosudarstvennoe pravo. Sostavil B. A. Kistiakovsky." Vasylenko, "Akademik Kistiakivs'kyi," p. xxvii. The *Komissiia po organizatsii domashnego chteniia* was started in the mid-1890s in Moscow with the purpose of establishing a self-education program. See P. Miliukov, "Komissiia po organizatsii domashnego chteniia v Moskve," *MB,* May 1894: 231–36.

[91] Vasylenko, "Akademik Kistiakivs'kyi," p. xxviii. This article, published in the *Politicheskaia èntsiklopediia,* was the precursor to his well-known article in the 1909 collection, M. O. Gershenzon, ed., *Vekhi, Sbornik statei o russkoi intelligentsii* (Moscow, 1909), cited below in more detail.

[92] Vasylenko, "Akademik Kistiakivs'kyi," pp. xxvi–xxviii.

[93] Gershenzon, *Vekhi. Sbornik statei o russkoi intelligentsii.*

[94] Kistiakovsky described *Vekhi* as a market success: "Three thousand copies were sold wholesale in 19 days. The second edition came out on May 28, and 2,200 copies were sold in the first 3 days. The last copy of the second edition was sold on June 16, 1909." Kistiakovsky to his mother, 28 June 1909, TsDIA, Kyiv, fond 263, opys 1.

[95] The conservative minister of national education, Lev Aristidovich Kasso, had dismissed the rector of the university. P. I. Novgorodtsev, "Russian Universities and Higher Technical Schools During the War," in *Russian Schools and Universities in the World War/Economic and Social History of the World War,* (New Haven, Conn., 1929), pp. 129–51 [=Russian Series]. Cited in Walicki, *Legal Philosophies,* p. 297.

[96] Vasylenko, "Akademik Kistiakivs'kyi," p. xxx. It had been edited by Sergei Andreevich Muromtsev in its earlier incarnation.

[97] Muromtsev was elected chairman of the First State Duma in 1906. Kistiakovsky, *Sotsial'nye nauki i pravo,* pp. 338–39.

[98] N. A. Kablukov, "V Moskovskom iuridicheskom obshchestve," in *Sergei Andreevich Muromtsev,* ed. D. I. Shakhovskoi (Moscow, 1940), pp. 116–40; Vucinich, *Social Thought,* p. 141.

[99] Kistiakovsky, "V zashchitu prava," pp. 126–32, 155.

[100] Vasylenko, "Akademik Kistiakivs'kyi," p. xxviii.

[101] Andriewsky, "The Politics," pp. 396–97.

[102] Vasylenko, "Akademik Kistiakivs'kyi," pp. xxxvi–xxxix.

[103] Andriewsky, "The Politics," pp. 107–114. See also George Shevelov, "The Language Question in the Twentieth Century, 1900–1941," *Harvard Ukrainian Studies* 10(1/2) June 1988: 71–170.

[104] Borys Krupnyckyj, *Geschichte der Ukraine*, 3rd ed. (Wiesbaden, 1963), pp. 271–72; Allen, *The Ukraine*, p. 255.

[105] A. Ia. Avrekh, *Tsarizm i tret'eiunskaia sistema* (Moscow, 1966), pp. 81–82; Krupnyckyj, pp. 272–74; Ben-Cion Pinchuk, *The Octobrists in the Third Duma, 1907–1912* (Seattle, 1974), pp. 177–78; Allen, p. 255. The rise of Great Russian chauvinism will be discussed in greater detail below.

[106] B. A. Kistiakovsky, "K voprosu o samostoiatel'noi ukrainskoi kulture," *Russkaia mysl'* 32 (May, 1911): 131–46. See also Krupnyckyj, *Geschichte der Ukraine*, pp. 272–73; Allen, *The Ukraine*, p. 255; von Rauch, *Russland*, pp. 163–64.

[107] Kistiakovsky, "V zashchitu prava," pp. 125–55; S. N. Harper, *The New Electoral Law for the Russian Empire* (Chicago, 1908); Alfred Levin, "3 June 1907, Action and Reaction," *Essays in Russian History,* [A collection dedicated to George Vernadskii], ed. A. D. Ferguson and A. Levin (Hamden, Conn., 1964), pp. 231–74; Geoffrey Hosking, *The Russian Constitutional Experiment, Government and Duma, 1907–1914* (Cambridge, 1973), pp. 14–56; Pinchuk, pp. 177–78; Avrekh, *Tsarizm i tret'eiunskaia sistema*, p. 255; Krupnyckyj, *Geschichte der Ukraine*, pp. 272–74.

[108] B. A. Kistiakovsky, *Stranitsy proshlogo* (Moscow, 1912) was actually a response to Vasilii Iakovlevich Bogucharskii, *Iz istorii politicheskoi bor'by v 70kh i 80kh gg. XIX veka* (Moscow, 1912). Bogucharskii claimed that Dragomanov had been duped by a government clique when he published *Vol'noe slovo* in Geneva in 1883. This debate will be discussed below. See also Vasylenko, "Akademik Kistiakivs'kyi," pp. xxxiv–xxxv.

[109] Vasylenko, "Akademik Kistiakivs'kyi," pp. xxxvi–xxxix.

[110] "Istoricheskaia Pol'sha i Velikorusskaia demokratiia," in M. P. Drahomanov [Dragomanov], *Sobranie politicheskikh sochinenii*, vol. 1 (Paris, 1905–1906), p. 253.

[111] B. A. Kistiakovsky, "Chto takoe natsionalizm?" *Natsional'nye problemy* 1 (May, 1915): 1-2.

[112] Vasylenko, "Akademik Kistiakivs'kyi," pp. xxxix–lx. See also the editorial notes on volumes 2 and 3 of *Natsional'nye problemy* that reported the first official attempt to close the journal.

[113] Vasylenko, "Akademik Kistiakivs'kyi," pp. xxxv–xxxvi. Kistiakovsky's earlier interest in the Russian revolutionary history was evident in his book *Stranitsy proshlogo*.

[114] Kistiakovsky, *Sotsial'nye nauki i pravo*, p. 346. For a synopsis of Kistiakovsky's thesis in *Sotsial'nye nauki i pravo,* see Vucinich, *Social Thought*, pp. 125–52.

[115] TsDIA, Kyiv, fond 263, opys 1, ed. kh. 69.

[116] Vasylenko, "Akademik Kistiakivs'kyi," p. xxxi; *Pravo* 13 (2 May 1917). As mentioned above, Kistiakovsky earned his first doctorate in Germany in 1899.

[117] Richard Pipes, *The Formation of the Soviet Union* (New York, 1968), p. 53–54.

[118] Emanuel Sarkisyanz, "Russian Imperialism Reconsidered," in *Russian Imperialism from Ivan the Great to the Revolution*, ed. Taras Hunczak (New Brunswick, 1974), p. 71; Alexander Motyl, *Will the Non Russians Rebel?* (Ithaca, 1987), p. 45.

[119] John S. Reshetar, *The Ukrainian Revolution, 1917–1920* (Princeton, 1952), pp. 166–67.

[120] Igor Kistiakovsky's earlier career was distinguished by his work as a close associate of Sergei A. Muromtsev, the lawyer and president of the First State Duma. "The 42-year-old liberal had formerly enjoyed wide popularity in Kiev and Moscow, where he served on the law faculties of both city's universities, and developed a broad civil practice. Now even some former associates thought him shockingly unprincipled. German arms, his energy and his 'evil genius,' according to one observer, kept the Hetman in power." William G. Rosenberg, *Liberals in the Russian Revolution* (Princeton, 1974), pp. 321–22. See also A. A. Goldenwieser [Gol'denveizer], "Iz kievskikh vospominanii," *Arkhiv Russkoi Revoliutsii* 6 (1922): 223–24.

[121] Stempowski, *Spohady,* p. 127.

[122] Igor Kistiakovsky's involvement in the Skoropads'kyi government was controversial enough to have been omitted from the extensive obituary-biography that Vasylenko wrote for the *Bulletin of the Socio-Economic Division of the Ukrainian Academy of Sciences* in 1923. Vasylenko, "Akademik Kistiakivs'kyi," p. ix. Reshetar, *The Ukrainian Revolution*, pp. 3–4, 160–70.

[123] *Rosiis'ko-ukraïns'kyi slovnyk pravnychoï movy*, cited in Mytropolyt Ilarion [Ivan Ohijenko], *Istoriia ukraïns'koï literaturnoï movy* (Winnipeg, 1949–1950), p. 350.

[124] Vasylenko, "Akademik Kistiakivs'kyi," pp. viii–ix.

[125] Ibid., p. ix. Reshetar, *The Ukrainian Revolution*, pp. 3–4, 160, 170. Interview with Professor George B. Kistiakowsky of Harvard University on March 19 and 20, 1976.

[126] Depenchuk, *Bohdan Kistiakivs'kyi,* p. 127.

[127] Kistiakovsky's widow could have been harmed or imprisoned as a part of the reaction to Igor Kistiakovsky's involvement with the Skoropadskii government; she was saved by the personal intervention of Nadezhda Krupskaia, Lenin's wife. Krupskaia's aid to Maria Berenshtam Kistiakovsky was a gesture from an old friend and cohort from their days as members of a St.

Petersburg workers organization as well as in respect for what Kistiakovsky and his wife had done in the struggle for human rights. Interview with Professor George B. Kistiakowsky of Harvard University on March 19 and 20, 1976.

Notes to Chapter 2

[1] Pavel Novgorodtsev, "K voprosu o sovremennykh filosofskikh iskaniiakh. (Otvet L. I. Petrazhitskomu)," in *Voprosy filosofii i psikhologii* 14(1) 66 (January-February 1903): 124.

[2] George Kline, "Changing Attitudes toward the Individual," in *The Transformation of Russian Society*, ed. Cyril Black (Cambridge: Harvard University Press, 1970), p. 606–608.

[3] Arnold Brecht, *Political Theory* (Princeton, 1959), pp. 239–40. The Marburg neo-Kantians were more concerned with transcendental questions of value—the "*a priori*"—than the Heidelberg School's members.

[4] Ibid., p. 239.

[5] Boris Landau, "Uchennia B. O. Kistiakivs´koho pro derzhavu," *Zapysky sotsial'no-ekonomichnoho viddilu, Ukraïns'ka Akademiia nauk,* vol. 1 (Kyiv, 1923), p. 108.

[6] B. A. Kistiakovsky, *Sotsial'nye nauki i pravo* (Moscow, 1916), p. 620.

[7] Landau, "Uchenie B. A. Kistiakovskogo," p. 108.

[8] B. A. Kistiakovsky [Dr. Theodor Kistiakowski], *Gesellschaft und Einzelwesen* (Berlin, 1899), p. v; Kistiakovsky, *Sotsial'nye nauki i pravo*, pp. 15–16; Alexander Vucinich, "A Sociological Synthesis: B. A. Kistiakovsky," in *Social Thought in Tsarist Russia* (Chicago, 1976), pp. 132–33. See also Andrzej Walicki, *Legal Philosophies of Russian Liberalism* (Oxford, 1989), pp. 349–50.

[9] Swoboda, "The Philosophical Thought," pp. 67–86. Swoboda provides an impressive survey of German neo-Kantianism and neo-Kantianism in Russia in the 1890s and beyond.

[10] Brecht, *Political Theory*, p. 9.

[11] Kistiakovsky, *Gesellschaft und Einzelwesen*, pp. v–vi; Frederick S. J. Copleston, *A History of Philosophy*, vol. 3 (New York, 1965), p. 135; Max Weber, "Objectivity in Social Science and Social Policy," in *The Methodology of the Social Sciences*, trans. Shils and Finch (New York, 1949); Brecht, *Political Theory*, pp. 206–215.

[12] Judith Zimmerman, "Sociological Ideas in Pre-Revolutionary Russia," *Canadian-American Slavic Studies* 9(3) Fall 1975: 319–21. See also Andrew Arato, "The Neo-Idealist Defense of Objectivity," *Telos* 21 (Fall 1974): 108–161.

[13] He was opposed to defining sociology as an extension of the natural sciences that treated society as an organism in a biological sense. Kistiakovsky, *Gesellschaft und Einzelwesen*, pp. 19–42; Zimmerman, "Sociological Ideas," p. 321.

[14] Kistiakovsky, *Gesellschaft und Einzelwesen,* p. 20–23; Vucinich, "A Sociological," p. 242.

[15] B. A. Kistiakovsky, "V zashchitu nauchno-filosofskogo idealizma," in *Sotsial'nye nauki i pravo*, p. 193. The article was originally published in *Voprosy filosofii i psikhologii* (1907).

[16] Weber, "Objectivity," p. 53. The *Archiv für Sozialwissenschaft und Sozialpolitik* became a major forum for neo-Kantians at the turn of the century.

[17] Kistiakovsky, "V zashchitu nauchno-filosofskogo idealizma," pp. 190–93; Wolfgang Friedmann, *Legal Theory*, third edition (London, 1953), p. 98.

[18] Kistiakovsky, "Prava cheloveka i grazhdanina," *Voprosy zhizni* 1 (January 1905): 122.

[19] Kistiakovsky, "Prava cheloveka i grazhdanina," enlarged and revised version of the 1905 article, in *Sotsial'nye nauki i pravo*, p. 497.

[20] Kistiakovsky, "V zashchitu nauchno-filosofskogo idealizma," p. 193. See also N. Berdiaev, "O novom russkom idealizme," in *Sub specie Aeternitatis* (St. Petersburg, 1907), pp. 152–90, for a definition of elements common among idealists—their rejection of positivism and Marxism.

[21] By 1904, there were nine Russian full members and two associate members of the Institut international de sociologie; five of these had served as vice-presidents of the institute—the historian Nikolai Kareev (1899), Maksim Kovalevskii (1895), Nikolai Mikhailovskii (1904), Jacques Novicow (1893–1894), and Evgenii de Roberty (1903). Zimmerman, "Sociological Ideas," pp. 305–306.

[22] Ibid., p. 307.

[23] Kistiakovsky, "Russkaia sotsiologicheskaia shkola i kategoriia vozmozhnosti pri reshenii sotsial'no-eticheskikh problem," in *Problemy idealizma,* ed. P. L. Novgorodtsev (Moscow, 1902), pp. 295–391; reprinted in Kistiakovsky, *Sotsial'nye nauki i pravo.*

[24] N. K. Mikhailovskii, *Sochineniia N. K. Mikhailovskogo*, vol. 4 (St. Petersburg, 1891), pp. 949, 952. See James H. Billington, *Mikhailovsky and Russian Populism* (London, 1958) and Thomas G. Masaryk, *The Spirit of Russia*, trans. E. and G. Paul, vol. 2 (New York, 1955), pp. 136–90.

[25] Vucinich, "A Sociological," pp. 37–38.

[26] Kistiakovsky, "Russkaia sotsiologicheskaia shkola," p. 72; Vucinich, "A Sociological," p. 58; Thomas G. Masaryk, *The Spirit of Russia*, vol. 2, pp. 140–42.

[27] Kistiakovsky, "Russkaia sotsiologicheskaia shkola," p. 64.

[28] Kistiakovsky, "Prava cheloveka i grazhdanina," in *Sotsial'nye nauki i pravo*, p. 497.

[29] His criticism of Mikhailovskii and the Russian Subjectivist School was sometimes focused too much on Mikhailovskii's imprecise use of terms and penchant for inventing phrases and terms. B. A. Chagin, ed., *Sotsiologicheskaia mysl' v Rossii* (Leningrad, 1978), p. 264.

[30] N. I. Kareev, review of *Sotsial'nye nauki i pravo*, by B. A. Kistiakovsky, in *Golos minuvshego* 11–12 (1917): 347–49; Also quoted in Vucinich, "A Sociological," pp. 138–39.

[31] Ibid. Kareev as quoted in Vucinich.

[32] Kistiakovsky, "Prava cheloveka i grazhdanina," in *Sotsial'nye nauki i pravo*, p. 508.

[33] Kistiakovsky, *Gesellschaft und Einzelwesen*, pp. 8–16, 32–34; P. L. Novgorodtsev, "Nravstvennyi idealizm v filosofii prava," in *Problemy idealizma*, pp. 294–95; Friedmann, *Legal Theory,* p. 84; H. B. Acton, "Introduction," in G. W. F. Hegel, *Natural Law* (Philadelphia, 1975), p. 15.

[34] Kistiakovsky, *Gesellschaft und Einzelwesen*, pp. 77–79; Emil Lask, "Rechtsphilosophie," in *Die Philosophie im Beginn des zwantigsten Jahrhunderts*, ed. Wilhelm Windelband, vol. 2 (Heidelberg, 1905), pp. 34–35; Brecht, *Political Theory*, pp. 215–31; Carl J. Friedrich, *The Philosophy of Law in Historical Perspective* (Chicago, 1958), pp. 165–77.

[35] Kistiakovsky, *Gesellschaft und Einzelwesen,* pp. 71–74; Emil Lask, "Rechtsphilosophie," pp. 34–37.

[36] Friedmann, *Legal Theory,* pp. 256–67. To be sure, not all neo-Kantians who accepted the idea of separating "what is" from "what should be," perceived law as a cultural phenomenon. Hans Kelsen, one of the most influential legal theorists in the early part of this century, rejected the idea that there was any connection between the normative laws (*Sollen*) and social realities (*Sein*). Unlike the neo-Kantians seeking a social theory of law, Kelsen developed a pure theory of law through which he hoped to solve normative problems by excluding all social reality and foregoing any attempt to connect law with social reality. *Der sociologische und der juristische Staatsbegriff* (Tübingen, 1928) is his major work on a social theory of law. See also Kelsen, *Reine Staatslehre* (Tübingen, 1934).

[37] Kistiakovsky, *Gesellschaft und Einzelwesen,* p. 33. He based his analysis of natural law and laws of nature on "Geschichte und Naturwissenschaft" (1894), in Wilhelm Windelband, *Praludien*, third edition (Tübingen, 1907), p. 217. See also Weber, "Objectivity," pp. 51–52.

[38] Kistiakovsky, *Gesellschaft und Einzelwesen,* p. 34.

[39] Kistiakovsky, *Sotsial'nye nauki i pravo*, pp. 346–47.

40 Ibid., p. 355; Vucinich, "A Sociological," p. 143.

41 Ibid., pp. 321–26.

42 Friedmann, *Legal Theory,* pp. 256–57.

43 Kistiakovsky, *Sotsial'nye nauki i pravo*, pp. 338, 346; N. S. Timasheff, *An Introduction to the Sociology of Law*, vol. 3 (Cambridge, Mass., 1939), p. 24.

44 Friedrich, *Philosophy of Law,* p. 88; Kelsen, *Der Soziologische und der Juristiche Staatsbegriff,* p. 109.

45 Kistiakovsky, *Gesellschaft und Einzelwesen*, pp. 32–34; Kistiakovsky, *Sotsial'nye nauki i pravo*, p. 321; P. L. Novgorodtsev, "Nravstvennyi idealizm v filosofii prava," in *Problemy idealizma*, p. 294. See also idem, *Krizis sovremennogo pravosoznaniia* (Moscow, 1909).

46 Kistiakovsky, *Sotsial'nye nauki i pravo*, pp. 344–46; Vucinich, "A Sociological," pp. 128–29.

47 Kistiakovsky, "Kategorii neobkhodimosti i spravedlivosti pri issledovanii sotsial'nykh iavlenii," in *Sotsial'nye nauki i pravo*, p. 173.

48 Rudolf Stammler, *Die Lehre von dem Richtigen Rechte* (Berlin, 1902), p. 39.

49 Kistiakovsky, "Kategoriia neobkhodimosti i spravedlivosti," p. 176.

50 Ibid., p. 179.

51 Kistiakovsky, *Gesellschaft und Einzelwesen*, p. v, pp. 72–79; Georg Jellinek, *System der subjektiven Öffentlichen Rechte* (Freiburg, 1892). See Alexander Hollerbach, "Georg Jellinek," *The International Encyclopedia of the Social Sciences*, vol. 8 (New York, 1968), pp. 252–54.

52 Kistiakovsky, *Gesellschaft und Einzelwesen*, p. 77.

53 N. N. Alekseev, "Sotsial'naia filosofiia Rudol'fa Shtammlera," *Voprosy filosofii i psikhologii* 96 (1909): 2–15 (secion Z); "Nravstvennyi idealizm v filosofii prava," pp. 255, 194–96; and Novgorodtsev, "Kant kak moralist," *Voprosy filosofii i psikhologii* 76 (1905): 29–35; Vucinich, "A Sociological," pp. 147–59.

54 P. N. Miliukov, "Sergei Andreevich Muromtsev: Biograficheskii ocherk," in K. K. Arsen'ev et al., *Sergei Andreevich Muromtsev. Sbornik statei,* ed. D. I. Shakhovskoi (Moscow 1911), p. 37.

55 Vucinich, "A Sociological," p. 140.

56 Kistiakovsky, *Sotsial'nye nauki i pravo*, pp. 338–39.

57 Ibid., pp. 334, 338–39. But the Russian regime suppressed efforts at studying the empirical social and political foundations of law, as well as discussions of law and politics.

Kistiakovsky was acutely aware of the government's repressive acts, for he was chosen as editor of the *Juridical Courier* when it was reopened for publication in 1912. The Moscow Juridical Society was ordered to close by the minister of education in 1899. In 1884 Sergei Andreevich Muromtsev had been dismissed from his position as professor of law at Moscow University. In 1912 when Kistiakovsky became the new editor of the Moscow Juridical Society's journal, he wrote his mother that he was honored to fill the position once held by Muromtsev. Mykola Vasylenko, "Akademik Bohdan Oleksandrovych Kistiakivs'kyi," in *Zapysky sotsial'no-ekonomichnoho viddilu, Ukraïns'ka Akademiia nauk*, vol. 1 (Kyiv, 1923), p. xxxix.

[58] Kistiakovsky, *Sotsial'nye nauki i pravo*, p. 323; "Real'nost' ob'ektivnogo prava," pp. 257–337, Kistiakovsky's critique of Petrazhitskii's psychological approach to law. Kistiakovsky's commitment to studying the social foundations of law was not shared by either Lev Iosifovich Petrazhitskii (1867–1931) or Nikolai Mikhailovich Korkunov (1853–1904), the jurist, political theorist, and professor of law at St. Petersburg University.

[59] Novgorodtsev, "Nravstvennyi idealizm," pp. 255–57, 296.

[60] Kistiakovsky, "Problema i zadacha sotsial'no-nauchnogo poznaniia," *Sotsial'nye nauki i pravo*, p. 27.

[61] Kistiakovsky, "Kategoriia neobkhodimosti i spravedlivosti pri issledovanii sotsial'nykh iavlenii," *Sotsial'nye nauki i pravo*, pp. 120–88.

[62] Vucinich, "A Sociological," pp. 150–51.

[63] Kistiakovsky, *Sotsial'nye nauki i pravo*, pp. 346–48.

[64] Kistiakovsky, *Sotsial'nye nauki i pravo*, p. 28; Vladimir Starosolskyj, "Bogdan Kistiakovskyj und das Russische soziologische Denken," in *Sonderabdruck aus Abhandlungen des Ukrainisch-Wissenschaftlichen Institutes*, vol. 2 (Berlin, 1929), p. 123. Kistiakovsky acknowledged his debt to Marxist methodology, while he emphatically rejected all forms of monist theories, materialistic or idealistic. All monist theories, in his view, had to become metaphysical in the end, for they developed the direction and goals of a study instead of providing the point of departure and method, which were the directions of Kistiakovsky's inquiry; Kistiakovsky, *Gesellschaft und Einzelwesen*, p. v. Kistiakovsky explained that he did not embark on a full analysis of the problem of social monism because he considered it an epistemological problem that would have interfered with his presentation of a methodological scheme.

[65] Kistiakovsky, *Sotsial'nye nauki i pravo*, pp. 645–59; Max Rheinstein, ed., *Max Weber on Law in Economy and Society* (New York, 1954), pp. 63, 299. Translated from Max Weber, *Wirtschaft und Gesellschaft* (Tübingen, 1928).

[66] Max Weber, "Objective Possibility and Adequate Causation in Historical Explanation," in his *The Methodology of the Social Sciences*, trans. and ed. by Edward A. Shils and Henry A. Finch (New York, 1949), pp. 164–87; Kistiakovsky, "Kategorii neobkhodimosti i spravedlivosti," pp. 120–88; Vucinich, "A Sociological," pp. 136–37.

[67] Vucinich, "A Sociological," p. 137.

[68] There is no evidence that Kistiakovsky and Max Weber worked closely with one another after their collaboration on Weber's two articles on Russian constitutionalism. However, Kistiakovsky traveled to Germany every year to maintain contact with the neo-Kantians in Heidelberg. In addition, there is some evidence that Weber read Kistiakovsky's work in Russian; he praised Kistiakovsky's criticism of the subjective school of sociology represented by Mikhailovskii. Perhaps, those connections are sufficient to explain some of the similarities that placed both of them in the ranks of the pioneers in the field of sociology and the social foundations of law. Kistiakovsky used the concept "ideal type" when he wrote, " . . . pure forms of the state very rarely coincide with concrete reality, as real facts. But they should be theoretically established in the sense of ideal types, according to their complete image, fullness and perfection." Vucinich, "A Sociological," p. 137.

Although Weber was not the only social theorist to use the concept of an ideal type, he is indeed one of those philosophical and sociological thinkers Kistiakovsky mentioned in his footnote to that quotation. Kistiakovsky referred to Weber's article, "Die 'objectivität' socialwissenschaftlicher und sozialpolitischer Erkenntnis," in *Archiv für Sozialwissenschaft und Sozialpolitik*, Bd. xix, S. 22, ff *bes*, 64 ff.

[69] Kistiakovsky, *Gesellschaft und Einzelwesen*, pp. 197–205; Kistiakovsky's optimistic view of the natural unity in society did not mean that he took no note of the tensions between the individual and society. However, his mention of potential conflict was limited. At one point he wrote, "Kant used his comparison of the society with the forest in this way. He showed that the trees in a forest grew much straighter and taller as a result of the crowding and the mutual constricting of their free development in much the same way as the talents and successes of individuals are stimulated by social antagonisms." Kistiakovsky, *Gesellschaft und Einzelwesen*, p. 132.

[70] Ibid., p. 83.

[71] Kistiakovsky, "Prava cheloveka i grazhdanina," *Sotsial'nye nauki i pravo*, pp. 514–15.

[72] Friedrich, *Philosophy of Law*, pp. 124–25; Georgii Gurvich, *Russo i deklaratsiia prav* (Petrograd, 1918), pp. 85–89; Novgorodtsev, "Nravstvennyi idealizm v filosofii prava," pp. 281–96; Friedmann, *Legal Theory,* pp. 69–77. See also Georges Gurvitch, *L'Idée du Droit Social* (Paris, 1931).

[73] Gurvich, *Russo i deklaratsiia prav*, pp. 85–89; Kistiakovsky's notion of a form of general will, which also provided the theoretical basis for his ideal of socialism and socialistic individualism, will be discussed in the next chapter.

[74] Max Weber, "Objectivity in the Social Sciences and Social Policy," p. 52.

[75] Ibid., p. 101.

[76] *The Legal Philosophies of Lask, Radbruch, and Dabin*, trans. Kurt Wilk (Cambridge, Mass., 1950), p. xxx.

[77] Kelsen, *Der Soziologische und der Juristiche Staatsbegriff*, pp. 106–113.

[78] Kistiakovsky, *Sotsial'nye nauki i pravo*, p. 249.

Notes to Chapter 3

[1] Marc Raeff, *Understanding Imperial Russia, State and Society in the Old Regime* (New York, 1984), p. 22.

[2] For a full discussion of the complex system of *sosloviia*, see Gregory Freeze, "The *Soslovie* (Estate) Paradigm and Russian Social History," *American Historical Review* 96(1) March 1986: 11–36; David Macey, *Government and Peasant in Russia, 1861–1906* (De Kalb, Ill., 1987), p. 339.

[3] Freeze, "Soslovie," p. 27.

[4] Francis Wcislo, "*Soslovie* or Class? Bureaucratic Reformers and Provincial Gentry in Conflict, 1906–1908," *The Russian Review* 47 (1988): 23. See also Leopold Haimson, "Conclusion: Observations on the Politics of the Russian Countryside (1905–1914)," in *The Politics of Rural Russia*, ed., Leopold Haimson (Bloomington, 1979), pp. 261–300; idem, "The Parties and the State: The Evolution of Political Attitudes," in Cyril E. Black, ed., *The Transformation of Russian Society* (Cambridge, Mass., 1969); Roberta Manning, *The Crisis of the Old Order* (Princeton, 1982), chapter 14; V. S. D'iakin, *Samoderzhavie, burzhuaziia i dvorianstvo v 1907-1911 gg.* (Leningrad, 1978).

[5] Abraham Ascher, *The Revolution of 1905: Authority Restored* (Stanford, Calif., 1992), pp. 337–68, provides a comprehensive account of the court intrigue leading to the dissolution of the Duma and the rewriting of the electoral laws to guarantee the limitation of hostile anti-government representatives from the Duma debates.

[6] Gosudarstvennaia duma, Vtoroi sozyv, *Zakonodatel'nye materialy* (St. Petersburg, 1907), p. 265.

[7] Peter Struve, "My contacts and conflicts with Lenin," *Slavonic and East European Review* 12 (1933/34): 573.

[8] "Ot redaktora," *Osvobozhdenie* 1 (1 July 1902): 2.

[9] Richard Pipes, *Struve, Liberal on the Left* (Cambridge, Mass., 1970), pp. 308–337; Shmuel Galai, *The Liberation Movement in Russia 1900–1905* (Cambridge, 1973), pp. 157–74.

[10] *Osvobozhdenie* 17 (1903): 291. (Miliukov signed his name "S. S.")

[11] Kistiakovsky to Struve, 6 April 1903, RTsKhIDNI (Rossiiskii tsentr khraneniia i izucheniia dokumentov noveishei istorii), fond 279 (Redaktsiia "Osvobozhdeniie"), opis' 1, delo 80, pp. 122–23. Cited in K. F. Shatsillo, *Russkii liberalism na kanune revolutsii 1905–1907 gg.* (Moscow, 1985), pp. 152–53, under old archival name—TsPA (Tsentral'nyi partiinyi arkhiv pri TsK KPSS, fond 279).

[12] Ibid, p. 153.

[13] Ivan Il'ich Petrunkevich and his wife (Tver'), Dmitrii Ivanovich Shakhovskoi (Iaroslavl'), N. N. L'vov (Saratov), P. Dolgorukov (Kursk), N Kovalevskii (Kharkiv), S. A. Kotliarevskii (Saratov), D. E. Zhukovskii, the organizer of the Schaffhausen meeting, Fedor Ismailovich Rodichev (Tver') and V. I. Vernadskii (Tambov); intelligentsia writers and activists such as Petr Struve, Nikolai Aleksandrovich Berdiaev, Sergei Nikolaevich Bulgakov, Bogdan Kistiakovsky and Semen Liudvigovich Frank who were all contributors to the collection *Problems of Idealism* in 1902. Some of the intelligentsia academics, including Pavel Ivanovich Novgorodtsev (professor of philosophy, Moscow University), Ivan Mikhailovich Grevs (professor of history, St. Petersburg University), Vasilii Vasil'evich Vodovozov; and socialists outside of the Social Democratic Party, Ekaterina Dmitrievna Kuskova and Sergei Nikolaevich Prokopovich. Shatsillo, *Russkii liberalism*, pp. 158–59; I. Petrunkevich, *Iz zapisok obchshestvennogo deiatelia* (Berlin, 1934), pp. 135–55. The *zemstvo* and non-*zemstvo* categories were misleading because the differences within those groups were far too great. Some of those in the *zemstvo* category—Rodichev, Vernadskii, and Kotliarevskii—were not landowners, but professionals. George Fischer, *Russian Liberalism* (Cambridge, Mass., 1958), p. 141. See also Galai, *The Liberation Movement*, p. 177; Pipes, *Struve, Liberal on the Left*, p. 333.

[14] Petrunkevich, *Iz zapisok*, pp. 339–92; Gregory Freeze, "A National Liberation Movement and the Shift in Russian Liberalism, 1901–1903," *Slavic Review* 28(1): 90.

[15] *Listok Osvobozhdenia* 17 (19 November 1904): 2.

[16] Ibid.

[17] Pipes, *Struve, Liberal on the Left*, pp. 375–76.

[18] Terence Emmons, *The Formation of Political Parties and the First National Elections in Russia* (Cambridge, Mass., 1983), p. 42. See also Judith Zimmerman, "Between Revolution and Reaction: The Russian Constitutional Democratic Party, October 1905 to June 1907," Ph.D. dissertation (Columbia University, 1967), chapter 4.

[19] Article 3 was based on the discussions at the September *zemstvo* congress, which had substantial representation from non-*zemstvo* provinces. Petitions from various nationalities, including Poles, Ukrainians, and Lithuanians, among others, led to a response for Kadet support in the national borderlands. Emmons, *The Formation*, p. 42; William Rosenberg, *Liberals in the Russian Revolution*, (Princeton, 1974), p. 13.

[20] Emmons, *The Formation*, p. 43; *Otchet Tsentral'nogo Komiteta Konstitutsionno-demokraticheskoi partii (Partiia narodnoi svobody) za dva goda s 18 oktiabria 1905 g. po oktiabr' 1907 g.* (St. Petersburg, 1907), pp. 17–18.

[21] B. A. Kistiakovsky, *Sotsial'nye nauki i pravo* (Moscow, 1916), p. 620.

[22] B. A. Kistiakovsky, "Prava cheloveka i grazhdanina," *Voprosy zhizni* 1 (January 1905): 118.

[23] Ibid., p. 119.

[24] Ibid., pp. 119–22.

[25] Ibid., pp. 121–25; Kistiakovsky noted Georg Jellinek's important model for individual rights that had a profound effect on his concept of human rights. Georg Jellinek, *Die Erklärung der Menschen und Bürgerrechte* (Leipzig, 1895). However, Kistiakovsky's dedication to socialist rights and socialism were not a part of Jellinek's formula.

[26] Kistiakovsky, "Prava cheloveka i grazhdanina," pp. 125–26; idem, "Gosudarstvo i lichnost," *Sotsial'nye nauki i pravo*, p. 573; Anton Menger, *Das Recht auf den vollen Arbeitersertrag in geschichtlicher Darstellung* (Stuttgart, 1886). See also George Gurvich, "Anton Menger," *Encyclopedia of the Social Sciences,* vol. 10 (New York, 1933), p. 310; Karl Grünberg, *Anton Menger, Sein Leben und Lebenswerk* (Vienna–Leipzig, 1909).

[27] Kistiakovsky, "Prava cheloveka i grazhdanina," pp. 125–26; Kistiakovsky, "Gosudarstvo sotsialisticheskoe i pravovoe," *Voprosy filosofii i psikhologii* 85 (November-December 1906): 495–96; Kistiakovsky, *Sotsial'nye nauki i pravo*, p. 321; Friedmann, *Legal Theory*, pp. 232, 284–85; Karl Renner, *The Institutions of Private Law and their Social Functions*, ed. O. Kahn-Freund (London, 1949). The French theorist Leon Duguit rejected the public-private law distinction on the basis of his conception of the society as a social organism, and from that position, he rejected the whole idea of private rights.

[28] Kistiakovsky, "Prava cheloveka i grazhdanina," pp. 125–26; Georg Jellinek, *System der Subjektiven Öffentlichen Rechte* (Freiburg, 1892).

[29] Kistiakovsky, *Sotsial'nye nauki i pravo*, p. 526.

[30] Ibid., p. 121. This example was first used by the nineteenth-century legal theorist Rudolf von Jhering in defining the nature of individual rights. Hans Kelsen and his followers in the Vienna School of neo-Kantian Marxists held that individual rights in fact should be derivative. In their view, Marxism contained a theoretical justification for a possibility of subordinating some individuals to the wishes of the collective; thus, it is understandable that Marxist-influenced legal theorists, such as Kelsen, did not stress the importance of inalienable rights. Hans Kelsen and his followers actually recognized no legal rights for the individual, except as a technical device which the law may or may not adopt in order to carry out legal transactions. Kelsen maintained that there was no concrete connection between the normative and positive in laws, for law was exclusively normative (a statement of ideals). Therefore, he argued that legal duties were of essence in the law, but legal rights were only an incidental aspect the law might dispense with. Hans Kelsen, *The General Theory of Law* (Boston, 1909); Friedmann, *Legal Theory,* pp. 87–89.

[31] Kistiakovsky, "Prava cheloveka i grazhdanina," p. 120.

[32] Ibid., pp. 125–26; Kistiakovsky, *Sotsial'nye nauki i pravo*, pp. 547–48.

[33] Kistiakovsky, "V zashchitu prava," in *Vekhi, Sbornik Statei o russkoi intelligentsii*, ed. M. O. Gershenzon (Moscow, 1909), p. 125. The combination of economic and political rights changed the world view on human rights and became the basis of the United Nations Universal Declaration of Human Rights in 1948.

[34] Kistiakovsky, "Gosudarstvo sotsialisticheskoe i pravovoe," pp. 495–96.

[35] Ibid.

[36] Kistiakovsky, "Prava cheloveka i grazhdanina," *Sotsial'nye nauki i pravo*, p. 496.

[37] Kistiakovsky, "Prava cheloveka i grazhdanina,"(1905), p. 126.

[38] Kistiakovsky, "Gosudarstvo sotsialisticheskoe i pravovoe," p. 495.

[39] Kistiakovsky, *Sotsial'nye nauki i pravo*, p. 577.

[40] Ibid., p. 590.

[41] Ibid., p. 581.

[42] Ibid., p. 551.

Notes to Chapter 4

[1] Richard Wortman, *The Development of a Russian Legal Consciousness* (Chicago, 1976), p. 285; Andrzej Walicki, *Legal Philosophies of Russian Liberalism* (Oxford, 1987), p. 21.

[2] See Wortman, *Development*.

[3] Mikhail Speranskii was appointed secretary of state, in charge of the activities of the State Council. He became the second most powerful man in the empire next to Alexander I. In March 1812, Alexander gave in to negative public opinion on Speranskii and dismissed him. Marc Raeff, *Michael Speransky: Statesman of Imperial Russia, 1772–1839* (The Hague, 1969), pp. 6–78; Wortman, *Development*, pp. 36–39.

[4] Wortman, *Development,* pp. 1–44.

[5] Marc Raeff, "The Bureaucratic Phenomenon of Imperial Russia," *American Historical Review* 84(2) 1979: 409.

[6] David Macey, *Government and Peasant in Russia, 1861–1909* (De Kalb, Ill., 1987), p. xv.

[7] As mentioned above, the Russian judiciary was not considered far inferior to the European judicial systems, though there was interference with the system on the part of the state. Walicki, *Legal Philosophies*, pp. 102–103; A. A. Goldenweiser [Gol'denveizer], *V zashchitu prava* (New York, 1952), pp. 211–12.

[8] Goldenweiser [Gol'denveizer], *V zashchitu,* pp. 211–12; W. Lednicki, *Pamiatniki,* vol. 1 (London, 1963), p. 309.

[9] Jane Burbank, "Legal Culture, Citizenship, and Peasant Jurisprudence: Perspectives from the Early Twentieth Century," in Peter Solomon, ed., *Reforming Justice in Russia, 1864–1996* (Armonk, 1997), pp. 88–90.

[10] Cathy Frierson, "Of Red Rooster, Revenge, and the Search for Justice: Rural Arson in European Russia in the Late Imperial Era," in Peter Solomon, ed., *Reforming Justice in Russia, 1864–1996* (Armonk, 1997), pp. 106–130. See also idem, "Rural Justice in Public Opinion: The Volost' Court Debate 1861–1912," *Slavonic and East European Review* 64(4) October 1986: 526–45; idem, "'I must always answer to the laws . . . ': Rules and Response at the Reformed *Volost* Court," *Slavonic and East European Review* 75, no. 2 (April, 1997; 308–334; and idem, *Peasant Icons: Representations of Rural People in Late Nineteenth Century Russia* (New York, 1993).

[11] Lional Kochan and Richard Abraham, *The Making of Modern Russia* (London, 1983), p. 182.

[12] Moshe Lewin, *The Making of the Soviet System* (New York, 1985), p. 73.

[13] Ibid., p. 72; David Macey, *Government and Peasant in Russia,* pp. 15–19.

[14] Leonard Schapiro, "The Pre-Revolutionary Intelligentsia and the Legal Order," in Ellen Dahrendorf, ed., *Russian Studies* (New York, 1987), pp. 58–60.

[15] The *zemstvo* movement cannot be fully discussed here. There is extensive literature describing the movements among the nobility to defend their interests and the gradual development of their group identity. See Seymour Becker, *Nobility and Privilege in Late Imperial Russia* (De Kalb, Illinois, 1985); Roberta Manning, *Crisis of the Old Order in Russia* (Princeton: Princeton University Press, 1982); Terrence Emmons and W. S. Vucinich, eds., *The Zemstvo in Russia: Experiment in Local Self-Government* (New York, 1982).

[16] A. F. Koni, *Sobranie sochinenii,* vol. 2 (Moscow, 1966), pp. 171–73, 180–81; See Wortman, *Development,* pp. 282–83.

[17] N. A. Troitskii, *"Narodnaia Volia" pered tsarskim sudom, 1880–1891 gg.* (Saratov, 1971), p. 24–25; see also Wortman, *Development,* p. 283.

[18] The State Council (*Gosudarstvennyi sovet*) was first established in 1810—its members appointed to draft legislative bills and advise the monarch; the council was limited in that it could take no legislative initiative. George Yaney, *The Systematization of the Russian Government* (Chicago, 1973), pp. 194–95. On February 20, 1906, the details of the revived and revised role of the State Council—Statutes for the State Council—were announced. Insofar as the State Council had not been mentioned in the October Manifesto, the proclamation of the role of the State Council as the upper house of parliament was generally interpreted as a reactionary act on the part of the autocracy. P.

N. Miliukov, *Vospominaniia (1859–1917)*, vol. 1 (New York, 1955), pp. 362–63, as quoted in Geoffrey Hosking, *The Russian Constitutional Experiment, Government and Duma, 1907–1914* (Cambridge, 1973), p. 11.

[19] The Council of Ministers was first established in 1857 by Tsar Alexander II, but from 1882 to 1904, it did not play a significant role in coordinating the ministers. Yaney, p. 251; the Council of Ministers was first revived in the decree of February 18, 1905, to draft legislation and to carry out constitutional reforms. The council worked on some reforms until another decree issued on August 6, 1905, relieved it of those duties. *(Tret'e) Polnoe sobranie zakonov Rossiiskoi imperii* (St. Petersberg, 1885–1916), no. 25853 and no. 26657.

In October 1905, the *Ukaz* issued to consolidate the activities of the Council of Ministers defined the revised functions of the council and its ministers. G. G. Savich, *Novyi Gosudarstvennyi stroi Rossii. Spravochnaia kniga* (St. Petersburg, 1907), pp. 28–31.

[20] The Lesehalle was founded in 1862 by Nikolai Ivanovich Pirogov, a famous doctor after whom the reading room was named. Max Weber, *Zur Russischen Revolution von 1905*, ed. Wolfgang J. Mommsen and Dittmar Dahlmann (Tübingen, 1989), pp. 5–6 [=*Max Weber Gesamtausgabe,* 10]; Fedor Stepun, *Vergangenes und Unvergängliches aus meinem Leben*. Vol. 1. *1884–1914* (München, 1947); Robert C. Williams, "Russians in Germany: 1900–1914," *The Journal of Contemporary History* 1(4) 1966: 121–49; and Claudie Weill, "Les étudiants russes en Allemagne," *Cahiers du Monde Russe et Soviétique* 20 (1979): 203–225.

[21] Bogdan Kistiakovsky and Max Weber corresponded extensively, though only one or two letters and numerous postcards Weber wrote to Kistiakovsky have been found. Otdelenie pis'mennykh istochnikov GIM, fond 108, contains Kistiakovsky's personal archive. None of the letters and other materials found in the archive were written by Kistiakovsky. See also "Arkhiv B. A. Kistiakovskogo," *Problemy sotsiologii* 1(1) 1992: 157–64.

[22] Weber, *Zur Russischen Revolution,* p. 7.

[23] Nachlass Max Weber-Schäfer, Privatbesitz, Bayerische Staatsbibliotek, Handschriftenabteilung, München; Weber, *Zur Russischen Revolution,* p. 17.

[24] Max Weber, "Russlands Übergangang zum Scheinkonstitutionalismus," in his *Zur Russischen Revolution,* p. 228.

[25] Kistiakovsky, "Konstitutsiia darovannaia i konstitutsiia zavoevannaia," *Poliarnaia zvezda* 11 (26 February 1906): 748. Kistiakovsky's writings in this period included three short newspaper articles: "Konstitutsiia darovannaia i konstitutsiia zavoevannaia," "Tret'e zasedanie gosudarstvennoi dumy i amnestiia," *Duma* 1 (27 April 1906): 747–54; and "Gosudarstvennaia duma i osnovnye zakony," *Duma* 2 (11 May 1906); Kistiakovsky's longer journal articles in 1905–1906 were: "Prava cheloveka i grazhdanina," *Voprosy zhizni* 1 (January 1905): 116–42; "Kabinet ministrov," Parts 1, 2. *Svoboda i kultura,* 2 (10 April 1906): 95–105; 3 (16 April 1906): 139–58; "Kak osushchestvit'

edinoe narodnoe predstavitel'stvo?" Parts 1–3. *Russkaia mysl'* 28 (March, April, June 1907) 3: 113–134; 4: 49–71; 6: 156–68; "Gosudarstvo pravovoe i sotsialisticheskoe," *Voprosy filosofii i psikhologii* 85 (November-December 1906): 469–507; "Nashe politicheskoe obrazovanie," *Svoboda i kultura* 6 (7 May 1906): 415–22.

26 Kistiakovsky, "Konstitutsiia darovannaia i konstitutsiia zavoevannaia," p. 745.

27 Marc Szeftel, *The Russian Constitution of April 23, 1906: Political Institutions of the Duma Monarchy* (Brussels, 1976).

28 Kistiakovsky, "Konstitutsiia darovannaia i konstitutsiia zavoevannaia," p. 747.

29 Ibid.

30 Kistiakovsky, "Gosudarstvennaia duma i osnovnye zakony," p. 2.

31 Ibid.

32 Ibid.

33 Kistiakovsky, "Gosudarstvo pravovoe i sotsialisticheskoe," p. 488.

34 Kistiakovsky, "Kabinet ministrov," Part 2, p. 158.

35 See chapter 6 for a full discussion.

36 Max Weber, "Zur Lage der bürgerliche Demokratie in Russland," *Zur Russischen Revolution,* p. 335. See also Richard Pipes, "Max Weber and Russia," *World Politics* 6(3) April 1955: 371–401.

37 Kistiakovsky, *Stranitsy proshlogo. K istorii konstitutsionnogo dvizheniia v Rossii* (Moscow, 1912), pp. 80–81.

38 Kistiakovsky, "Gosudarstvo pravovoe i sotsialisticheskoe," p. 489.

39 Ibid.

40 Kistiakovsky, "Gosudarstvo i lichnost'," *Sotsial'nye nauki i pravo,* p. 592.

41 Kistiakovsky, "Gosudarstvo pravovoe i sotsialisticheskoe," pp. 491–95.

42 Kistiakovsky, "Gosudarstvo i lichnost'," pp. 591–92.

43 Kistiakovsky, "V zashchitu prava," in *Vekhi, Sbornik statei o russkoi intelligentsii,* ed. M. O. Gershenzon (Moscow, 1909), p. 137.

44 Kistiakovsky, "Gosudarstvo i lichnost'," p. 565.

45 Kistiakovsky, "V zashchitu prava," p. 136.

46 Kistiakovsky, "Gosudarstvo pravovoe i sotsialisticheskoe," p. 483; idem, "Gosudarstvo i lichnost'," p. 565.

47 Kistiakovsky, "V zashchitu prava," pp. 135–36.

48 Kistiakovsky, "Gosudarstvo i lichnost'," p. 566.

49 Kistiakovsky, "Kak osushchestvit' edinoe narodnoe predstavitel'stvo?" Part 1, p. 165.

50 Ibid.

51 Kistiakovsky, "Gosudarstvo pravovoe i sotsialisticheskoe," p. 485.

52 Alfred Levin, "3 June 1907, Action and Reaciton," in *Essays in Russian History,* ed. A. D. Ferguson and A. Levin (Hamden, Conn., 1964), pp. 231–74; Hosking, *The Russian Constitutional Experiment,* pp. 14–56; Abraham Ascher, *The Revolution of 1905. Authority Restored* (Stanford, 1992), pp. 354–68.

Notes to Chapter 5

1 B. A. Kistiakovsky, "Gosudarstvo pravovoe i sotsialisticheskoe," *Voprosy filosofii i psikhologii* 85 (November–December 1906): 488–89.

2 Kistiakovsky, "Nashe politicheskoe obrazovanie," *Svoboda i kul'tura* 3 (16 April 1906): 415. See also Jeffrey Brooks, *When Russia Learned to Read: Literacy and Popular Culture, 1861–1917* (Princeton, 1985).

3 Ibid.

4 Kistiakovsky, "Gosudarstvo pravovoe i sotsialisticheskoe," p. 492.

5 Ibid., p. 490.

6 L. I Petrazhitskii, "Teoriia gosudarstva i prava," in *Law and Morality,* trans. H. W. Babb (Cambridge, Mass., 1955), p. 99.

7 Aleksandr Herzen, "Du développement des idées révolutionnaires en Russie," in *Sobranie sochinenii,* vol. 6 (Moscow, 1956), p. 121, as quoted in B. A. Kistiakovsky, "V zashchitu prava," in *Vekhi, Sbornik statei o russkoi intelligentsii,* ed. M. O. Gershenzon (Moscow, 1909), p. 130. In the translation and edited version of Kistiakovsky's *Vekhi* article, Marshall S. Shatz and Judith Zimmerman note that Kistiakovsky's citation of Herzen was inaccurate. See B. Kistiakovsky, "In Defense of Law (The Intelligentsia and Legal Consciousness)," in Shatz and Zimmerman, eds., *Vekhi: A Collection of Articles on the Russian Intelligentsia,* p. 40 [= *Canadian Slavic Studies* 4(1) Spring 1970]. This translation was republished in book form as Shatz and Zimmerman, eds. *Vekhi = Landmarks. A Collection of Articles on the Russian Intelligentsia* (Armonk, N.Y., 1994). See also Bogdan Kistiakovsky, "In Defense of Law," in *Landmarks, A Collection of Essays on the Russian Intelligentsia, 1909,* ed. Boris Schragin and Albert Todd (New York, 1977), pp. 112–38.

8 Kistiakovsky. "V zashchitu prava," pp. 130–32, 148, 154.

9 Leopold Haimson, "The Problem of Social Stability in Urban Russia," in *Slavic Review* 8(4) December 1964: 619–42, treats this work as a sign of the developing crises of the elite *(krizis verkhov)* in which the unity and, thus, the leadership of the intelligentsia began to break down.

[10] S. L. Frank, *Biografiia P. B. Struve* (New York, 1956), p. 81; and "O Vekhakh," in P. B. Struve, *Patriotica. Politika, kul'tura, religiia, sotsializm* (St. Petersburg, 1911), p. 229; Susan Heuman, "*Vekhi*, A Collection of Essays on the Russian Intelligentsia," unpublished essay for the Russian Institute of Columbia University, 1968. See also Andrzej Walicki, *Legal Philosophies of Russian Liberalism* (Oxford, 1987), pp. 374–76.

[11] M. O. Gershenzon, *Vekhi, Sbornik statei o russkoi intelligentsii* (Moscow, 1909), p. iii.

[12] In a footnote added to his article for the second edition of *Vekhi*, A. S. Izgoev stated that the basic unity among the authors was fragmented by the variety of their motivations: "I consider it a duty to make reservations in relation to the 'platform' formulated in the foreword to this book; I whole-heartedly accept the basic thesis set down there, but I differ with the authors in their basic motivation." Ibid., p. 577.

[13] George F. Putnam, *Russian Alternatives to Marxism. Christian Socialism and Idealistic Liberalism in Twentieth-Century Russia* (Knoxville, 1976), pp. 56–92.

[14] See chapter 1, pp. 22–24, for a discussion of *Problems of Idealism*. Leonard Schapiro, "The Vekhi Group and the Mystique of Revolution," in *Slavonic and East European Review* 34 (December 1955–1956): 56–57.

[15] N. Poltoratskii, "Lev Tolstoy and Vekhi," p. 332.

[16] N. Poltoratskii, "Vekhi i russkaia intelligentsia," *Mosty* 10 (1963): 298.

[17] Ibid., pp. 298–99.

[18] Ibid., pp. 296–97.

[19] K. Arsen'ev et al., *Intelligentsiia v Rossii. Sbornik statei s predisloviem I. I. Petrunkevicha* (St. Petersburg, 1910), p. x.

[20] V. I. Lenin, *Sochineniia*, vol. 14 (Moscow, 1929); Struve, "O Vekhakh," p. 218.

[21] A. Ia. Avrekh, *Tsarism i tret'ieiun'skaia sistema* (Moscow, 1966), p. 8.

[22] Ia. Bechev (pseudonym for Viktor Chernov), "Pravovye idei v russkoi literature," in *Vekhi kak znamenie vremeni* (Moscow, 1910), pp. 174–75.

[23] Christopher Read, *Religion, Revolution and the Russian Intelligentsia 1900–1912* (London, 1979), p. 161; Walicki, *Legal Philosophies,* p. 389.

[24] Pavel Miliukov, "Intelligentsiia i istoricheskaia traditsiia," in *Intelligentsiia v Rossii*, (Moscow, 1991), p. 187.

[25] Walicki, *Legal Philosophies,* p. 393.

[26] V. A. Maklakov, *The First State Duma*, trans. M. Belkin (Bloomington, 1964), p. 243 [=Indiana University Publications Russian and East European Series, 30].

[27] Miliukov, "Intelligentsiia i istoricheskaia traditsiia," p. 134; Ia. Vechev, pp. 174–75.

[28] W. E. Butler, "Civil Rights in Russia: Legal Standards in Gestation," in *Civil Rights in Imperial Russia*, ed. Olga Crisp and Linda Edmondson (Oxford, 1989), pp. 4–10; Walicki, *Legal Philosophies*, pp. 384–85.

[29] Kistiakovsky, "V zashchitu prava," p. 148. My translations of excerpts from this article by Kistiakovsky are based on Shatz and Zimmerman's translation entitled "B. A. Kistiakovsky, 'In Defense of Law (The Intelligentsia and Legal Consciousness),'" in *Vekhi* = *Landmarks*.

[30] There is a pronounced continuity in the major themes of individualism, human rights, constitutionalism, and socialism in Bogdan Kistiakovsky's earlier writings and his 1909 *Vekhi* article. This later article was more programmatic and polemical than his article in *Problemy idealizma* and his articles published in 1906 just after the October Manifesto was proclaimed. In the 1909 article, "In Defense of Law," Kistiakovsky moved from his focus on the philosophical concerns of Western Europe and Russia to the concrete social, economic, and political problems of life in the Russian Empire. His deeper involvement and familiarity with Russian conditions had led him to a more integrated approach to his conception of the role of law and legal consciousness and its significance in the context of the Russian Empire. Kistiakovsky, "V zashchitu prava," pp. 126–55.

[31] Ibid., p. 126.

[32] Ibid., p. 132.

[33] Ibid. Kistiakovsky, "V zashchitu nauchno-filosofskogo idealizma," *Sotsial'nye nauki i pravo,* p. 193; Kistiakovsky, "Prava cheloveka i grazhdanina," *Voprosy zhizni* 1 (January 1905): 497.

[34] Kistiakovsky, "V zashchitu prava," pp. 130–32, 148, 154.

[35] Ibid., p. 155.

[36] Ibid.

[37] Ibid., p. 144.

[38] Ibid., pp. 145–48.

[39] Ibid., p. 145.

[40] Ibid., p. 127.

[41] Ibid., p. 132.

[42] Ibid., p. 134; N. K. Mikhailovskii, *Sochineniia N. K. Mikhailovskogo,* vol. 4 (St. Petersburg, 1897), p. 949.

[43] N. I. Kareev, review of *Sotsial'nye nauki i pravo* by B. A. Kistiakovsky, *Golos minuvshego,* 11–12 (1917): 348–49; also quoted in Alexander Vucinich, *Social Thought in Tsarist Russia. The Quest for a General Science of Society* (Chicago, 1976), pp. 138–39. See also pp. 44–47 above.

[44] B. A. Kistiakovsky, *Sotsial'nye nauki i pravo* (Moscow, 1916), pp. 132–33.

[45] *Sobranie sochinenii K. D. Kavelina*, vol. 2 (St. Petersburg, 1898), pp. 894–95, as cited in Leonard Schapiro, *Russian Studies* (New York, 1988), p. 62.

[46] Ibid.; Leonard Schapiro, "The Pre-Revolutionary Intelligentsia and the Legal Order," in *The Russian Intelligentsia,* ed. Richard Pipes (New York, 1961), p. 27. See also Darrel P. Hammer, "Two Russian Liberals: The Political Thought of B. N. Chicherin and K. D. Kavelin," Ph.D. dissertation, Columbia University, 1962–1963.

[47] Kistiakovsky, "V zashchitu prava," p. 138.

[48] Ibid., p. 141.

[49] Ibid., p. 142.

[50] Ibid., p. 145.

[51] Ibid., pp. 139–40; See Complete Text of the Protocols. Russian Social-Democratic Workers' Party, Second Regular Congress. *Polnyi tekst protokolov S-D R.P.* (Geneva, 1903), pp. 169–70.

[52] Ibid., p. 149.

[53] Ibid.; Richard Wortman, *The Development of a Russian Legal Consciousness,* (Chicago, 1976), pp. 282–83; Samuel Kucherov, *Courts, Lawyers and Trials Under the Last Three Tsars* (New York, 1953), p. 205. For the court martial system, see William Fuller, "The Russian Revolution of 1905 and Military Justice," chapter 6 of *Civil Military Relations in Imperial Russia, 1881–1914* (Princeton, 1985). See also N. V. Cherkasova, *Formirovanie i razvitie advokatury v Rossii* (Moscow, 1987); V. I. Smoliarchuk, *Giganty i charodei slova* (Moscow, 1984), which deals with legal orators at the turn of the century. N. V. Cherkasova, N. V. Davidov, and N. N. Polianskii, *Sudebnaia reforma,* 2 vols.(Moscow, 1915).

[54] Kistiakovsky, "V zashchitu prava," pp. 148–49.

[55] Ibid., p. 154.

[56] Ibid., pp. 148–49.

[57] Ibid.

[58] This decree was controversial because it was another political infringement on the independent realm of the judiciary, and, more noteworthy, it resulted in the execution of about one thousand people in the eight months that the law was in effect. Ibid., p. 154; Samuel Kucherov, *Courts, Lawyers and Trials,* pp. 205–212.

[59] Kistiakovsky, "V zashchitu prava," p. 151.

[60] William G. Wagner, "Civil Law, Individual Rights, and Judicial Activism in Late Imperial Russia," in Peter Solomon, ed., *Reforming Justice in Russia,* p. 24. See also William G. Wagner, *Marriage Property and Law in Late Imperial Russia* (Oxford, 1994).

[61] Kistiakovsky, "V zashchitu prava," p. 143.

[62] Bogdan Kistiakovsky's interest in the codification of peasant customs and common law was undoubtedly influenced by his father Alexander Kistiakovsky's extensive work on this subject, including *Programma dlia sobraniia iuridicheskikh obychaev i narodnye vozzreniia po ugolovnomu pravu* (Kyiv, 1894).

[63] Kistiakovsky, "V zashchitu prava," p. 143.

[64] Ibid., p. 154.

[65] The courts provided even more freedom for political speeches than the legislative chambers did; Samuel Kucherov, *Courts, Lawyers and Trials*, pp. 213–14; Anatole Leroy-Beaulieu, *The Empire of the Tsars and the Russians*, vol. 2 (New York, 1969), p. 49.

[66] Kistiakovsky, "V zashchitu prava," pp. 153–54.

[67] Kistiakovsky, "Nashi zadachi," *Iuridicheskii vestnik* 1 (January 1913): 12.

[68] Ibid., p. 4.

[69] Ibid., p. 6.

[70] Ben-Cion Pinchuk, *The Octobrists in the Third Duma 1907–1912* (Seattle, 1974), p. 56.

[71] Ibid. See also G. L. Yaney, "The Concept of the Stolypin Land Reform," *Slavic Review* 23: 275–93.

[72] Kistiakovsky, "Nashi zadachi," p. 8.

[73] Ibid., p. 10.

[74] Ibid., p. 11–12.

[75] Ibid., p. 14.

[76] Ibid., pp. 15–17.

[77] Kistiakovsky, "Politicheskoe i iuridicheskoe znachenie manifesta 17 Oktiabra 1905 goda," *Iuridicheskii vestnik* 3 (March 1915): 110.

Notes to Chapter 6

[1] Oscar Jaszi, *The Dissolution of the Hapsburg Monarchy* (Chicago, 1929), pp. 3–32; Richard Pipes, *The Formation of the Soviet Union* (New York, 1968), pp. 1–49; cf. Georg von Rauch, *Russland: Staatliche Einheit und nationale Vielfalt* (München, 1953); Robert A. Kann, *The Multinational Empire: Nationalism and National Reform in the Hapsburg Monarchy 1848–1918*, 2 vols.(New York, 1950).

[2] B. A. Kistiakovsky, "Russkie oppozitsionnye partii i ukraintsy," *Osvobozhdenie* 77 (September 1905): 467–70.

[3] Ibid., p. 468.

[4] Kistiakovsky to N. Vasilenko [M. Vasylenko], 1907, as quoted in Yevhen Pyzhur [Eugene Pyziur], "Bohdan Oleksandrovych Kistiakivs'kyi," *Ukraïns'ka literaturna hazeta* 34 (April 1958): 8.

[5] Kistiakovsky, "Russkie oppozitsionnye partii i ukraintsy," p. 470.

[6] Ibid., pp. 467–68.

[7] Kistiakovsky, "M. P. Dragomanov i vopros o samostoiatel'noi ukrainskoi kul'ture," *Ukrainskaia zhizn'* 6 (June, 1912): 23.

[8] In the Russian Empire the figures for the same years were respectively 951 and 7,214, of which 5,147 were rural cooperatives. E. M. Kayden, "Consumers' co-operation," in *Cooperative Movement in Russia During the War,* E. M. Kayden and A. N. Antsiferov, (New Haven, Conn., 1929), p. 40; see also Gerold T. Robinson, *Rural Russia Under the Old Regime* (Berkeley and Los Angeles, 1967), pp. 255–56; Hugh Seton-Watson, *The Decline of Imperial Russia* (New York, 1962), p. 304; cf., Anita Bredahl Peterson, "The Development of Cooperative Credit in Rural Russia, 1871–1914," Ph.D. dissertation, Cornell University, 1973, for a general discussion of the cooperative movement and its theory in Russian and European contexts.

[9] Kistiakovsky, "M. P. Dragomanov i vopros," p. 23.

[10] Ibid., p. 25.

[11] See s.v. "Co-operative movement," written by V. Holubnychny and I. Vytanovych, in the *Encyclopedia of Ukraine,* ed. Volodymyr Kubijovyč, vol. 1 (Toronto, 1984), pp. 582–87.

[12] Ibid., p 582; Olga Andriewsky, "The Politics of National Identity: The Ukrainian Question in Russia, 1904–1912," Ph.D. dissertation, Harvard University, 1991, pp. 127–30.

[13] Andriewsky, "The Politics of National Identity," p. 128.

[14] B. A. Kistiakovsky, "Predislovie," in *Sobraniie politicheskikh sochinenii M. P. Dragomanova,* vol. 2 (Paris, 1906), p. liv.

[15] See Karl Renner [Rudolf Springer], *Staat und Nation* (Vienna, 1899); idem, *Der Kampf der Österreichischen Nationen um den Staat* (Leipzig, 1902); idem, *Das Selbstbestimmungsrecht der Nationen,* vol. 1, *Nation und Staat* (Leipzig-Vienna, 1918) and Otto Bauer, *Die Nationalitätenfrage und die Sozialdemokratie* (Vienna, 1907), [=Marx Studien, 2]; idem, "Die Bedingungen der nationalen Assimilation," *Der Kampf* 6 (March 1912): 246–63, contains a restatement of Bauer's views.

[16] Pipes, *Formation of the Soviet Union,* p. 27.

[17] In 1899, at the Bruenn Congress of Austrian Social Democrats, the idea of extraterritorial or personal national cultural autonomy was first raised; however, it was not passed as the formal position of the party. *Verhandlungen des Gesamtpartietages der Sozialdemokratie in Österreich* (Vienna, 1899), pp. 74–75. The idea or extraterritorial or personal national cultural autonomy

was further developed in the first decade of this century by Karl Renner and Otto Bauer; Pipes, *Formation of the Soviet Union,* pp. 24–28; Jaszi, *Dissolution of the Hapsburg Monarchy,* pp. 177–84.

[18] Each nation was to be treated as a union of individuals rather than a territorial corporation; each of the nationalities should be entered—with the names of all citizens who considered themselves a part of that national group—in a national register. In this way, the people of each national group would begin to administer their cultural affairs independently. Otto Bauer, *Die Nationalitätenfrage,* p. 353; see also Pipes, *Formation of the Soviet Union,* pp. 26–27.

[19] Karl Renner [Rudopf Springer], *Grundlagen und Entwicklungen der Österreichisch-Ungarischen Monarchie* (Vienna and Leipzig, 1906), pp. 206–208.

[20] Bauer, *Die Nationalitätenfrage,* pp. 353–62.

[21] Renner, *Grundlagen,* p. 206; cf. idem, *Das Selbstbestimmungsrecht der Nationen,* Part 1.

[22] Kistiakovsky's clearest statement of national rights and the movement toward socialism is in his article "Chto takoe natsionalism," in *Natsional'nye problemy* 1 (May 1915). In this article, he clearly distinguishes between the national chauvinism of a group in a ruling position, such as the Great Russians, and the nationalism of suppressed peoples who are striving for equality, democracy, and, in general, social progress. He also stresses the negative aspects of nationalism as an end in itself in his article "M. P. Dragomanov i vopros," pp. 10–36. Kistiakovsky shared the Austrian socialists' view on nationalism.

Bauer wrote of his and Renner's plan for the minority nationalities: " . . . the advance of the classes shall no longer be hindered by national struggles . . . The field shall be free for the class struggle." Bauer, *Die Nationalitätenfrage,* p. 362, as noted in Pipes, *Formation of the Soviet Union,* p. 27.

[23] *Stenograficheskie otcheti, 1906 god, Sessiia pervaia,* vol. 1 (St. Petersburg, 1906), pp. 75–76. In this address the Kadet and peasant majority called for the equality of all citizens in the empire; that is, they proposed that all nationalities be equal to the Great Russians and openly stated the need for each nationality to develop its own way of life. The resolution was passed unanimously by the Duma.

[24] Alfred Levin, "3 June 1907, Action and Reaction," in *Essays in Russian History,* ed. A. D. Ferguson and A. Levin (Hamden, Conn., 1964), pp. 231–74; Geoffrey A. Hosking, *The Russian Constitutional Experiment, Government and Duma, 1907–1914* (Cambridge, 1973), pp. 14–56.

[25] A. Ia. Avrekh, *Tsarism i tret'ieiun'skaia sistema* (Moscow, 1966), p. 81; Dmytro Doroshenko, *Narys istoriï Ukraïny* (Munich, 1966), p. 184.

[26] See *Obshchii svod po imperii resultatov razrabotki dannykh pervoi vseobshchei perepisi naseleniia, proizvedennoi 28 Ianvaria 1897,* 2 vols.

(St. Petersburg, 1905); volume 1 contains the figures for the geographic distribution of population according to language; cf. A. G. Rashin, *Naselenie Rossii za 100 let (1811–1913 gg.)* (Moscow, 1956).

[27] Hosking, *Russian Constitutional Experiment,* p. 218; Avrekh, *Tsarism i tret'ieiun'skaia sistema,* p. 83.

[28] Hosking, *Russian Constitutional Experiment,* pp. 14–56, 116–20; Ben-Cion Pinchuk, *The Octobrists in the Third Duma 1907–1912* (Seattle, 1974), pp. 111–12.

[29] Andriewsky, "The Politics of National Identity," p. 325.

[30] B. A. Kistiakovsky, "Kholmshchina i Ukraina," *Moskovskii ezhenedel'nik* 19 (13 May 1908): 32–46 and 20 (20 May 1908): 17–28; idem, "Mizh shuitseiu i desnitseiu," *Rada* 31 December 1908; E. Chmielewski, *The Polish Question in the Russian State Duma* (Knoxville, 1970), pp. 117–20; Andriewsky, "The Politics of National Identity," p. 334.

[31] Andriewsky, "The Politics of National Identity," pp. 334–36.

[32] B. A. Kistiakovsky [Ukrainets], "K voprosu o samostoiatel'noi ukrainskoi kul'ture," *Russkaia mysl'* 5 (May 1911): 136. Unlike the official Great Russian nationalism, the Kadet position was a form of nationalism cushioned by being placed in a constitutional context—a constitutional nationalism.

[33] Kistiakovsky, "M. P. Dragomanov i vopros," p. 36.

[34] *Ukrainskaia zhizn'* was published by the Moscow Society of Slavic Culture's Ukrainian Section in which Kistiakovsky had been an active member since 1910. *Russkaia mysl'* was the liberal journal closest to the Kadet Party's political position; it was edited by P. B. Struve after 1907. Kistiakovsky's articles in *Ukrainskaia zhizn* included: "M. P. Dragomanov i *Vol'noe slovo*," 1 (January 1912): 10–35; [A. Khatchenko], "Gertsen i Ukraina," 4 (April 1912): 22–30; [A. Khatchenko], "M. P. Dragomanov i vopros o samostoiatel'noi ukrainskoi kulture," 6 (November 1912): 10–35; "Iurii Iur'evich Tsvetkovskii kak obshchestvennyi deiatel' (Pamiati odnogo iz poslednikh ukrainofilov)," 7–8 (July–August, 1913).

[35] Kistiakovsky, "M. P. Dragomanov i vopros," p. 25; idem, "K voprosu o samostoiatel'noi ukrainskoi kulture," pp. 133–34.

[36] Aleksandr Herzen was actually half German and half Russian, but in the Russian Empire he was classified as a Russian. Kistiakovsky, "Gertsen i Ukraina," p. 22.

[37] Alexander Herzen, "The Russian People and Socialism, An Open Letter to Jules Michelet," in *From the Other Shore* (New York, 1956), pp. 175–76.

[38] Alexsander Herzen, "Rossiia i Pol'sha," in *Kolokol*, as quoted in Kistiakovsky, "Gertsen i Ukraina," p. 24.

[39] Ibid., p. 25.

[40] Kostomarov signed the letter *Ukrainets*, a pseudonym that Kistiakovsky later adopted to avoid reprisals. Kistiakovsky, "Gertsen i Ukraina," p. 24.

[41] Ibid., p. 29.

[42] Ibid., p. 27.

[43] Ibid., p. 24.

[44] Kistiakovsky, "M. P. Dragomanov i vopros," p. 24.

[45] For a full bibliography on these polemics, see Boris Rogosin, "The Politics of Mikhail P. Dragomanov: Ukrainian Federalism and the Question of Political Freedom in Russia," Ph.D. dissertation, Harvard University, 1967.

[46] Both Volodymyr Antonovych and Mykhailo Drahomanov took part in the publication *Hromada*, which Drahomanov edited.

[47] Kistiakovsky published the following works to refute Bogucharskii: *Stranitsy proshlogo* (Moscow, 1912); "Organ zemskogo soiuza 'Vol'noe slovo' i legenda o nem," *Russkaia mysl'* (November, 1912). Kistiakovsky, "M. P. Dragomanov i Vol'noe slovo," *Ukrainskaia zhizn* 1 (January 1912): 10–35, supplemented the debate.

[48] In fact, by 1886, an irreperable split developed between Drahomanov and the Kyiv *Hromada* that feared that Drahomanov's activities abroad could provoke even more repression of Ukrainian life. Beyond the allegations that Drahomanov was politically compromised, some members of *Hromada* disagreed with Drahomanov's socialist and constitutionalist politics as well as his attacks on the authoritarian tactics of the Russian revolutionary movement. The *Hromada* finally denied Drahomanov financial resources and he was left isolated. *Encyclopedia of Ukraine*, s.v. "Mykhailo Drahomanov."

[49] Kistiakovsky, *Stranitsy proshlogo*, p. 84.

[50] Ibid., p. 118.

[51] Mykola Vasylenko, "Akademik Bohdan Oleksandrovych Kistiakivs'kyi," in *Zapysky sotsial'no-ekonomichnoho viddilu, Ukraïnska akademiia nauk*, vol. 1 (Kyiv, 1923), pp. xxxii–xxxiii.

[52] Kistiakovsky, "M. P. Dragomanov i vopros," p. 24. Kistiakovsky noted that Drahomanov " . . . turned to the Galician Ukrainians and insisted that the Ukrainian intelligentsia should facilitate the emergence and growth of various forms of economic organization among the people." Drahomanov considered it impossible to recommend similar work among the Russian Ukrainians. Kistiakovsky and other disciples of Drahomanov, on the other hand, did advocate working among Russian Ukrainians in the 1880s.

Notes to Chapter 7

[1] Benedict Anderson, *Imagined Communities* (London, 1983), p. 16.

[2] Ivan Rudnytsky, *Essays in Modern Ukrainian History* (Edmonton and Cambridge, Mass., 1987), p. 384.

[3] See Robert Edelman, *Gentry Politics on the Eve of the Russian Revolution* (New Brunswick, N.J., 1980).

[4] Geoffrey Hosking, *The Russian Constitutional Experiment, Government and Duma, 1907–1914* (Cambridge, 1973), p. 216.

[5] P. B. Struve, "Velikaia Rossiia," in *Patriotica. Politika, kul'tura, religiia, sotsializm. Sbornik za piat' let (1905–1910 gg.)* (St. Petersburg, 1911), also published as "A Great Russia," in *The Russian Review* 2(4) November 1913: 17.

[6] Struve, "Velikaia Rossiia," p. 18.

[7] Ibid., p. 28.

[8] Ibid.

[9] Ibid., p. 146.

[10] Patricia Herlihy, *Odessa: A History, 1794–1914* (Cambridge, Mass., 1986), p. 251.

[11] Struve, "A Great Russia," p. 20.

[12] P. B. Struve, "Intelligentsiia i natsional'noe litso," *Slovo* 10 (10 March 1909).

[13] Richard Pipes, *Struve, Liberal on the Right, 1905–1944* (Cambridge, Mass., 1980), p. 210; Olga Andriewsky, "The Politics of National Identity: The Ukrainian Question in Russia, 1904–1912," Ph.D. dissertation, Harvard University, 1991, p. 278.

[14] Struve, "Intelligentsiia i natsional'noe litso," reprinted in *Patriotica*; Jeffrey Brooks, "*Vekhi* and the *Vekhi* Dispute," *Survey* 86 (1973): 232–33.

[15] Struve, "Intelligentsiia i national'noe litso," in *Patriotika*, p. 371.

[16] Ibid.

[17] P. B. Struve, "Ofitsial'nyi natsionalizm i ego protivorechiia," *Russkaia mysl'* 1910 (June): 137. Struve argued that the population should accept the state and state power in his article "O gosudarstve," in Struve, *Patriotika*, p. 100.

[18] Andriewsky, "The Politics of National Identity," pp. 370–76.

[19] V. E. Jabotinsky [Zhabotinsky], "Evreistvo i ego nastroenie," *Russkaia mysl'* 1911 (January): 99–114.

[20] Vladimir Jabotinsky, "Memoirs by My Typewriter," in Lucy Dawidowicz, *The Golden Tradition: Jewish Life and Thought in Eastern Europe* (New York, 1967) p. 398.

[21] Olga Andriewsky, "*Medved' iz berlogi:* Vladimir Jabotinsky and the Ukrainian Question, 1904–1914," *Harvard Ukrainian Studies* 14(3/4) December 1990: 253–54.

[22] Ibid., p. 253.

[23] Jabotinsky, "Evreistvo i ego nastroenie," p. 114, as cited by Andriewsky, "Jabotinsky and the Ukrainian Question," pp. 255–56.

[24] P. B. Struve, "Na raznye temy—Chto zhe takoe Rossiia?" *Russkaia mysl'* 1911 (January): 185.

[25] Ibid.

[26] Ibid., pp. 184–85.

[27] Pipes, *Liberal on the Right*, p. 211.

[28] Ibid., p. 187.

[29] B. A. Kistiakovsky, "K voprosu o samostoiatel'noi ukrainskoi kul'ture," *Russkaia mysl'* 32 (May, 1911): 132.

[30] Ibid., p. 133.

[31] Ibid., p. 135.

[32] Ibid., p. 134. Ivan Mazepa was the hetman of Left-Bank Ukraine (i.e., to the east of the Dnipro and under Russian overlordship) beginning in 1687. Mazepa hoped to unite divided Ukraine and attempted to make Ukraine an independent and united state by allying himself with Charles XII of Sweden against Peter I during the Great Northern War. When his attempt failed, the autonomy of Ukraine was further diminished by the forced installation of Russian-nominated hetmans. Catherine II coerced the last hetman to resign in 1764, and Left-Bank Ukraine was divided into three provinces (*gubernii*). As a result of the Partition of Poland in 1793 and 1795, Ukraine was once again left divided. Parts of the Right-Bank and all of the Left-Bank territories, along with the Black Sea littoral and the Sea of Azov fell under Russian rule, while Galicia (with Bukovina) became part of the Hapsburg Empire. See Zenon Kohut, *Russian Centralism and Ukrainian Autonomy: Absorption of the Hetmanate, 1760s–1830s* (Cambridge, Mass., 1988).

[33] Kistiakovsky, "K voprosu," p. 134.

[34] Kistiakovsky expressed his dismay at the lack of interest in the minority nationalities among the Great Russians: " . . . the only Russian society which is interested in the Ukrainians and is ready to defend their interests is the Society of Slavic Cultures in Moscow." Kistiakovsky himself was a member of the Ukrainian section of its Russian organization, which published *Ukrainskaia zhizn'*. Ibid., p. 135.

[35] Ibid., p. 138; Andriewsky, "The Politics of National Identity," p. 403n174, points out that the Ukrainian Orthodox Church formally became subject of the patriarch of Moscow in 1686 and official censorship can be traced to that date.

[36] Kistiakovsky, "K voprosu," pp. 138–39.

[37] Ibid., p. 136. The issue of teaching non-Russian languages was a major subject of controversy in the 1910 Duma discussion on the reform of the educational system. Ben-Cion Pinchuk, *The Octobrists in the Third Duma*

1907–1912 (Seattle, 1974), pp. 124–36, discusses the 1910 debates on the teaching of non-Russian languages in schools in the chapter on the Nationalist Coalition.

[38] As mentioned above, Little Russia (*Malorossia*) is an archaic usage to designate Ukraine.

[39] Volapük is a world language, like Esperanto, composed of a mixture of languages.

[40] Kistiakovsky, "K voprosu," p. 142.

[41] Ibid., p. 135.

[42] Ibid., p. 142.

[43] Ibid., p. 146.

[44] Ibid., p. 132.

[45] Ibid.

[46] Ibid, p. 141.

[47] P. B. Struve, "Obshcherusskaia kul'tura i ukrainskii partikularizm," *Russkaia mysl'* 33 (January, 1911): 86.

[48] Ibid., p. 76.

[49] Ibid., p. 66.

[50] Ibid.

[51] P. B. Struve, "Neskol'ko slov po ukrainskomu voprosu," *Russkaia mysl'* 34 (January 1913): 11.

[52] Ibid.

[53] Struve, as cited in Pipes, *Struve, Liberal on the Right*, p. 216. The debate on the Ukrainian question broadened to include Kadets, such as Miliukov, Kokoshkin and Gredeskul who objected to Struve's views. P. N. Miliukov, "Ukrainskii vopros i P. B. Struve," *Rech'* 303 (9 November 1914). See the November and December 1914 issues of *Rech'*.

[54] Pipes, *Struve, Liberal on the Right*, pp. 217–18. See *Den'* 157 (June 10): 1915.

[55] Pipes, *Struve, Liberal on the Right*, pp. 218–19.

[56] B. A. Kistiakovsky, "Chto takoe natsionalism," *Natsional'nye problemy* 1 (May 1915): 2.

[57] Ibid., p. 1.

[58] Ibid., p. 2.

[59] Ibid., p. 1.

[60] Ibid., p. 2.

[61] Ibid.

Notes to the Conclusion

[1] Among the many articles on the subject, V. Kudriavtsev, E. A. Lukasheva, "Sotsialisticheskoe pravovoe gosudarstvo" in *Kommunist* 1988 (11) and "Perestroika i prava cheloveka" in *Nedelia* 42(2) 1987. See also Susan Heuman, "Transforming Subjects into Citizens" in Al Schmidt, ed., *The Impact of Perestroika on Soviet Law* (Dordrecht, 1990). Peter Juviler and Bertram Gross, editors, *Human Rights for the 21st Century* (Armonk, N.Y., 1993). See A. A. Gol'tsblat, "Pravovoe gosudarstvo ili diktatura. K voprosu o meste teorii pravovogo gosudartsvo v politicheskoi praktike Rossii," in *Konstitutsionnyi vestnik* 4 (Moscow, 1990): 25–39; O. F. Skakun, "Teoriia pravovogo gosudarstva v dorevoiutsionnoi Rossii," in *Sovetskoe gosudarstvo i pravo* 1990 (2); V. V. Sonin, V. P. Fedorov, "Pravoponimanie v dorevoliutsionnoi nemarksistkoi iuridicheskoi mysli Rossii," in *Gosudarstvennyi stroi i politiko-pravovye idei Rossii vtoroi poloviny XIX stoletiia*, M. G. Korotkikh, V. V. Iachevskii, eds. (Voronezh, 1987); and E. V. Kuznetsov, *Filosofiia prava v Rossii* (Moscow, 1989).

[2] Jane Burbank argues that the courts, especially the local courts, might have become an effective arena where ideas of national citizenship could have developed. Jane Burbank, "Legal Culture, Citizenship, and Peasant Jurisprudence: Perspectives from the Early Twentieth Century," in Peter Solomon, ed., *Reforming Justice in Russia*, pp. 91–99. See also C. A. Frierson, "Rural Justice in Public Opinion: The *Volost'* Court Debate 1861–1912," *Slavonic and East European Review* 64(4) October, 1986: 545.

[3] Alfred Rieber, "Landed Property, State Authority and Civil War," *Slavic Review* 47(1) Spring 1988. See also Leopold Haimson: "The Problem of Social Identities in Early Twentieth Century Russia" and William G. Rosenberg: "Identities, Power, and Social Interaction in Revolutionary Russia" which, together with Reiber's article, make up the "Discussion" in *Slavic Review* 47(1).

[4] Alfred Rieber, "The Sedimentary Society," *Russian History* 16(2–4) 1989: 356.

[5] Kistiakovsky, "Prava cheloveka i grazhdanina," *Sotsial'nye nauki i pravo*, pp. 481–551.

Select Bibliography

Archival Sources

Tsentral′nyi derzhavnyi istorychnyi arkhiv Ukraïny, Kyiv (TsDIA, Kyiv), Fond 263, 274.

Tsentral′nyi derzhavnyi istorychnyi arkhiv Ukraïny, L′viv (TsDIA, L′viv), Fond 663.

Otdelenie pis′mennykh istochnikov, Gosudarstvennyi istoricheskii muzei, Moscow (OPI GIM), Fond 108.

Rossiiskii tsentr khraneniia i izucheniia dokumentov noveishei istorii (RTsKhIDNI), Fond 279, "Osvobozhdenie."

Bayerische Staatsbibliotek, Handschriftenabteilung, Munich, Nachlass Max Weber-Schäfer.

Works by Bogdan Aleksandrovich Kistiakovsky

Kistiakovsky, B. A. [T. S.]. "Vmesto predisloviya ko vtoromu izdaniiu." In A. F. Kistiakovsky, *Issledovanie o smertnoi kazni*. 2d edition, pp. v–xlv. St. Petersburg, 1896.

——. "Agrarii v Germanii." *Novoe slovo* 11–12 (2) July-August 1897: 152– 79.

——. "Iuveleinaia vystavka Beklina v Bazele." *Novoe slovo* 3(2) November 1897: 79–95.

—— [Dr. Theodor Kistiakowski]. *Gesellschaft und Einzelwesen. Eine Methodologische Studie*. Berlin, 1899.

——. "Ideia ravenstva s sotsiologicheskoitochki zreniia." *Mir bozhii*. 4 (1900) 1: 160–69.

——. "Russkaia sotsiologicheskaia shkola i kategoriia vozmozhnosti pri reshenii sotsial′no-eticheskikh problem." In *Problemy idealizma*, ed. P. I. Novgorodtsev. Moscow, 1903.

——. "Prava cheloveka i grazhdanina." *Voprosy zhizni* 1 (January 1905): 116–42.

——. "Russkie oppozitsionnye partii i ukraintsy." *Osvobozhdenie* 77 (September 1905): 467–70.

————. "Konstitutsiia darovannaia i konstitutsiia zavoevannaia." *Poliarnaia zvezda* 11 (26 February 1906): 747–54.

————. "Kabinet ministrov." Part 1. *Svoboda i kul'tura* 2 (10 April 1906): 95–105.

————. "Kabinet ministrov." Part 2. *Svoboda i kul'tura* 3 (16 April 1906): 139–58.

————. "Tret'e zasedanie gosudarstvennoi dumy i amnistiia." *Duma* 1 (27 April 1906):

————. "Nashe politicheskoe obrazovanie." *Svoboda i kul'tura* 6 (7 May 1906): 415–22.

————. "Gosudarstvennaia duma i osnovnye zakony." *Duma* 2 (28 April/11 May 1906):

————. "Gosudarstvo pravovoe i sotsialisticheskoe." *Voprosy filosofii i psikhologii* 85 (November-December 1906): 469–07.

————. "Predislovie." In *Sobranie politicheskikh sochinenii M. P. Dragomanova*, ed. B. A. Kistiakovsky, vol. 2, pp. vii–lix. Paris, 1906.

————. "Kak osushchestvit' edinoe narodnoe predstavitel'stvo?" Part 1. *Russkaia mysl'* 28 (March 1907): 113–34.

————. "Kak osushchestvit' edinoe narodnoe predstavitel'stvo?" Part 2. *Russkaia mysl'* 28 (April 1907): 49–71.

————. "Kak osushchestvit' edinoe narodnoe predstavitel'stvo?" Part 3. *Russkaia mysl'* 28 (June 1907): 156–68.

————. "M. P. Dragomanov. Ego politicheskie vzgliady, literaturnaia deiatel'nost' i zhizn'." In *Politicheskie sochineniia M. P. Dragomanova*, ed. I Grevs and V. Kistiakovsky. Moscow, 1908.

————. "Kholmshchina i Ukraina." *Moskovskii ezhenedel'nik* 19 (13 May 1908): 32–46 and 20 (20 May 1908): 17–28.

————. "Mizh shuitseiu i desnitseiu." *Rada* 31 December 1908.

————. "V zashchitu prava." In *Vekhi. Sbornik statei o russkoi intelligentsii*, ed. M. O. Gershenzon. Moscow, 1909.

————. Review of *Ocherki po teorii statistiki*, by A. A. Chuprov. *Voprosy prava* 1 (1910): 183–200.

————. "Georg Jellinek kak myslitel' i chelovek." *Russkaia mysl'* 32 (March 1911): 77–86.

————. "K voprosu o samostoiatel'noi ukrainskoi kul'ture." *Russkaia mysl'* 32 (May 1911): 131–146.

————. "M. P. Dragomanov po ego pis'mam." *Russkaia mysl'* 32 (September 1911) 2: 132–50.

————. *Stranitsy proshlogo. K istorii konstitutsionnogo dvizheniia v Rossii.* Moscow, 1912.

————. "M. P. Dragomanov i 'Vol'noe slovo.'" *Ukrainskaia zhizn'* 1 (January 1912): 97–119.

———— [Khatchenko, A.]. "Gertsen i Ukraina." *Ukrainskaia zhizn'* 4 (April 1912): 22–30.

————. "M. P. Dragomanov i vopros o samostoiatel'noi ukrainskoi kul'ture." *Ukrainskaia zhizn* 6 (June 1912): 10–35.

————. "Organ zemskogo soiuza 'Vol'noe slovo' i legenda o nem." *Russkaia mysl'* 33 (November 1912): 47–103.

————. "Nashi zadachi." *Iuridicheskii vestnik* 1 (January 1913): 1–15.

———— [Khatchenko]. "Iurii Iur'ievich Tvetkovskii kak obshchestvennyi deiatel'" *Ukrainskaia zhizn'* 7/8 (July-August 1913): 94–111.

————. "Politicheskoe i iuridicheskoe znachenie manifesta 17 oktiabria 1905 goda." *Iuridicheskii vestnik* 3 (March 1915): 107–111.

————. "Chto takoe natsionalizm." *Natsional'nye problemy* 1 (May 1915): 1–2.

————. *Sotsial'nye nauki i pravo. Ocherki po metodologii sotsial'nykh nauk i obshchei teorii prava.* Moscow, 1916.

————. "In Defense of Law (The Intelligentsia and Legal Consciousness)," in *Vekhi: A Collection of Articles on the Russian Intelligentsia,* ed. Marshall S. Shatz and Judith Zimmerman (Montreal, 1970) [= Canadian Slavic Studies 4(1) Spring 1970]. This translation was republished in book form as Shatz and Zimmerman, eds. *Vekhi = Landmarks. A Collection of Articles on the Russian Intelligentsia* (Armonk, N.Y., 1994).

————. "In Defense of Law," in *Landmarks, A Collection of Essays on the Russian Intelligentsia, 1909,* ed. Boris Schragin and Albert Todd (New York, 1977), pp. 112–38.

Secondary Literature on Kistiakovsky's Life and Times

Ageev, Iu. I. "Voprosy prava, gosudarstva i kul'tury v traktovke russkogo dorevolutionnogo pravoveda B. A. Kistiakovskogo." In *Voprosy teorii i istorii gosudarstva i prava* 58 (1969): 72–90.

Alekseev, N. N. "Sotsial'naia filosofiia Rudol'fa Shtammlera." *Voprosy filosofii i psikhologii* 96 (1909) 2: 1–26.

————. *Nauki obshchestvennye i estestvennye v istoricheskom vzaimootno-shenii ikh metodov.* Moscow, 1912.

Andriewsky, Olga. *"Medved' iz berlogi:* Vladimir Jabotinsky and the Ukrainian Quesion, 1904–1914." *Harvard Ukrainian Studies* 14(3/4) December 1990: 253–54.

————. "The Politics of National Identity: The Ukrainian Question in Russia, 1904–1912," Ph.D. dissertation, Harvard University, 1991.

Arsen'ev, K. et al. *Intelligentsiia v Rossii. Sbornik statei.* St. Petersburg, 1910.

Avksent'ev, N. et al. *Vekhi kak znamenie vremeni.* Moscow, 1910.

Avrekh, A. Ia. *Tsarizm i tret'eiunskaia sistema.* Moscow, 1966.

Berdiaev, N. A. "O novom russkom idealizme." *Sub specie Aeternitatis,* pp. 152–90. St. Petersburg, 1907.

————. *Dukhovnyi krizis intelligentsii. Stat'i po obshchestvennoi i religioznoi psikhologii (1907–1909).* St. Petersburg, 1910.

Bogucharskii, V. Ia. *Iz istorii politicheskoi bor'by v 70kh i 80kh gg. XIX veka.* Moscow, 1912.

————. "Zemskii soiuz ili sviaschchennaia druzhina." *Russkaia mysl'* 33 (September 1912): 74–120.

————. "V zakliuchenie polemiki." *Russkaia mysl'* 34 (February 1913) 2: 125–31.

Bochachevsky-Chomiak, Martha. *Feminists Despite Themselves: Women in Ukrainian Community Life.* Edmonton, 1988.

Brooks, Jeffrey. "Vekhi and the *Vekhi* Dispute." *Survey* 86 (1973): 21–50.

Chagin, B. A., ed. *Sotsiologicheskaia mysl' v Rossii: Ocherki nemarksistskoi sotsiologii poslednei treti XIX–nachala XX veka.* Leningrad, 1978.

Depenchuk, Larysa. *Bohdan Kistiakivs'kyi.* Kyiv, 1995.

Diehl, Karl. Review of *Gesellschaft und Einzelwesen,* by Dr. Theodor Kistiakowski. *Jahrbücher für Nationalökonomie und Statistik* 3(22) 1901: 878–79.

"Disput' B. A. Kistiakovskogo v Kharkovskom Universitete." *Pravo* 13 (2 May 1917): 787–98.

Drahomanov, M. P. *Istoricheskaia Pol'sha i Velikorusskaia demokratiia.* Geneva, 1882.

————. *Lysty do Ivana Franka i inshykh.* Vol. 1. L'viv, 1906.

————. *Sobranie politicheskikh sochinenii M. P. Dragomanova,* ed. B. A. Kistiakovsky. Vol. 2. Paris, 1905–1906.

Ernst, Paul. "Zur Methodologieder Soziologie." *Beilage zur Allgemeinen Zeitung* 73 (29 March 1900).

Fischer, George. *Russian Liberalism.* Cambridge, Massachusetts, 1958.

Frank, S. L. *Biografia P. B. Struve.* New York, 1956.

Gershenzon, M. O., ed. *Vekhi. Sbornik statei o russkoi intelligentsii.* Moscow, 1909.

Gurvich, Georgii [George]. "Kistiakovsky, Bogdan Alexandrovich (1868–1920)." *Encyclopedia of the Social Sciences,* 1st ed., vol. VII-VIII, pp. 575–78. New York, 1963.

—————. *Russo i deklaratsiia prav.* Petrograd, 1918.

Heuman, Susan Eva. "*Vekhi,* A Collection of Essays on the Russian Intelligentsia." Unpublished essay for the Russian Institute of Columbia University, 1968.

—————. "A Socialist Conception of Human Rights: A Model from Prerevolutionary Russia." In *Human Rights: Cultural and Ideological Perspectives,* ed. Adamantia Pollis and Peter Schwab, pp. 44–59. New York, 1979.

—————. "Perspectives on Legal Culture in Prerevolutionary Russia." In *Revolution in Law: Contributions to the Development of Soviet Legal Theory, 1917–1938,* ed. Piers Beirne, pp. 3–16. Armonk, New York, 1990.

Himka, John-Paul. *Socialism in Galicia.* Cambridge, Massachusetts, 1983.

Hollerhach, Alexander. "Jellinek, Georg." *International Encyclopedia of the Social Sciences,* vol. 7–8, pp. 252–253. New York, 1968.

Jabotinsky, V. E. [Zhabotynskii]. "Evreistvo i ego nastroenie." *Russkaia mysl'* 32 (January 1911: 95–114.

—————. "Memoirs by My Typewriter." In Lucy Dawidowicz, comp., *The Golden Tradition: Jewish Life and Thought in Eastern Europe,* pp. 394–401. New York, 1967.

Jellinek, Georg. *System der Subjektiven Öffentlichen Rechte.* Freiburg, 1892.

—————. *Die Erklärung der Menschen und Bürgerrechte. Ein Beitrag zur modernen Verfassungsgeschichte.* Leipzig, 1895.

—————. *Konstitutsii, ikh istoriia i znachenie v sovremennom prave.* St. Petersburg, 1905 [Translated from the original German].

—————. *Deklaratsiia prav cheloveka i grazhdanina. Biblioteka dlia samoobrazovaniia.* Ed. A. A. Bykin, A. A. Kizewetter, Dr. M. I. Konovalov, P. N. Miliukov, Dr. P. I. Novgorodtsev, V. D. Sokolov, and Dr. A. I. Chuprov. 3d ed. Vol. 4. Moscow, 1906 [Translation ed. A. E. Vorms].

—————. *Allgemeine Staatslehre.* 3d ed. Berlin, 1929.

Kalynovych, V. I. *Politychni protsesy Ivana Franka ta ioho tovaryshiv.* L'viv, 1967.

Kantsstudien. V. 1900, pp. 252–55.

Karsev, N. I. Review of *Sotsial'nye nauki i pravo,* by B. A. Kistiakovsky. *Golos minuvshego* 11/12 (1917): 345–51.

Kelsen, Hans. *Der Sociologische und der Juristische Staatsbegriff.* Tübingen, 1928.

Koch, Gottfried. Review of *Gesellschaft und Einzelwesen: Eine Methodologische Studie,* by Dr. Theodor Kistiakowski. *Archiv für Öffentliches Recht* 16 (1901): 144–46.

Koni, A. F. *Sobranie sochinenii.* Vol 2. Moscow, 1966.

Landau, Boris. "Uchennia B. O. Kistiakivs'koho pro derzhavu." In *Zapysky sotsial'no-ekonomichnoho viddilu, Ukraïns'ka akademiia nauk.* Vol. 1, pp. 15–20. Kyiv, 1923.

Landmarks, A Collection of Essays on the Russian Intelligentsia, 1909, ed. Boris Shragin and Albert Todd. New York, 1977 [Translated from the original Russian].

Lask, Emil. "Rechtsphilosophie." In *Die Philosophie im Beginn des zwanzigsten Jahrhunderts. Festschrift für Kuno Fischer,* vol. 2, ed. Wilhelm Windelband, pp. 269–320. Heidelberg, 1905.

L'vov, S. A. "Kritika 'Filosofii tsennostei' v Russkoi burzhuaznoi politiko-pravovoi mysli" (B. A. Kistiakovskii). Ph.D. dissertation. Leningrad, 1983.

Maklakov, V. A. *The First State Duma,* trans. M. Belkin. Bloomington, Indiana, 1964 [=Indiana University Publications Russian and East European Series, 30].

Menger, Anton. *Das Recht auf den vollen Arbeitsertrag in gesichtlicher Darstellung.* Stuttgart, 1886.

————. *Neue Staatslehre.* 2d ed. Jena, 1904.

————. *Novoe uchenie o gosudarstve.* Trans. P. Markovich. St. Petersburg, 1906.

Miliukov, P. N. "Ukrainskii vopros i P. B. Struve." *Rech'* 303 (9 November 1914).

————. *Vospominaniia (1859–1917).* Vol. 1. New York, 1955.

Mommsen, Wolfgang J. *Max Weber und die deutsche Politik, 1890–1920.* Tübingen, 1959.

Mytropolyt Ilarion [Ivan Ohijenko]. *Istoriia ukraïns'koï literaturnoï movy.* Winnipeg, 1949–1950.

Novgorodtsev, P. I., ed. *Problemy idealizma. Sbornik statei.* Moscow, 1903.

————. "K voprosu o sovremennykh filosofskikh iskaniiakh. (Otvet L. I. Petrazhitskomu)." *Voprosy filosofii i psikhologii* 14 (I) 66 January- February 1903: 124.

————. *Krizis sovremennogo pravosoznaniia.* Moscow, 1909.

Oberländer, Gisela. *Die Vechi—Diskussion (1909–1912)*. Inaugural-Dissertation zur Erlangung des Doktorgrades der Philosophischen Fakultät der Universität Köln. Köln, 1965.

Oleinikov, Iu. "Ot legal'nogo marksizma k 'Vekham.'" In *Uchenye zapiski Gosudarstvennogo pedagogicheskogo instituta imeni A. I. Gertsena*, vol. 2, ed. N. P. Andreev et al., pp. 137–78. Leningrad, 1936.

Petrazycki, Leon [L. I. Petrazhitskii], "Teoriia gosudarstva i prava." In his *Law and Morality*, trans. H. W. Babb. Cambridge, Massachusetts, 1955.

Petrunkevich, I. I. *Iz zapisok obshchestvennogo deiatelia. Arkhiv russkoi revolutsii*. Prague, 1934.

Pipes, Richard. "Max Weber and Russia." *World Politics* 7(3) April 1955: 371–401.

————. *Struve, Liberal on the Left, 1870–1905*. Cambridge, Massachusetts, 1970.

————. *Struve, Liberal on the Right, 1905–1944*. Cambridge, Massachusetts, 1980.

Pollard, Alan. "The Russian Intelligentsia: The Mind of Russia." *California Slavic Studies* 3 (March 1964): 1–32.

Poltoratsky, N. "*Vekhi* i russkaia intelligentsia." *Mosty* 10 (1963): 298.

Pyziur, Eugene. "Bohdan Oleksandrovich Kistiakivs'kyi." *Ukraïns'ka literaturna hazeta* 33 (March 1958): 2, 9 and 34 (April 1958): 4, 8.

Read, Christopher. *Religion, Revolution and the Russian Intelligentsia 1900–1912: The* Vekhi *Debate and its Intellectual Background*. London, 1979.

Renner, Karl. *Staat und Nation*. Vienna, 1899.

————. *Das Selbsbestimmungsrecht der Nationen*. Vol. 1, *Nation und Staat*. Leipzig-Vienna, 1918.

Ringer, Fritz K. *The Decline of the German Mandarins. The German Academic Community 1890–1933*. Cambridge, Massachusetts, 1969.

Rogosin, Boris I. "The Politics of Mikhail P. Dragomanov: Ukrainian Federalism and the Question of Political Freedom in Russia." Ph.D. dissertation, Harvard University, 1967.

Savel'ev, A. "O Bogdane Aleksandroviche Kistiakovskom." *Nashe nasledie* 4(16) 1990:11–12.

Schapiro, Leonard. "The Vekhi Group and the Mystique of Revolution." *The Slavonic and East European Review* 34 (December 1955/1956): 56–76.

————. "The Pre-Revolutionary Intelligentsia and the Legal Order." In *The Russian Intelligentsia*, edited by Richard Pipes, pp. 19–39. New York, 1961.

Shamshurin, V. I. "Chelovek i gosudarstvo v russkoi filosofii estestvennogo prava." *Voprosy filosofii* 6: 136–40.

Shatsillo, K. F. *Russkii liberalism na kanune revolutsii 1905–1907 gg.* Moscow, 1985.

Starosolskyj, Vladimir. "Bogdan Kistiakovskyj und das Russische soziologische Denken." *Sonderabdruck des Ukrainisch-Wissenschaftlichen Institutes in Berlin.* Vol. 2. Berlin, 1929.

Stempowski, Stanisław "Uryvok z spohadiv." *Spohady.* Vol. 8, pp. 126–32. Warsaw, 1932 [=Pratsi Ukraïnskoho naukovoho institutu].

Struve, P. B. "Intelligentsiia i natsional'noe litso." *Slovo* 10 (10 March 1909).

————. "Ofitsial'nyi natsionalizm i ego protivorechiia." *Russkaia mysl'* 31 (June 1910): 137.

————. "Parlamentskii sud nad oktiabristami—ofitsial'nyi natsionalizm i ego protivorechiia." *Russkaia mysl'* 31 (June 1910): 168–78.

————. "Na raznye temy—Chto zhe takoe Rossiia?" *Russkaia mysl'* 32 (January 1911): 184–87.

————. *Patriotika. Politika, kul'tura, religiia, sotsializm. Sbornik statei.* St. Petersburg, 1911.

————. "Obshcherusskaia kul'tura i ukrainskii partikuliarizm." *Russkaia mysl'* 33 (January 1912): 65–86.

————. "Neskol'ko slov po ukrainskomu voprosu." *Russkaia mysl'* 34 (January 1913): 10–11.

————. "A Great Russia." *The Russian Review* 2(4) November 1913: 11–30.

Swoboda, Philip. "The Philosophical Thought of S. L. Frank, 1902–1915: A Study of the Metaphysical Impulse in Early Twentieth-Century Russia." Ph.D. Dissertation, Columbia University, 1992.

Timasheff, N. S. *An Introduction to the Sociology of Law.* Cambridge, Massachusetts, 1939 [=Harvard Sociological Studies, 3].

Tuchaps'kyi [rus. Tuchapskii], P. L. *Iz perezhitogo, devianostye gody.* Odesa, 1923.

"Ukraïns'ki hurtky v Kyivi druhoï polovyny 1880-ykh ta pochatku 1890-ykh rokiv." In *Za sto lit.* Vol. 3. Kyiv, 1928.

Vasylenko, Mykola [Nikolai Vasilenko]. "Akademik Bohdan Oleksandrovych Kistiakivs'kyi." In *Zapysky sotsial'no-ekonomichnoho viddilu, Ukraïns'ka Akademiia Nauk.* Vol. 1, pp. viii–xli. Kyiv, 1923.

Vierkandt, A. Review of *Gesellschaft und Einzelwesen,* by Dr. Theodor Kistiakowski. *Zeitschritt für Sozialwissenschaft* 3 (1900): 748–49.

Volkov, F. K. et al., ed. *Ukrainskii narod v ego proshlom i nastoiashchem.* St. Petersburg, 1914.

von Beyme, Klaus. *Politische Soziologie im zaristischen Russland.* Wiesbaden, 1965.

Vucinich, Alexander. "A Sociological Synthesis: B. A. Kistiakovskii." In his *Social Thought in Tsarist Russia: The Quest for a General Science of Society, 1861–1917,* pp. 125–52. Chicago, 1976.

Wasilewski, Leon [Lev Vasylivs'kyi]. "Moja Wspomnenia Ukrainskie." *Spohady,* pp. 5–35. Warsaw, 1932 [=Pratsi Ukraïns'koho naukovoho institutu, 8].

Weber, Marianne. *Max Weber—Ein Lebensbild.* Tübingen, 1926.

Weber, Max. *Max Weber Gesamtausgabe. Briefe 1906–1908.* Abteilung II: Briefe, Band 5. Ed. M. Rainer Lepsius and Wolfgang J. Mommsen. Tübingen, 1990.

————. "Russlands Übergang zum Scheinkonstitutionalismus." In *Zur Russischen Revolution von 1905: Schriften und Reden 1905–1912,* ed. Wolfgang J. Mommsen and Dittmar Dahlmann, pp. 281–684. Tübingen, 1989 [=*Max Weber Gesamtausgabe,* 10].

————. "Zur Lage der bürgerlichen Demokratie in Russland." In *Zur Russischen Revolution von 1905: Schriften und Reden 1905–1912,* ed. Wolfgang J. Mommsen and Dittmar Dahlmann, pp. 71–280. Tübingen, 1989 [=*Max Weber Gesamtausgabe,* 10].

Zimmerman, Judith E. "Sociological Ideas in Pre-Revolutionary Russia." *Canadian-American Slavic Studies* 9 (Fall 1975): 302–323.

————. "The Political Views of the Vekhi Authors." *Canadian-American Slavic Studies* 10(3) Fall 1976: 307–327.

————. "Russian Liberal Theory,1900–1917." *Canadian-American Slavic Studies.*14 (Spring 1980): 1–20.

Intellectual and Historical Context

Acton, H. B. Introduction to G. W. F. Hegel, *Natural Law.* Philadelphia, 1975.

Allen, W. E. D. *The Ukraine.* Cambridge, 1940.

Anderson, Benedict. *Imagined Communities.* London, 1986.

Arato, Andrew. "The Neo-Idealist Defense of Subjectivity." *Telos* 21 (Fall 1974): 108–161.

Ascher, Abraham. *The Revolution of 1905.* Vol. 1. Stanford, 1988.

————. *The Revolution of 1905.* Vol. 2. Stanford, 1992.

Baberowski, Jorg. "*Das Justizwesen* in späten Zarenriech zum Problem von Rechtsstaatlichkeit, politischen Justiz und Rückständigkeit in Russland," *Zeitschrift für neue Rechtsgeschichte* 3–4 (1991): 156–72.

Bauer, Otto. *Die Nationalitätenfrage und die Sozialdemokratie.* Vienna, 1907 [=*Marx–Studien* 2].

―――――. "Die Bedingungen der nationalen Assimilation." *Der Kampf* 5(6) March 1912: 246–63.

Becker, Seymour. *Nobility and Priviliege in Late Imperial Russia.* De Kalb, Illinois, 1985.

Bendix, Reinhardt. *Max Weber.* Garden City, New York, 1960.

Berlin, Isaiah. *The Crooked Timber of Humanity.* New York, 1991.

Billington, James H. *Mikhailovsky and Russian Populism.* London, 1958.

Borysenko, V. I. *Borot'ba demokratychnykh syl za narodnu osvitu na Ukraïni v 60–90-ykh rokakh XIX st.* Kyiv, 1980.

Brecht, Arnold. *Federalism and Regionalism in Germany. The Division of Prussia.* New York, 1945.

―――――. *Political Theory.* Princeton, 1959.

Brooks, Jeffrey. *When Russia Learned to Read: Literacy and Popular Culture, 1861–1917.* Princeton, 1985.

Burbank, Jane. "Legal Culture, Citizenship, and Peasant Jurisprudence: Perspectives from the Early Twentieth Century." In Peter Solomon, ed., *Reforming Justice in Russia, 1864–1996,* pp. 82–106. Armonk, New York, 1997.

Chalidze, Valerii. *Prava cheloveka i Sovetskii Soiuz.* New York, 1974.

Cherkasova, N. V. *Formirovanie i razvitie advokatury v Rossii.* Moscow, 1987.

Chernov, Victor. *The Great Russian Revolution.* New Haven, 1936.

Chmielewski, E. *The Polish Question in the Russian State Duma.* Knoxville, 1970.

Copleston, Frederick S. J. *A History of Philosophy.* Vol. 3. New York, 1965.

Coser, Lewis A. *Masters of Sociological Thought.* New York, 1977.

Crisp, Olga and Linda Edmondson, ed. *Civil Rights in Imperial Russia.* Oxford, 1989.

Dan, Theodore. *The Origin of Bolshevism.* New York, 1970.

Doroshenko, Dmytro. *Istoriia Ukraïny.* 2 vols. Uzhhorod, 1932.

―――――. *Narys istoriï Ukraïny.* Munich, 1966.

―――――, Mykola Holybets', Ivan Kryp'iakevych, and Iaroslav Pasternak. *Velyka istoriia Ukraïny.* L'viv, 1948.

Dzyuba, Ivan. *Internationalism or Russification? A Study in the Soviet Nationalities Problem.* Preface by Peter Archer. 2nd edition. London, 1968 [Translated from the original Ukrainian].

Efimenko, A. Ia. *Istoriia ukrainskogo naroda.* St. Petersburg, 1906.

Emmons, Terence. *The Formation of Political Parties and the First National Elections in Russia.* Cambridge, Massachusetts, 1983.

Engelstein, Laura. "Combined Underdevelopment: Discipline in the Law in Imperial and Soviet Russia." *American Historical Review* 98(2) April 1993: 338–53.

————. "Reply." *American Historical Review* 98(2) April 1993: 376–81.

————. *The Keys to Happiness. Sex and the Search for Modernity in Fin-de-Siècle Russia.* Ithaca, New York, 1992.

Eroshkin, N. P. *Ocherki istorii gosudarstvennykh uchrezhdenii dorevoliutsionnoi Rossii.* Moscow, 1960.

Ferenczi, Caspar. "Funktion und Bedeutung der Presse in Russland vor 1914." *Jarbücher Für Geschichte Östeuropas* 30(3) 1982: 362–98.

Franko, Ivan. *Beiträge zur Geschichte und Kultur der Ukraine,* ed. E. Winter and P. Kirchner. Berlin, 1963.

Freeze, Gregory L. "A National Liberation Movement and the Shift in Russian Liberalism. 1901–1903." *Slavic Review* 28(1) March 1969: 80–89.

————. "The *Soslovie* (Estate) Paradigm and Russian Social History." *American Historical Review* 96(1) March 1986: 11–36.

Friedmann, Wolfgang. *Legal Theory.* 3rd ed. London, 1953.

————. *Law in a Changing Society.* Abridged edition. London, 1964.

Friedrich, Carl Joachim. *The Philosophy of Law in Historical Perspective.* Chicago, 1958.

Frierson, Cathy. "'I Must Always Answer to the Laws . . . ': Rules and Response at the Reformed *Volost* Court." *Slavonic and East European Review* 75(2) April 1997: 308–334.

————. "Of Red Rooster, Revenge, and the Search for Justice: Rural Arson in European Russia in the Late Imperial Era." In Peter Solomon, ed., *Reforming Justice in Russia, 1864–1996,* pp. 106–130. Armonk, New York, 1997.

————. *Peasant Icons. Representations of Rural People in Late Nineteenth-Century Russia.* New York, 1993.

————. "Rural Justice in Public Opinion: The Volost' Court Debate 1861–1912." *Slavonic and East European Review* 64(4) October 1986: 526–45.

Fuller, William C. *Civil-Military Conflict in Imperial Russia, 1881–1914.* Princeton, 1985.

Galai, Shmuel. *The Liberation Movement in Russia 1900–1905*. Cambridge, 1973.

Gol'denveizer, A. A. *V zashchitu prava*. New York, 1952.

Gol'tsblat, A. A. "Pravovoe gosudarstvo ili diktatura. K voprosu o meste teorii pravovogo gosudarstva v politicheskoi praktike Rossii." *Konstitutsionnyi vestnik* 4 (Moscow, 1990): 25–39.

Grünberg, Karl. *Anton Menger, Sein Leben und Lebenswerk. Sonder-Abdruck aus der Zeitschrift für Volkswirtschaft, Sozialpolitik und Verwaltung*. Vol. 18. Vienna-Leipzig, 1909.

Gruzenberg, O. O. *Yesterday: Memoirs of a Russian-Jewish Lawyer*. Berkeley, 1981.

Gurvich Georgii [Gurvitch, Georges]. *L'Idée du Droit Social*. Paris, 1931.

—————. *Sociology of Law*. International Library of Sociology and Social Reconstruction, ed. Dr. Karl Mannheim. London, 1947.

Hagen, Manfred. *Die entfaltung Politischer Öffentlichkeit in Russland, 1906–1914*. Wiesbaden, 1982 [=Quellen und Studien zur Geschichte des Östlichen Europa, 16].

Haimson, Leopold H. "The Problem of Social Identities in Early Twentieth Century Russia." *Slavic Review* 47(1): 1–20.

—————. "The Problem of Social Stability in Urban Russia." *Slavic Review* 23 (December 1964): 619–42.

—————. *The Russian Marxists and the Origins of Bolshevism*. Cambridge, Massachusetts, 1955 [Reprint=Boston, 1966].

—————. "Conclusion: Observations on the Politics of the Russian Countryside (1905–1914)." In *The Politics of Rural Russia*, pp. 261–300. Bloomington, 1979.

Hammer, Darrel P. "Two Russian Liberals: The Political Thought of B. N. Chicherin and Ḳ. D. Kavelin." Ph. D. dissertation, Columbia University, 1962–1963.

Harper, S. N. *The New Electoral Law for the Russian Empire*. Chicago, 1908.

Hecker, Julius, F. *Russian Sociology*. New York, 1915.

Herlihy, Patricia. *Odessa: A History, 1794–1914*. Cambridge, Massachusetts, 1986.

Herzen, Aleksandr. *From the Other Shore* and *The Russian People and Socialism: An Open Letter to Jules Michelet*. Introduction by Isaiah Berlin. New York, 1956.

Hessen, Sergius. "The Rights of Man in Liberalism, Socialism and Communism." In *Human Rights: Comments and Interpretations. A Symposium*, intro. Jacques Maritain, pp. 108–142. New York, 1949.

Hosking, Geoffrey A. *The Russian Constitutional Experiment, Government and Duma, 1907–1914.* Cambridge, 1973.

Hrushevs'kyi, Mykhailo S. [M. S. Grushevskii]. *Ocherk istorii ukrainskogo naroda.* 2d ed. St. Petersburg, 1906.

Hughes, H. Stuart. *Consciousness and Society.* New York, 1958.

"Iur'evskii universitet." *Entsiklopedicheskii slovar'* (Brokgaus-Efron), vol. 41, pp. 435–37. St. Petersburg, 1904.

Jaszi, Oscar. *The Dissolution of the Habsburg Monarchy.* Chicago, 1921 [Reprint= University of Chicago Press, "Phoenix Books," 1961].

Juviler, Peter and Bertram Gross, eds. *Human Rights for the 21st Century.* Armonk, New York, 1993.

Kablukov, N. A. "V Moskovskom iuridicheskom obshchestve." In *Sergei Andreevich Muromtsev,* ed. D. I. Shakhovskoi, pp. 116–40. Moscow, 1911.

Kann, Robert A. *The Multinational Empire, Nationalism and National Reform in the Habsburg Monarchy 1848–1918.* Vol 2. New York, 1950.

Kappeler, Andreas. *Russland als Vielvölkerreich.* Munich, 1993.

Katalog der Böcklin Jubileiums Austellung. Basel, 1897.

Kayden, E. M. "Consumers' Co-operation." In *Co-operative Movement in Russia During the War,* ed. E. M. Kayden and A. N. Antsiferov, pp. 1–231. New Haven, 1929.

Keep, J. L. H. *The Rise of Social Democracy in Russia.* Oxford, 1963.

Kindersley, Richard. *The First Russian Revisionists: A Study of "Legal Marxism" in Russia.* Oxford, 1962.

Kline, George L. "Changing Attitudes toward the Individual." In *The Transformation of Russian Society,* ed. Cyril Black, p. 606–608. Cambridge, 1970.

————. "Kolakowski and the Revision of Marxism." in *European Philosophy Today,* ed. George L. Kline, pp. 117–63. Chicago, 1965.

————. "Socialist Legality and Communist Ethics." *Natural Law Forum. American Journal of Jurisprudence* 8 (August 1963): 20–28.

Kohn, Hans. *The Idea of Nationalism.* Toronto, 1967.

Kohut, Zenon *Russian Centralism and Ukrainian Autonomy: Imperial Absorption of the Hetmanate, 1760s–1830s.* Cambridge, Massachusetts, 1988.

Krupnyckyj, Borys. *Geschichte der Ukraine.* 3d ed. Wiesbaden, 1963.

Kucherov, Samuel. *Courts, Lawyers and Trials Under the Last Three Tsars.* Foreword by Michael Karpovich. New York, 1953.

Kuznetsov, E. V. *Filosofiia prava v Rossii.* Moscow, 1989.

Lednickii, W. *Pamiatniki.* Vol. 1. London, 1963.

Leikina-Svirskaia, B. R. *Intelligentsiia v Rossii vo vtoroi polovine XIX veka.* Moscow, 1929.

Lenin, V. I. *Sochineniia.* Vol. 14. Moscow, 1929.

Leontovitsch, Victor. *Geschichte des Liberalismus in Russland.* Frankfurt am Main, 1957.

Leroy-Beaulieu, Anatole. *The Empire of the Tsars and the Russians.* Vol. 2. *The Institutions.* New York, 1969 [Translated from the 3d French edition by Zenaide A. Ragozin].

Levin, Alfred. "3 June 1907, Action and Reaction." In *Essays in Russian History* (A Collection dedicated to George Vernadsky), ed. A. D. Ferguson and A. Levin, pp. 231–74. Hamden, Conn., 1964.

Lewin, Moshe. *The Making of the Soviet System.* New York, 1985.

Macey, David A. J. *Government and Peasant in Russia, 1861–1906.* De Kalb, Illinois, 1987.

Macpherson, C. B. *The Political Theory of Possessive Individualism, Hobbes to Locke.* London, 1962.

Malia, Martin. *Alexander Herzen and the Birth of Russian Socialism, 1812–1855.* Cambridge, Massachusetts, 1961.

Manning, Roberta. *Crisis of the Old Order in Russia.* Princeton, 1982.

Mannheim, Karl. *Ideology and Utopia.* Trans. Louis Wirth and Edward Shils. New York, 1936.

Masaryk, Thomas Garrigue. *The Spirit of Russia.* Vol. 2, trans. Eden and Cedar Paul. New York and London, 1961.

Mendel, Arthur, P. *Dilemmas of Progress in Tsarist Russia.* Cambridge, Massachusetts, 1961.

Menger, Anton. *Anarkhizm, individualisticheskoe i kommunisticheskoe gosudarstvo,* ed. K. L. Olenin. Odesa, 1905.

Mikhailovskii, N. K. *Sochineniia N. K. Mikhailovskogo.* Vol. 4. St. Petersburg, 1891.

Miliukov, Paul et al. *History of Russia.* Vol. 3 *(1855–1932),* trans. Charles Lam Markmann. New York, 1969.

Mommsen, Hans. *Die Sozialdemokratie und die Nationalitätenfrage im Habsburgischen Vielvölkerstaat.* Vol. 1. Vienna, 1963.

Mommsen, Wolfgang J. *The Age of Bureaucracy. Perspectives on the Political Sociology of Max Weber.* New York, London, 1974.

Motyl, Alexander. *Will the Non Russians Rebel?* Ithaca, 1987.

Nol'de. Boris E. *Ocherki russkogo gosudarstvennogo prava.* St. Petersburg, 1911.

Novgorodtsev, P. I. *Istoricheskaia shkola iuristov: ee proiskhozhdenie i sud'ba.* Moscow, 1896.

—————. *Kant i Gegel' v ikh ucheniiakh o prave i gosudarstve.* Moscow, 1901.

—————. *Ob obshchestvennom ideale.* 3d ed. Moscow, 1921.

Oberländer, Erwin, George Katkov, Nikolaus Poppe, and Georg von Rauch, eds. *Russia Enters the Twentieth Century.* New York, 1971.

Obshchii svod po imperii resultatov razrabotki dannykh i vseobshchei perepisi naseleniia, proizvedennoi 28 Ianvaria 1897. 2 vols. St. Petersburg, 1905.

Park, Robert Ezra. *Race and Culture.* New York, 1950.

Pinchuk, Ben-Cion. *The Octobrists in the Third Duma 1907–1912.* Seattle, 1974.

Pipes, Richard. *The Formation of the Soviet Union.* Cambridge, Massachusetts, 1954 [Revised edition=New York, 1968].

Poliakov, A. V. and I. Iu. Kozlikhin, ed. *Vlast' i pravo, iz istorii russkoi pravovoi mysli.* Leningrad, 1990.

Protokoly konferentsii rossiiskikh natsional'no-sotsialisticheskikh partii. St. Petersburg, 1908.

Putnam, George F. "The Russian Non-Revolutionary Intelligentsia Evaluates its Relation to the Russian Folk (1900–1910)." Ph.D dissertation, Harvard University, 1961.

—————. *Russian Alternatives to Marxism. Christian Socialism and Idealistic Liberalism in Twentieth-Century Russia.* Knoxville, 1977.

Raeff, Marc. "Russia's Perception of her Relationship with the West." *Slavic Review* March 1964: 13–19.

—————. *Plans for Political Reform in Imperial Russia.* Englewood Cliffs, New Jersey, 1966.

—————. *Michael Speransky: Statesman of Imperial Russia, 1772–1839.* The Hague, 1969.

—————. "Patterns of Russian Imperial Policy Toward the Nationalities." In *Soviet Nationality Problems,* ed. Edward Allworth, pp. 22–42. New York, 1971.

—————. "The Bureaucratic Phenomenon of Imperial Russia." *American Historical Review* 84(2) 1979: 409.

—————. *The Well Ordered Police State.* New Haven, 1983.

—————. *Understanding Imperial Russia, State and Society in the Old Regime.* New York, 1984.

Read, Christopher. *Religion,Revolution and the Russian Intelligentsia 1900–1912.* London, 1979.

Rashin, A. G. *Naselenie Rossii za 100 let (1811–1913 gg.).* Moscow, 1956.

Renner, Karl [Rudolf Springer]. *Der Kampf der Österreichischen Nationen um den Staat.* Leipzig, 1902.

————. *Grundlagen und Entwicklungen der Österreichisch-Ungarishen Monarchie.* Wein–Leipzig, 1906.

————. *The Institutions of Private Law and their Social Functions,* ed. O. Kann-Freund. London, 1949.

Reshetar, John S. *The Ukrainian Revolution 1917–1920.* Princeton, 1952.

Rheinstein, Max, ed. *Max Weber on Law in Economy and Society.* New York, 1954.

Rieber, Alfred. "Landed Property, State Authority and Civil War." *Slavic Review* 47(1) Spring 1988: 29–38.

————. "The Sedimentary Society." *Russian History* 16(2–4) 1989: 353–76.

Robinson, Gerold Tanquary. *Rural Russia Under the Old Regime.* Berkeley and Los Angeles, 1967.

Rosenberg, William G. "Identities, Power, and Social Interaction in Revolutionary Russia." *Slavic Review* 47(1): 21–28.

————. *Liberals in the Russian Revolution.* Princeton, 1974.

Rudnytsky, Ivan L., ed. *Mykhailo Drahomanov. A Symposium and Selected Writings.* New York, 1952.

————. *Essays in Modern Ukrainian History,* ed. Peter L. Rudnytsky. Edmonton, 1987.

Sarkisyanz, Emanuel. "Russian Imperialism Reconsidered." In *Russian Imperialism from Ivan the Great to the Revolution,* ed. Taras Hunczak. New Brunswick, New Jersey, 1974.

Savich, G. G. *Novyi Gosudarstvennyi stroi Rossii. Spravochnaia kniga.* St. Petersburg, 1907.

Scheibert, Peter. "Die Petersburger religiös-philosophischen Zusammenkünfte von 1902 und 1903." *Jahrbücher für Geschichte Osteuropas* 12 (1964): 513–60.

Seton-Watson, Hugh. *The Decline of Imperial Russia.* New York, 1952.

Shatz, Marshall S. and Judith Zimmerman, eds. and trans. *Vekhi = Landmarks. A Collection of Articles on the Russian Intelligentsia.* Armonk, New York, 1994.

Shokhol', K. "K voprosu o razvitii vysshego zhenskogo obrazovaniia v Rossii." *Zhurnal ministerstva narodnogo prosveshcheniia* 40 (August 1912): 153–95.

Simmons, E. J., ed. *Continuity and Change in Russian Thought*. Cambridge, Massachusetts, 1955.

Skakun, O. F. *Politicheskaia i pravovaia mysl' na Ukraine (1861–1917)*. Kharkiv, 1987.

————. "Teoriia pravovogo gosudarstva v dorevoliutsionnoi Rossii." *Sovetskoe gosudarstvo i pravo* 1990 (2): 113–20.

Smoliarchuk, V. I. *Giganty i charodei slova*. Moscow, 1984.

Solomon, Peter H., ed. *Reforming Justice in Russia, 1864–1996*. Armonk, New York, 1997.

Sonin, V. V. and V. P. Fedorov. "Pravoponimanie v dorevoliutsionnoi nemarksistkoi iuridicheskoi mysli Rossii." In M. G. Korotkikh, V. V. Iachevskii, eds. *Gosudarstvennyi stroi i politiko-pravovye idei Rossii vtoroi poloviny XIX stoletiia*. Voronezh, 1987, pp. 60–68.

Sorokin, Pitirim. *Contemporary Sociological Theories*. New York, 1928.

Stammler, Rudolf. *Die Lehre von dem Richtigen Rechte*. Berlin, 1902.

Stenograficheskie otchety, 1906 god, Sessiia pervaia. Vol. 1. St. Petersburg, 1906.

Stepun, Fedor. *Vergangenes und Unvergängliches aus meinem Leben*. Vol. 1. *1884–1914*. Munich, 1947.

Szeftel, Marc. *The Russian Constitution of April 23, 1906: Political Institutions of the Duma Monarchy*. Brussels, 1976.

Trainin, I. P. "The Relationship Between State and Law." In V. I. Lenin, et al., *Soviet Legal Philosophy*, pp. 433–56. Cambridge, Massachusetts, 1951.

Treadgold, Donald W. *Lenin and His Rivals*. New York, 1955.

"Ukraina." *Entsiklopedicheskii slovar'* (Brokgaus-Efron), vol. 34, pp. 633–35. St. Petersburg, 1902.

"Ukrainofil'stvo." *Entsiklopedicheskii slovar'* (Brokgaus-Efron), vol. 34, pp. 635–38. St. Petersburg, 1902.

Venturi, Franco. *Roots of Revolution*. New York, 1966.

Vladimirskii-Budanov, Mikhail. *Obzor istorii russkogo prava*. 6th ed. St. Petersburg, Kyiv, 1909 [Reprint ed.=Russian Reprint Series. The Hague, 1966].

Von Beyme, Klaus. *Die Parlamentarischen Regierungsysteme in Europa*. Munich, 1970.

Von Rauch, Georg. *Russland: Staatliche Einheit und nationaleVielfalt*. Munich, 1953.

Vucinich, W. S., ed. *The Zemstvo in Russia: Experiment in Local Self-Government*. New York, 1982.

Wagner, William G. *Marriage, Property, and Law in Late Imperial Russia.* Oxford, 1994.

————. "Civil Law, Individual Rights, and Judicial Activism in Late Imperial Russia." In Peter Solomon, ed. *Reforming Justice in Russia, 1864–1996,* pp. 21–43. Armonk, New York, 1997.

Walicki, Andrzej. *Legal Philosophies of Russian Liberalism.* Oxford, 1987.

Walkin, Jacob. *The Rise of Democracy in Pre-Revolutionary Russia.* New York, 1962.

Wcislo, Francis W. "*Soslovie* or Class? Bureaucratic reformers and Provincial Gentry in Conflict, 1906–1908." *The Russian Review* 47 (1988): 1–24.

Weber, Max. *Wirtshchaft und Gesellschaft.* Tübingen, 1928.

————. *The Methodology of the Social Sciences.* Trans. and ed. Edward A. Shils and Henry A. Finch. New York, 1949.

————. *Max Weber on Law in Economy and Society,* ed. Max Rubenstein. New York, 1954.

Weill, Claudie. "Les étudiants russes en Allemagne." *Cahiers du Monde Russe et Soviétique* 20 (1979): 203–225

Whittaker, Cynthia, H. "The Women's Movement During the Reign of Alexander II: A Case Study in Russian Liberalism." *Journal of Modern History* 48(2) June 1976: 35–70.

Wilk, Kurt, trans. *The Legal Philosophies of Lask, Radbruch, and Dabin.* Cambridge, Massachusetts, 1950.

Williams, Robert C. "Russians in Germany: 1900–1914." In *1914: The Coming of the First World War.* Ed. Walter Laqueur and George Mosse, pp. 254–83. New York, 1966 [=Journal of Contemporary History, 3].

Wittram, R. *Geschichte der baltischen Deutschen.* Stuttgart, 1938.

Wortman, Richard S. *The Development of a Russian Legal Consciousness.* Chicago, 1976.

Yaney, George L. *The Systematization of Russian Government.* Chicago, 1973.

Zenkovsky, V. V. *A History of Russian Philosophy.* Vol. 2. New York, 1953 [Authorized translation from the Russian by George L. Kline].

————, ed. *Sbornik pamiati Semena Liudvigovicha Franka.* Munich, 1954.

Index

Advanced Courses for Women (*Vysshie zhenskie kursy*), 25, 29, 162n86

agrarian legislation of 1906–1907, 109–110

Alexander I, Tsar, 76

Alexander II, Tsar, 7, 78, 120, 154n6
assassination of (1881), 10

anarchy, 12, 86

Anderson, Benedict, *Imagined Communities,* 129

Andriewsky, Olga, 135

Antonovych, Volodymyr, 8, 9, 10, 125, 155n8, 187n46

"Back to Kant" movement, 42

Baden School, *see* Heidelberg (or Baden) School

"Banquet movement," 27

Basic Law of 1906, 59

Bauer, Otto, 117, 118, 185n17, 185n22

Bechev, Ia., 98

Berdiaev, Nikolai Aleksandrovich, 4, 23, 26, 27, 40, 95, 96–97, 157n51, 161n79, 173n13

Berenshtam, Viliam, 9, 25

Berlin, Isaiah, *The Crooked Timber of Humanity*, 3

Berlin, University of, 20, 22

Bernstein, Eduard, 157n37

Black Hundreds [*Rus.* Chernye sotni] 130

Bloody Sunday, 64

Böcklin, Arnold, 21, 158n52

Bogolepov, Nikolai Pavlovich, 32

Bogucharskii, Vasilii Iakolevich, 27, 125–26, 164n108

Brecht, Arnold, 42

Bulgakov, Sergei Nikolaevich, 4, 23, 26, 27, 96–97, 161n79, 173n13

Bund, 117

Chernov, Viktor, 99

Chicherin, Aleksei, 81

Chicherin, Boris Nikolaevich, 3, 39

Chełm [*Ukr.* Kholm], 120–21

Club of Russian Nationalists, 130, 142

Cohen, Hermann, 42, 148n53

Commission for the Organization of Reading at Home, 30, 31

Committee for Popular Enlightenment, 93

Comte, Auguste, 43–44, 93

Constitutional Democratic Party (Kadets), 30, 32 33, 64 65, 82, 96, 98, 115, 119, 143, 173n19, 185n23, 186n32

Constitutionalism, 11, 35, 83–87, 113
Kistiakovsky's concept of, 30, 34, 59, 81, 87–92, 151

Cooperative Movement, cooperatives, 115–16, 118

Council of Ministers, 76, 82, 121, 177n19

Courts, 77–78, 148
role of, in establishment of law, 106–109

customary law, 8, 78, 79, 102, 148

Cyril and Methodius Brotherhood, 8–9, 12, 122, 123

Das Kapital (Marx), 18

decentralization, 13

Degen, Sergei, 15–16

Demidov Lyceum, 31

Depenchuk, Larysa, 5, 160n71

Dolgorukov, P., 173n13

Dorpat (Tartu, Estonia), *see* Tartu (Dorpat), Estonia

Dorpat University, 17–20, 22, 127, 156n32, 157n39

"Draft Constitution for the Ukrainian Society Free Union" (1884), 12, 35

Drahomanov, Mykhailo Petrovych, 3, 4, 5, 8, 9, 11, 15, 83, 153n10, 160n75, 187
and constitutionalism, 34, 87, 124–26
"Draft Constitution for the Ukrainian Society Free Union," 12, 35
and federalism, 34, 124–126, 142
influence of, 11–13
Kistiakovsky's publication of political writings of, 27–28, 124
as mentor for Kistiakovsky, 87, 124–27
Vol'noe slovo, 26, 125, 126

Duguit, Leon, 174n27

Duma, 30, 136, 163n89, 189n37

economic rights, 2, 66–68, 74

electoral reforms, 34, 88, 91, 94, 119, 130

Ems Ukaz (1876), 10, 33, 130, 147

Engel, Friedrich, 117

Erfurt Program, 18, 157n37

extra-territorial organization of nationalities, 118

federalism, 11–13, 34, 81, 117–18, 122, 142, 151

Filosofov, Dmitrii Vladimirovich, 97

First State Duma, 29, 53, 60, 91, 94, 119, 130

Frank, Semen Liudvigovich, 23, 26, 27, 30, 95–97, 173n13

Franko, Ivan, 15, 18

Free Union, 12–13

Frierson, Cathy, 78

Fundamental Laws of 1906, 82, 84–85, 91, 100, 109, 111

Galicia, 11, 13–16, 127, 135, 137–38, 142–43, 156n23, 156n25
Austrian, 19

Galician Ukrainian Peasant Radical Party, 15–16

General theory of law, 23, 52–58

Gershenzon, Mikhail Osipovich, 31, 95, 96

Gessen, Iosif, 23

Gessen, Sergei Iakovlevich, 23

Gippius, Zinaida Nikolaevna, 97

Great Reforms of 1861, 7, 32, 77, 78, 79

Great Russian chauvinism, 34–35, 91, 115, 118, 119, 145, 150

Greek Catholic Church, 13

Grevs, Ivan Mikhailovich, 173n13

Gurvich, Georgii, 25, 56

Hapsburg Monarchy, 12, 14, 113, 117, 127, 129. *See also* Galicia

Heidelberg, 23, 27, 29, 40
Russian students in, 23, 28, 29, 81, 82

Heidelberg (or Baden) School, 42, 45

Herzen, Aleksandr, 94–95, 122–24, 186n36
Kolokol [The Bell], 26, 122, 123–24

Historical Songs of the Little Russian People (Antonovych and Drahomanov), 8

Holy Brotherhood, 126

Hromada movement, 8–11, 25, 125, 187n48

Hrushevs'kyi, Mykhailo, 37

human rights, 1–2, 3, 10, 59–62, 74, 81, 174n25, 175n33
concept of, in Union of Liberation and Kadet Party, 62–66

idealism, 22, 23–24, 25, 42–44

Imperial Russian Geographic Society, 9

individualism, 1, 59
and neo–Kantianism, 40–44, 47

individual value judgments, 22, 41, 57

inorodtsy ("outsiders"), 129

intelligentsia, 1–2, 31, 32, 34, 37, 61, 92, 108
and cooperative movement, 116
at Dorpat University, 17–18
Drahomanov and, 11
and *Hromada* movement, 8–9
and legal consciousness, 99–105, 112
and neo–Kantianism, 24
role of, after 1913, 109–112, 150
and sociology, 44
and Union of Liberation, 26
Vekhi on, 95–99

Institut international de sociologie, 167n21

Intelligentsia v Rossii [The Intelligentsia in Russia], 98

Iuridicheskii vestnik [Juridical Courier], 32, 36, 109, 111

Izgoev, A. S., 95

Jabotinsky, Vladimir, 133–36

Jaffe, Edgar, 43

Jellinek, Georg, 23, 25, 28, 31, 48, 52, 68, 69, 174n25

Jhering, Rudolf von, 174n30

judicial reforms of 1864, 7, 77, 106

jurisprudence, 48, 50
analytical, 50, 52–53, 54
normative, 52, 53, 54, 57–58
psychological, 52, 53, 54
sociological, 51–52, 53–54

Kadets, *see* Constitutional Democratic Party

Kareev, Nikolai Ivanovich, 40, 47, 103, 167n21

Kasso, Lev, Aristidovich, 163n95

Kautskii, Karl, 157n37

Kavelin, Konstantin Dmitrievich, 103–104

Kelsen, Hans, 57–58, 68, 168n36, 174n30

Kennan, George, 13

Kharkiv University, 16, 36

*khlopomany,*158n8

Kholmshchyna, 120–21

Khomiakov, Nikolai, 62

Kievlianin [The Kyivan], 137

Kistiakovsky, Alexander [*Ukr.* Oleksander Fedorovych Kistiakivs'kyi, *Rus.* Aleksandr Fedorovich Kistiakovskii], 5, 7, 8, 9, 20–21, 154n2
legal and criminological work, 154n2

Kistiakovsky, Bogdan [*Ukr.* Bohdan Oleksandrovych Kistiakivs'kyi, *Rus.* Bogdan Aleksandrovich Kistiakovskii]
and constitutionalism, 30, 34, 59, 87–92, 151
family life of, 5, 7–8, 20–21, 25–26, 157n49
exile to Vologda, 25-26
in Germany, 20–21, 22, 23, 26, 27–28, 161n78, 165n116
legal views of, 2–3, 23, 47–58, 70–74, 183n62
and Moscow Juridicial Society, 169n57
and neo-Kantianism, 24–25, 160n68
and *Osvobozhdenie,* 26–27, 161n79
and Max Weber, 159n61, 162n83, 171n68, 177n21
works
"Chto takoe natsionalizm?" [What is Nationalism?], 144, 185n22
"Georg Jellinek kak mysliteľ i chelovek," 159n61
Gesellschaft und Einzelwesen [Society and the Individual], 22, 24, 36, 41, 52, 158n56, 170n64, 171n69
"Gosudarstvennaia duma i osnovnye zakony" [The State Duma and the Fundamental Laws], 85
"Kholmshchina i Ukraina" [The Kholm Region and Ukraine], 121
"M. P. Drahomanov i vopros o samostoiateľnoi ukrainskoi kuľture" [M. P. Drahomanov and the Question of an Independent Ukrainian Culture], 125

Kistiakovsky, Bogdan (works, *con't*)
  "Nashe politicheskoe obrazova-
  nie"[Our Political Education], 30–31
  "Prava cheloveka i grazhdanina" [The
  Rights of Man and the Citizen], 2, 66
  Sotsial'nye nauki i pravo [Social
  Sciences and Law], 32, 36, 52
  Stranitsy proshlogo [Pages from the
  Past], 34, 126
  "V zashchitu prava, Intelligentsiia i
  pravosoznanie" [In Defense of Law,
  The Intelligentsia and Legal Con-
  sciousness], 4, 5, 31, 95, 98, 99,
  181n30
Kistiakovsky, Igor [*Ukr.* Ihor Oleksan-
  drovych Kistiakivs'kyi, *Rus.* Igor'
  Aleksandrovich Kistiakovskii], 37–38,
  154n1, 165n20
Kistiakovsky, Maria Berenshtam [*Ukr.*
  Mariia Berenshtam Kistiakivs'ka, *Rus.*
  Mariia Berenshtam Kistiakovskaia],
  25, 27
  exile of, 25–26
Kistiakowsky, George, 5
Kistiakovsky, Vladimir [*Ukr.* Volodymyr
  Oleksandrovich Kistiakivs'kyi, *Rus.*
  Vladimir Aleksandrovich], 154n1
Kolokol [The Bell], 26, 122, 123–24
Koni, Anatolii Fedorovich, 3
Kostomarov, Mykola [*Rus.* Nikolai
  Ivanovich Kostomarov], 8–9, 123-24,
  187n40
Kotliarevsky, S. A., 26, 173n13
Kovalevskii, Maksim, 167n21
Kriticheskoe obozrenie [The Critical
  Review], 31
Kulish, Panteleimon, 8–9
Kuskova, Ekaterina Dmitrievna, 27,
  173n13
Kyiv *Hromada*, 8, 9–10, 155n8

Lask, Emil, 48, 57, 68
Lavrov, Petr, 24, 45
law
  general theory of, 23, 52–58

law (*con't*)
  natural, 2, 47–50, 56–57
  role of courts in establishment of, 106–
  109
  and social change, 70–74
  social theory of, 48, 51
  sociological basis of, 3, 4, 42
legal consciousness, intelligentsia and,
  99–105, 112
legal estates, 60–61, 79, 148
legal Marxists, 21, 23
legal reforms, *see* judicial reforms of
  1864
legal system, constructing, 77–81
Lenin, Vladimir Ililch, 1, 21, 27, 63, 97
"Lesehalle" (N. I. Pirogov Reading Room
  in Heidelberg) 82, 177n20
Libava (Liepaja, Libau), 20
"Liberation of Labor" (Marxist Political
  Group) 18, 157n40
Literaturno-naukovyi vistnyk [The
  Literary Scientific Herald], 33
"Little Russians," 9, 14, 135, 138–39,
  141
L'viv, 18, 143, 156n25
  University of, 14
L'vov, N. N., 26, 173n13

Maklakov, Vasilii, 98
Marburg School, 42, 45, 51
Marx, Karl, 15, 59, 93, 117
  Das Kapital, 18
Marxism, 17–18, 21–22, 23–24, 26, 41,
  58, 72, 93, 96–97, 149
Materialism, 41, 44
Mazepa, Ivan, 189n32
Menger, Anton, 67–68
Merezkovskii, Dmitrii Sergeevich, 97
Mikhailovsky, Nikolai Konstantinovich,
  24, 44–47, 103, 159n66, 167n21
Miliukov, Pavel Nikolaevich, 62, 97, 98,
  99

minority nationalities, 34, 113, 119, 121, 144, 150–51. *See also* Non–Russian nationalities *and* Ukrainian movement

Mohylians'kyi, Mykhailo, 32

Moscow Commercial Institute, 29

Moscow Commision for the Organization of Reading at Home, 30, 163n90

Moscow Juridical Society, 32, 53, 109

Moscow Society of Slavic Culture, 32, 34

Moskovskie vedomosti [The Moscow Gazette], 97

Moskovskii ezhenedel'nik [The Moscow Weekly], 97, 121

multifaceted sociological method, 52

multinational empire, 34, 59, 81, 113, 115, 118–19, 121, 136, 141

Muromtsev, Sergei Andreevich, 32, 44, 53, 54, 163n97, 165n120, 170n56

Narod [The People], 18–19

Nashe nasledie [Our Heritage], 4

National autonomy, 9, 117, 118–19, 124, 128

nationalism, Russian, 130–33

national self-determination, *see* self-determination

Natsional'nye problemy [National Problems], 35, 36, 144

natural rights, 47, 60

Natural law, 2, 56–57
positivism and, 47–50

Naumenko, Volodymyr Ia., 32, 35

Neo-Kantianism and Neo-Kantians, 5, 21–22, 27, 28, 29, 31, 101, 158n53, 168n36,171n68
Heidelberg School of, 42, 45, 166n3
individualism and, 40–44, 47
Kistiakovsky's return to Russia and Russian, 22–25
Marburg School of, 42, 45, 51, 163n3
Vienna school of, 57, 68, 153n3, 174n30

Neo-Slav Movement, 138

Neue Zeit, 18

Nicholas I, Tsar, 9

Nicholas II, Tsar, 84, 91

non-Russian nationalities, 10, 11, 28, 33, 114, 118–20, 122, 128, 129–30, 146
Kistiakovsky's position on, 13, 34–36, 91–92, 140
Struve's position on, 137. *See also* Minority nationalities

Novgorodtsev, Pavel Ivanovich, 3, 4, 23, 27, 39, 40, 53, 54, 173n13

Novicow, Jacques [Iakov Novikov], 167n21

Novoe slovo [The New Word], 21

Novoe vremia [The New Times], 97, 137

Obshchestvennaia mysl' [Social Thought], 44

October Manifesto (1905), 29, 33, 64, 84, 100, 109, 111, 128, 138
Kistiakovsky's reaction to, 81–82

Osvobozhdenie [Liberation], 2, 26, 27, 29, 62–63, 64, 96, 124, 136, 137, 161n78

Pan-Slavism, 9, 16, 120, 131

Pavlyk, Mykhailo, 15, 18

peasantry, 61, 78–79, 86, 104, 108–110, 124, 139, 142, 148
Ukrainian (Galician), 11, 115–16

Petrazhitskii, Lev Iosifovich, 3, 23, 53–54, 94, 159n60, 170n58

Petrograd, 36

Petrunkevich, Ivan Il'ich, 26, 98, 173n13

Pirogov, Nikolai Ivanovich, 177n20

Plekhanov, Georgii Valentinovich, 27, 105

Poliarnaia zvezda [The Polar Star], 30, 122, 136, 162n89

Polish national uprising (1863), 9, 10, 13, 127, 154n6

Polish Partition of 1772, 14

Political rights, 2, 66–68, 74

Politicheskaia èntsiklopedia [Political Encyclopedia], 30–31, 93
"Pomich narodu" [Aid to the People], 16
Populism, 24, 45, 102, 108
   Russian, 10, 15, 24
   Ukrainian, 10–11
Positivism, 41, 42, 43–44
   and natural law, 47–50
Pravo, 23
Problemy idealizma [Problems of Idealism], 23, 24, 83, 97
Prokopovich, Sergei Nikolaevich 27, 173n13
Proudhon, Pierre Joseph, 12

Rada, 37
Radbruch, Gustav, 31
Raeff, Marc, 76–77
Rechtstaat, 75, 76–77, 80, 88–89, 111–12, 147
Referenda, 71, 91
Religious-Philosophical Society, 97
Renner, Karl, 68, 117, 118, 185n17, 185n22
Rieber, Alfred, 149, 151
Roberty, Evgenii de, 167n21
Rodichev, Fedor Ismailovich, 26, 173n13
Rule-of-law state [*Rechtsstaat*], 61, 70, 80, 81, 88, 92, 94, 147–48
Russian Liberation movement, 21, 26–27, 28, 34, 61–62,137
Russian Revolution (1905), 29, 33, 60, 66, 82, 91, 93, 95, 124
Russian Revolution (1917), 36, 39, 148, 150
Russian Subjectivist School, 24, 47
Russkaia mysl' [Russian Thought], 35, 97, 122, 133, 135,136, 137, 186n34
"Ruthenians," 12, 13–15, 18

Schaffhausen, Switzerland, 26, 63
Scientific method, 41

scientific philosophical idealism, 42–43
Sein ("what is"), distinction between *Sollen* ("what should be") and, 25, 41, 42, 46, 48, 52, 53, 55–58, 80, 91, 168n36
self-determination, 46, 65, 69, 71, 73, 88, 93, 123, 149
   national, 113, 129, 144
self-government, 12, 13, 35, 65
Senate, Russian Imperial, 76, 80, 107
Shakhovskoi, Dmitrii Ivanovich, 173n13
Shevchenko, Taras, 8–9
Simmel, Georg, 22, 28, 31
Skoropads'kyi, Pavlo Petrovych, 37–38
Slavophiles, 62, 102, 108
Slovo [The Word], 97
social change, law and, 70–74
Social Democratic Party, Social Democrats, 26–27, 82, 96, 105, 116, 117–18
Socialist constitutional state, 61, 81, 87–90
Socialist Revolutionaries, 82, 98, 105
social science methodology, 22, 41–43, 54–55, 57–58, 91, 110, 149, 150, 152
social theory of law, 48, 51
Society of Slavic Reciprocity, 138
Society of Ukrainian Progressives, 36
sociology of law, 3, 4, 42
Sollen, see *Sein*
Soloviev, Vladimir, 3, 58, 96
Sombart, Werner, 43
Soslovie system, 60–61, 79, 148
Speranskii, Mikhail, 76, 175n3
Stakhovich, Mikhail, 62
Stammler, Rudolf, 51
State Council [*Gosudarstvennyi sovet*], Russian Imperial, 76, 82, 85, 109, 176n18
State Duma [*Gosudarstvennaia duma*], Russian Imperial, 82, 85–86, 107, 109, 121, 139
   First, 29, 53, 60, 91, 94, 119, 130
   Second, 34, 60, 91, 94, 107, 119, 130

State Duma (*con't*)
  Third, 34, 119
  Fourth, 119

Stempowski, Stanisław [Stanislaw Stempovsky], 17–18, 19, 20, 37–38

Stepun, Fedor, 23

Stolypin, Petr, 34, 60, 78, 88, 94, 98, 109–110, 119–20, 130

Struve, Petr Berngardovich, 2, 30, 40, 44, 61, 62–63, 83, 99, 132–33, 157n51, 173n13
  and debate on Ukrainian national question, 34–35, 133–43
  "A Great Russia," 131–32, 143
  "The Intelligentsia and Revolution," 95
  and legal Marxists, 21, 23
  on nationalism, 144, 145, 146
  and *Osvobozhdenie*, 26, 29, 96, 124
  and *Problemy idealizma*, 23, 24
  and publication of Drahomanov's political writings, 27–28, 124
  and *Russkaia mysl'*, 35, 97

subjective rights, 68–70

subjective sociology, 24–25, 44–47, 55

subjects, 59–60

Svoboda i kul'tura [Freedom and Culture], 30, 136, 162n89

Tartu (Dorpat), Estonia, 17

territorial organization of nationalities, 118

Tolstoy, Leo, 58, 97

Treaty of Periaslavl' (1654), 14

trial by jury, 77, 80, 106

Trubetskoi brothers, 97

Trudoviki, 119

Tuchaps'kyi, Pavlo [*Rus.* Pavel Tuchapskii], 15, 18

Ukraina, 35

"Ukrainets," 137, 140

Ukrainian Academy of Sciences, 5, 38

Ukrainian Central Council, 37

Ukrainian language, 9, 15, 114–15, 138–39, 141–42, 143, 151
  ban on, 10, 33–34, 130, 147

Ukrainian movement, 2, 8, 11, 14, 25, 28, 34
  course on, for Russians, 122–24
  debate over, 133–43
  defending, after 1907, 119–21
  Kistiakovsky and, 10, 23, 29, 33, 38, 59

Ukrainian Radical Party, 18, 37

Ukrainian Social Democrats, 116, 118

Ukrainian women's movement, 25

Ukrainophile, 32, 34
  Kistiakovsky as, 114–19

Ukrainskaia zhizn' [Ukrainian Life], 34, 122, 143, 186n34

Union of Liberation, 26, 27, 30, 83, 96, 105, 114, 115, 131,132
  concept of rights in, 63–65
  See also Osvobozhdenie

United Nations Universal Declaration of Human Rights, 2, 175n33

Vagner, U. N., 161n79

Vasylenko, Mykola, 32, 161n79

Vekhi [Landmarks], 4, 5, 31, 93, 101, 103, 136, 163n94
  on intelligentsia, 95–99

Vernadskii, Vladimir Ivanovich, 38, 173n13

Vesy [The Scales], 97

Vienna school of neo–Kantians, 57, 68, 174n30. *See also* Neo-Kantianism

Vodovozov, Vasilii Vasilevich, 161n79, 173n13

Vol'noe slovo [The Free Word], 26, 125, 126

Vologda, exile to, 25–26

Vucinich, Alexander, 4

Vysshie zhenskie kursy. See Advanced Courses for Women

Wagner, William G., 107

Walicki, Andrzej, 4

Wcislo, Frank, 60

Weber, Max, 4, 23, 28–29, 43, 55, 57, 82–84, 87, 90

Western Zemstvo Bill, 120

Windelband, Wilhelm, 22, 28, 42

Wortman, Richard, 75

Zasulich, Vera, 80

Zemstvo movement, 13, 26, 61, 62, 63, 65, 79–80, 120, 161n76, 173n19, 176n15

Zemstvo Union, 65, 125, 126, 161n76

Zhabotinsky, Vladimir, *see* Jabotinsky, Vladimir

Zheleznev, V. I., 161n79

Zhivago, Sergei I., 23

Zhukovskii, D. E., 173n13

Zimmerman, Judith, 44–45

Ukrainian Research Institute
HARVARD UNIVERSITY
Selected Publications

Nationalism, Marxism, and Modern Central Europe: A Biography of Kazimierz Kelles-Krauz (1872–1905). Timothy Snyder. Harvard Papers in Ukrainian Studies. Paperback, ISBN 0-916548-84-9.

The Great Soviet Peasant War. Bolsheviks and Peasants, 1917–1933. Andrea Graziosi. Harvard Papers in Ukrainian Studies. Booklet, ISBN 0-916458-83-0.

The Ukrainian Language in the First Half of the Twentieth Century (1900–1914). Its State and Status. George Shevelov. Harvard Series in Ukrainian Studies. Clothbound, ISBN 0-916458-30-X.

Socialism in Galicia: The Emergence of Polish Social Democracy and Ukrainian Radicalism (1860–1890). John-Paul Himka. Harvard Series in Ukrainian Studies. Paperback, ISBN 0-916458-07-5.

The Strategic Role of Ukraine: Diplomatic Addresses and Essays (1994–1997). Yuri Shcherbak. Harvard Papers in Ukrainian Studies. Paperback, ISBN 0-916458-85-7.

Odessa: A History, 1794–1914. Patricia Herlihy. Harvard Series in Ukrainian Studies. Clothbound, ISBN 0-916458-15-6; Paperback, ISBN 0-916458-43-1.

To receive a free catalogue of all Harvard Ukrainian Research Institute publications (including the journal *Harvard Ukrainian Studies* and the publications of the Harvard Ukrainian Business Initiative) please write, fax, or call to:

HURI Publications
1583 Massachusetts Avenue
Cambridge, MA 02138
USA
tel. 617-495-3692 *fax.* 617-495-8097

e-mail:
huri@fas.harvard.edu
on-line catalog:
http://www.sabre.org/huri (follow the publications path)

Typeset using Adobe PageMaker 6.0 for the Macintosh at the Harvard Ukrainian Research Institute in DCTimes and Adobe Minion.

Cover design: Jennie Bush, Designworks/Books by Design.

Printed on acid-free paper by Metrolitho Division, Trans-continental/Best Books, Canada.